PSYCHOMOTOR INDIVIDUALIZED EDUCATIONAL PROGRAMS for Intellectual, Learning, and Behavioral Disabilities

DOLORES GEDDES
University of Southern California

ALLYN AND BACON, INC.
Boston London Sydney Toronto

Library of Congress Cataloging in Publication Data
Geddes, Dolores, 1935–
Psychomotor individualized educational programs for intellectual, learning, and behavorial disabilities.
Bibliography: p.
Includes index.
1. Physical education for handicapped children. 2. Handicapped children—Education. 3. Individualized instruction. I. Title.
GV445.G36 371.9'044 80-24468
ISBN 0-205-07274-7

Printed in the United States of America

Printing number and year (last digits):
10 9 8 7 6 5 4 3 2 1 85 84 83 82 81

To my husband, Roger K. Burke, and our children, Brad, Kim, and Lynne

Contents

Preface

This book focuses upon developing and implementing the psychomotor component of the Individualized Educational Program (IEP) that must be provided by local school systems to handicapped students. IEPs are required by current federal legislation to ensure that all handicapped children have an appropriate free public education. Psychomotor performance levels usually are assessed by physical education teachers as members of the IEP team, and program recommendations are subsequently made during the IEP conference. This book is intended for use by physical education and other teachers who program for handicapped students, for students taking adapted physical education or special education college and university courses, for participants taking in-service training workshops, and for other persons interested in this subject.

An assessment model, the Geddes Psychomotor Inventory (GPI), and an accompanying psychomotor individualized educational program, the Geddes Psychomotor Development Program (GPDP), are provided in this book for use with students with handicapping conditions who are placed in special and regular physical education classes. The GPI and the GPDP also may be used with many other students who have handicapping conditions that are not discussed in this book. The GPI analyzes psychomotor performance competencies of individuals from infancy through young adulthood.

Since one of the most critical problems of teachers is their being inundated with time-consuming paperwork in developing the IEP, a format is provided to lessen much of the paperwork. This type of prepared program should be used as a foundation upon which to build and to modify, with many creative ideas from the teacher's own repertoire after consideration of each student's needs. The GPDP suggests activities for students functioning from primary through young adult levels in psychomotor performance. Since the GPDP presents activities to develop a wide range of competency levels, it was not practical to include all potential physical activities, such as in the areas of rhythms, dance, aquatics, movement exploration, relays, tag and game situations, and sports. Activities such as volleyball or basketball were not described since it was felt that physical education teachers already know how to teach these games. A separate section of physical fitness was not included since physical fitness factors are integral components of physical activities such as throwing a softball, running the six-hundred-yard run-walk, and performing the vertical jump. The GPI describes a combination of content-referenced and norm-referenced competencies from infancy through young adulthood.*

Nonorthopedic disabilities were chosen for this book because participants without primary physical impairments may be evaluated by psychomotor inventories for nonhandicapped populations. The handicapping conditions of subaverage intellectual function (mild, moderate, severe, and profound levels of impairment), specific learning disabilities, behavioral disabilities, and autistic-like conditions are given emphasis since these are prevalent, nonorthopedic problems demonstrated by students in both regular and adapted physical education classes. Although the autistic-like condition is a rare problem, it is included here because more autistic-like students are encountered in public schools now than in the past. A categorical approach in discussing the disabilities is employed since teachers need categorical information before they can be noncategorical in programming. It was not considered feasible to omit the research-clinical-program literature regarding persons with certain handicapping conditions and their motor performance.

I would like to acknowledge the artwork of my daughter Lynne Geddes in this book. Her perceptive line drawings contributed much to the understanding of the written word. My daughter Kimble Burke Morton also assisted me in the writing of this book with program suggestions drawn from her adapted physical education teaching experiences. My husband, Roger K. Burke, devoted a great amount of time to reviewing manuscript materials based upon his professional experiences in textbook writing. Special thanks to Kimberly Wood, Lisa Barkdull, Maurine Howell, Lorraine Kisselburgh, and Kathy Rogers for their contributions.

*Chronologic age references are given to assist teachers.

I

LEGISLATIVE MANDATES
The Need for Individualized Educational Programs

1

INTRODUCTION

One of the most significant trends in education today is that of providing educational programs for all individuals regardless of the type or severity of any handicapping condition. Increased numbers of individuals with various disabilities and handicapping conditions are being enrolled in both special and regular education programs. Many students in need of specially designed instruction are placed in special education settings. In addition, the regular program situation is greatly affected since mainstreaming procedures cause the integration of handicapped students into the regular classes.

Because of this trend, regular educators (including physical education teachers) and special educators (including adapted physical education teachers) are requesting information to aid them in programming for these students. One of the most urgent requests is for assistance in developing and implementing the Individualized Educational Program (IEP) required by federal legislation. The focus of this book is directed toward the specific request for assistance in developing and implementing IEPs in the psychomotor performance area as provided by physical education, special education, regular classroom, or related personnel.

Public Law (PL) 94–142, Education of All Handicapped Children Act, ensures that all handicapped children ages three to twenty-one years will receive a free and appropriate public education. Physical education clearly is required by PL 94–142 as part of the special educational programs that provide specially designed instruction. These programs must be offered at no cost to the parents or guardians in order to meet the unique needs of handicapped students. This legislation specifies that [high-] quality, individualized instruction, including physical education, must be provided to handicapped children.

Local educational agencies are charged with the responsibility for carrying out such programming. Due-process provisions are described concerning the right to a hearing, representation by counsel, and the right to call witnesses if grievances are filed by parents and children to secure the rights under the law.

Section 504 of the Rehabilitation Act of 1973 guarantees the civil and personal rights of handicapped persons in all programs for which sponsoring groups receive federal funds. Agencies operating public education programs are required to provide high-quality programs to each qualified handicapped child or face a potential loss of federal funds. Equal opportunities for and nondiscriminatory practices toward persons with handicapping conditions are required. Physical education and athletics must be provided in the most normal setting possible at the preschool, elementary, presecondary, secondary, and postsecondary school levels.[1]

The impact of this legislation combined with already existing state legislation and master education plans results in the requirement of high-quality individualized physical education programs for all handicapped persons from three to twenty-one years of age.[2] These persons must be placed in the least restrictive environment (most normal setting possible). Unfortunately there is a tremendous variation in the implementation procedures employed by local school systems in the nation. The implementation approaches range from highly sophisticated adapted physical education programs and well-designed mainstreaming plans to little effort on the part of the school systems to provide physical education in accordance with the mandates of federal legislation.

This book describes the pertinent requirements of PL 94–142 in relation to the psychomotor component of the IEP, describes an evaluation approach, suggests program activities, and reviews the related program and research literature for selected disabilities.

---

1. Physical Education and Recreation for the Handicapped; Information and Research Utilization Center (IRUC); P.E. and athletics emphasized in rehabilitation act rules, regs, IRUC Briefings 2(3):1, 8, 13, 1977.

2. For example, in California, physical education programs for handicapped students must be consistent with P L. 94–142, Section 504, and Senate Bill 1870 (enacted in 1980) that revises and implements the California Master Plan for Special Education. Teachers who provide such programming include physical education and classroom teachers.

2

PUBLIC LAW 94-142 AND THE REHABILITATION ACT OF 1973

Public Law (PL) 94–142, the Education of All Handicapped Children Act of 1975, in conjunction with section 504 of the Rehabilitation Act of 1973, state legislation, and master education plans, has had a far-reaching impact upon the education of handicapped students. PL 94–142 became fully effective in 1977 with provisions that were designed to:

- Ensure that all handicapped children have available to them a free appropriate public education.
- Ensure that rights of handicapped children and their parents are protected.
- Assist states and localities in providing for the education of handicapped children.
- Ensure that all handicapped children are educated to the maximum degree possible with their nonhandicapped peers in the least-restrictive environments.
- Assess and ensure the effectiveness of efforts to educate handicapped children. (IRUC, 1976)

Section 121a.14 of the final rules and regulations for implementing PL 94–142 (Federal Register 1977) defines special education as

> "specially designed instruction, at no cost to the parents or guardians, to meet the unique needs of a handicapped child, including classroom instruction, instruction in physical education, home instruction, and instruction in hospitals and institutions."

PHYSICAL EDUCATION

Physical education is part of the specially designed instruction that must be provided to each handicapped child at no cost to parents or guardians. The U. S. House of Representatives specified that (1977):

- Special education as set forth in the Committee bill includes instruction in physical education, which is provided as a matter of course to all nonhandicapped children enrolled in public elementary and secondary schools. The Committee is concerned that although these services are available to and required of all children in our school system, they are often viewed as a luxury for handicapped children.
- The Committee expects the Commissioner of Education to take whatever action is necessary to assure that physical education services are available to all handicapped children, and has specifically included physical education within the definition of special education to make clear that the Committee expects such services, specially designed where necessary, to be provided as an integral part of the educational program of every handicapped child.

Physical education includes: special physical education, adapted physical education, movement education, and motor development, and means the development of physical and motor fitness, fundamental motor skills and patterns, skills in aquatics, dance and individual and group games and sports, including intramural and lifetime sports (96th Congress, 1977).

Physical education provided to handicapped children must be comparable to services provided to nonhandicapped children. Physical education services must be received in compliance with the provisions for instruction in physical education specified in PL 94–142 (IRUC, 1977).

Each handicapped child must be given the opportunity to participate in the regular physical education program that is available to nonhandicapped children unless the handicapped child is enrolled full time in a separate facility, or the child needs specially designed physical education, as prescribed in the child's IEP (96th Congress, 1977).

Also, if specifically designed physical education is prescribed, the public agency responsible for the education of that child shall provide the services directly, or make arrangements for it to be provided through other public or private programs. A public agency administering a separate facility shall ensure that the child receives appropriate physical education services . . . (96th Congress, 1977).

INDIVIDUALIZED EDUCATIONAL PROGRAM (IEP)

An Individualized Educational Program (IEP) must be developed for every handicapped student in a meeting attended by teachers, parents, and other related personnel. Section 121a.346 (96th Congress, 1977) specified the components required in the student's IEP:

- A statement of the child's present levels of educational performance;
- A statement of annual goals, including short-term instructional objectives;
- A statement of the specific special education and related services to be provided to the child, and the extent to which the child will be able to participate in regular educational programs;
- The projected dates for initiation of services and the anticipated duration of the services; and
- Appropriate objective criteria and evaluation procedures and schedules for determining, on at least an annual basis, whether the short-term instructional objectives are being achieved.

Individualized planning conferences are to be held to develop each child's IEP, with a review of it at least annually. Complete reevaluation must be carried out at least every three years. The public agency shall ensure that each individualized planning conference includes a representative of the public agency, the child's teacher, one or both of the child's parents, the child (when appropriate) and other individuals at the discretion of the parent or agency (96th Congress, 1977).

Parents must be actively involved in the individualized planning conference to develop IEPs for their handicapped child. Public agencies are required to notify the parents of the purpose, time, location, and participants at the meeting; schedule the meeting at a mutually agreeable place and time; ensure that parents understand the process of the meeting, including arrangements for interpreters; and furnish a copy of the child's IEP to the parent upon request. The agency must document efforts to involve the parents in meetings and use individual or conference telephone calls only if active parental participation cannot be arranged.

In 1980, the Bureau of Education for the Handicapped interpreted the purposes and functions of IEPs:

- *extend procedural protections* guaranteed under existing laws to parents of children with handicapping conditions.
- *serve as management tools* to ensure that each child with a handicapping condition is provided special education and related services appropriate to his/her special learning needs.
- *provide compliance/monitoring documents* to determine whether a child with a handicapping condition is receiving a free appropriate public education.
- *set forth in writing commitments of resources* necessary to enable each child with a handicapping condition to receive needed special education and related services.
- *offer communication vehicles* among all participating parties to ensure that they know what the child's problems are, what will be provided, and what anticipated outcomes may be. (AAHPERD,[2] 1980)

DUE PROCESS

Due process attempts to ensure the fairness of educational decisions and the accountability of both the agency professionals and the parents (Turnbull, Strickland, and Brantley 1978):

- A due process hearing may be initiated by the parents or public agency as an impartial forum for presenting complaints regarding the child's identification, evaluation, and placement or for challenging decisions made by another party.
- Parents may obtain an independent educational evaluation (an evaluation conducted by a licensed examiner not employed by the state or local education agency and who does not routinely provide evaluations for these agencies) if they are dissatisfied with the evaluation obtained by the public agency. The independent evaluation must be conducted at public expense. . . .
- Parents must be provided with written notice prior to the public agency's proposal or refusal to initiate or change the child's identification, evaluation, or educational placement.
- Parental consent must be obtained prior to conducting the initial evaluation for placement in a program providing special education and related services.
- When the public agency is unable to identify the parents or discover their whereabouts, the agency has the duty to assign an individual to act as the surrogate for the parents. . . .

2. The American Alliance for Health, Physical Education and Recreation (AAHPER) became the American Alliance for Health, Physical Education, Recreation and Dance (AAHPERD) in 1979.

EVALUATION

Evaluation procedures must not discriminate against the handicapped child. These procedures and the assessment items or batteries must be selected on an individual basis in accordance with the particular needs of the student. The public agency must ensure that a member of the evaluation team or another representative familiar with the evaluation procedures participates in the planning conferences. The following requirements for evaluation are specified (96th Congress, 1977):

- Tests and other evaluation materials:
  1. are provided and administered in the child's native language or other mode of communication, unless it is clearly not feasible to do so;
  2. have been validated for the specific purpose for which they are used; and
  3. are administered by trained personnel in conformance with the instructions provided by their producer.
- Tests and other evaluation materials include those tailored to assess specific areas of educational need and not merely those which are designed to provide a single general intelligence quotient.
- Tests are selected and administered so as best to ensure that when a test is administered to a child with impaired sensory, manual, or speaking skills, the test results accurately reflect the child's aptitude or achievement level or whatever other factors the test purports to measure, rather than reflecting the child's impaired sensory, manual, or speaking skills. . . .
- No single procedure is used as the sole criterion for determining an appropriate educational program for a child, and
- The evaluation is made by a multidisciplinary team or group of persons, including at least one teacher or other specialist with knowledge in the area of suspected disability.
- The child is assessed in all areas related to the suspected disability, including, where appropriate, health, vision, hearing, social and emotional status, general intelligence, academic performance, communicative status, and *motor abilities* [emphasis added].

LEAST RESTRICTIVE ENVIRONMENT

PL 94–142 requires that handicapped children be placed in the least restrictive environment possible. This is interpreted as education of handicapped students with their nonhandicapped peers to the maximum possible extent. This could result in mainstreaming the handicapped student into a regular class. Handicapped students should be placed in separate facilities or special classes only if the severity or nature of the handicapping condition prevents them from successful participation in regular classes even with supplementary aids or services. Combinations of mainstreamed and regular classes also might be provided a handicapped student.

A continuum of alternative placement must be available to meet the needs of handicapped children for special education and related services. This continuum must:

- Include alternative placements such as instruction in regular classes, special classes, special schools, the home, hospitals and institutions, and
- Make provision for necessary supplementary services such as resource room or itinerant instruction if the child is placed in a regular class. (96th Congress, 1977)

ZERO REJECT PRINCIPLE

Currently PL 94–142 requires that all handicapped children be served as described above if they are between ages three and twenty-one. However, exceptions will be made in those states in which compulsory education legislation does not require education for certain ages. For example, if a state does not require compulsory education for preschool children, it would not be mandated for preschool handicapped children. Unless an exception is made because of age, PL 94–142 specifies a zero reject principle; this requires that all handicapped children be provided with a free, appropriate public education. This principle is implemented by conducting a child find program on an annual basis so that all handicapped children within each school system's jurisdiction are located, identified, and evaluated. The local education agency reports to the state department of education the number of handicapped children within age and disability categories so that federal funds are passed through the state agency to the local agency for programming. Top priority is given to (Turnbull, Strickland, and Brantley 1978):

- all handicapped children who are not receiving any education, and
- handicapped children within each disability area with the most severe handicaps who are receiving an inappropriate education.

Also,

- the public agency must insure that handicapped children have equal opportunities with nonhandicapped children to participate in nonacademic and extracurricular services including counseling sessions, athletics, transportation, health services, recreation, special interest groups and clubs, and employment.

Section 504 of the Rehabilitation Act of 1973, has many similar provisions regarding equal opportunity for and nondiscriminatory practices toward people with disabilities. In essence, these requirements guarantee the civil rights and personal fulfillment of disabled persons, including thorough physical education and athletics, from preschool to postsecondary school levels. Although a specific IEP is not described, section 504 requires that local school systems provide an appropriate education to each qualified handicapped child in the most normal setting possible. Federal funds will be withdrawn from agencies that do not comply with this legislation.

QUESTIONS AND ANSWERS ABOUT LEGISLATION FOR PHYSICAL EDUCATION: PL 94–142 AND SECTION 504, REHABILITATION ACT OF 1973

When is a student identified or considered handicapped (AAHPERD, July/August 1979)?

Under PL 94–142 two criteria must be satisfied before an individual is considered handicapped and eligible for services—the individual must possess an identifiable handicapping condition, conventionally determined through traditional categories, and he or she must have identified special educational needs.

What are responsibilities of individual schools and local education agencies in providing opportunities through participation in intramural activities for students with various handicapping conditions (AAHPERD, July/August 1979)?

The phrase "including intramural and lifetime sports" is part of the definition of physical education within PL 94–142. Therefore, development of skills to enable a student with a handicapping condition to participate actively in intramural programs and activities can be recommended through and included in the individualized planning process.

Two units in physical education are required for graduation from high school. How does PL 94–142 affect this requirement (AAHPERD, July/August 1979)?

PL 94–142 does not deal with statewide or local graduation requirements. If a student with a handicapping condition has no special physical or motor needs he or she is expected to meet physical education requirements in the same ways as able-bodied students. The school may have to make certain accommodations so the student can participate actively with classmates; this is not only expected but required by Section 504. This instruction cannot be less than that required of able-bodied students; individualized education programs can require more than basic state requirements depending on actual needs of a student.

How are placement differences or disagreements about programs that cannot be resolved in individualized planning meetings handled (AAHPERD, July/August 1979)?

Both parents in behalf of their child and the local education agency are guaranteed the same due process and appeal privilege. When differences arise the child remains in his or her current placement or program until the appeal is resolved. The child's current placement and the disagreeing party determine the appealing party.

An individual in our state education agency has stated that children with handicapping conditions do not have to be provided physical education if this is not a requirement for all students. This conflicts with other interpretations that have been provided about PL 94–142. Please clarify (AAHPERD, July/August 1979).

The physical and motor needs of all children with handicapping conditions must be assessed to determine whether the individual has any special physical and/or motor needs. If a child has no special physical and motor needs then he or she is governed by the same requirements as other students at the same grade level.

The individualized planning committee agrees that an individual child needs a service not available through the local education agency. Must this service be added to programs sponsored by the local education agency (AAHPERD, July/August 1979)?

PL 94–142, its rules and regulations, and interpretations have consistently stated that a local education agency is responsible for seeing that a needed service is made available to children who need such services. However, the law provides latitude and alternatives by which such services can be provided. For example, the service can be provided directly by the local education agency; it can also be contracted or subcontracted from some other agency or group; some combination of these and/or other approaches can be used.

Swimming and other aquatics activities are provided at a nearby YMCA as part of our public school required physical education program. All fourth grade students are bussed to the facility for this program. Unfortunately the pool at this YMCA is not accessible to individuals in wheelchairs or with various orthopedic conditions.

We have several fourth grade students who require an accessible pool. What must we do (AAHPERD, July/August 1979)?

Third party provisions within Section 504 mandate that recipients of federal funds not enter agreements or relationships with organizations or agencies which discriminate. While discrimination by the YMCA is not intentional, lack of accessibility to the pool is discriminatory. Therefore, the local education agency has several options—(1) encourage the YMCA to remove architectural barriers that make the pool inaccessible, (2) move the program to another pool that is accessible, or (3) eliminate the program.

Must outdoor education and camping opportunities be provided handicapped students (AAHPER, March 1978)?

Various circumstances affect answers to this question. If outdoor education and/or camping opportunities are provided to nonhandicapped students in a local school system, these same opportunities must be available to handicapped children and youth.

What are elements of physical education contained in the definition found in PL 94–142 (AAHPER, March 1978)?

By definition physical education means the development of (1) physical and motor fitness; (2) fundamental motor skills and patterns; and (3) skills in aquatics, dance, individual and group games, and sports, including intramural and lifetime sports. The term physical education includes special physical education, adapted physical education, movement education, and motor development.

Can a school district send itinerant teachers in to work just with special education children who are in a regular physical education class (AAHPER, March 1978)?

Rules and regulations of PL 94–142 include subparts dealing with a continuum of alternative placements and use of itinerant teachers to supplement regular class instruction. There are many organizational possibilities for this to be accomplished such as resource rooms and traditional itinerant approaches.

There is some talk that the specially trained physical education teacher could be replaced by classroom teachers with a supervisor or coordinator for the physical education program. Would this meet conditions of PL 94–142 (AAHPER, March 1978)?

Certification requirements and other considerations regarding personnel are strictly state matters. All that PL 94–142 rules and regulations state is that personnel serving children receiving special education and related services must meet state certification requirements or standards.

What motor ability tests are acceptable (AAHPER, March, 1978)?

Rules and regulations for PL 94–142 require that all tests and other evaluation materials must meet certain criteria. Since these criteria are couched in general terms, they must be interpreted when applied to assessment procedures designed to determine physical and motor functions. Among specifications in the rules and regulations that warrant specific mention are requirements that tests and other evaluation materials must (1) be validated by trained personnel in conformance with instructions provided by the producer of the instrument, (2) be tailored to assess specific areas of educational need and not merely those designed to provide a single general intelligence (motor) quotient, and (3) not be a single procedure as a single criterion for determining an appropriate educational program for a child. Within specified criteria total batteries designed to measure general and/or specific components of motor ability are appropriate as are single test items designed to measure specific components of motor ability even though taken from different batteries and sources. Instruments that are norm or criterion referenced can be used for these purposes.

Who pays for special wheelchairs needed by participants in sports programs (AAHPER, March 1978)?

As in so many questions of this type, different interpretations are being received from different individuals in monitoring agencies. Several factors must be considered. Individuals cannot be denied access to a program because of lack of equipment. Auxiliary aids to enable an individual to take part in a program are considered reasonable accommodations and means of making it possible for the program to be accessible for the individual to take part in the activity. If necessary equipment for participation in sports programs is provided nonhandicapped students, consistency must be maintained in ways these programs are administered for handicapped students.

Are Little League baseball, Pop Warner football, bitty basketball, age group swimming, junior hockey, youth soccer, and similar youth sport programs governed by Section 504 (AAHPERD, May 1979)?

Section 504 bars discrimination under any program receiving federal financial assistance from the Department of Health, Education, and Welfare (DHEW).

What is the probability of a wheelchair-confined paraplegic being placed in a public school physical education position (AAHPER, November 1977)?

Just as colleges and universities that receive federal funds are prohibited from discriminating against qualified handicapped individuals, so are public school systems. The same rules and regulations basically apply to public schools as to colleges and universities. As such, an individual cannot be denied a position, including in physical education, because he or she is confined to a wheelchair, can't see or hear, or has a past history of emotional difficulties.

Is the interscholastic football rule that bars anyone with an artificial hand, arm, or leg discriminatory (AAHPER, November 1977)?

It would appear that on its face this rule does discriminate against individuals with prosthetic hands, arms, or legs. The present prohibition is found under the section of the rules dealing with illegal equipment. Therefore, it is the contention of many individuals that the intent of the rule is not discriminatory but rather included for consistency and safety of all concerned, the individual player as well as teammates and opponents. It has been recommended to the rules committee that this specific prohibition be eliminated from the existing rule and that further emphasis be given to the fact that no one be permitted to play wearing any substance harder than sole leather (the basis of the the rule on illegal equipment). A clarification note has been recommended for consideration that states in effect that this rule derives from safety considerations so that anyone with a prosthesis made of legal material would not be prevented from participating. This seems consistent with the intent of both the football rules and Section 504.

Are academic eligibility requirements that require students to pass three (or sometimes more) subjects discriminating against mentally retarded students in special education programs (AAHPER, November 1977)?

Again, there seems little doubt that these requirements do discriminate against mentally retarded students in special education programs which are not organized or administered on the basis of subjects or units. Before Section 504 became effective different approaches were used by states to deal with students in these situations. Some states made special provisions through state high school athletic or activity association action to grant qualified mentally retarded students eligibility for interscholastic activities. At least one state has no academic eligibility requirement for any students, including those in special education. Other states base eligibility on participation in a state certified special education program. Some states still have unwritten understandings or procedures whereby these students can be declared eligible. Those states which still maintain rigid academic requirements based on passing a given number of subjects or Carnegie Units that make it impossible for mentally retarded students to gain eligibility for interscholastic sports would appear to be operating in a manner potentially contrary to the letter and intent of Section 504. In addition, PL 94–142 specifies that students receiving special education and related services must have access to extracurricular activities, including athletics, that are comparable to those received by their nonhandicapped classmates.

Can a state or local education agency prohibit an individual with one eye or one kidney or who is deaf or epileptic from taking part in athletics in general or specific sports in particular for their own health, welfare, and safety (AAHPER, November 1977)?

Not only are different interpretations being given to these questions but courts have ruled in opposite ways in cases that have come before them. A basketball player at Ohio University was granted an opportunity to try out for the basketball team despite having only one eye. The university had denied this because of possibilities of injury to the remaining good eye and a previous position of the American Medical Association recommending that individuals with only one of paired parts should do nothing to endanger that good part. While the court commended the university for its consideration, it ruled that the final decision was up to the individual and that to do otherwise was in conflict with Section 504 and denied basic due process guarantees of the Constitution. However, in two cases that are now in the appeal process, two junior high school students in different parts of New York state, each with only one of paired parts, were denied the opportunity to take part in contact activities in physical education classes. The courts ruled that it was perfectly within the responsibilities of the state education agency and local school boards to establish policies and procedures that considered the health and safety of their students. In addition, these students were afforded opportunities to take part in noncontact activities which should meet their needs. While there is no indication of how higher courts might rule, these conflicting judgments reveal the complexity of these situations and how unpredictable and inconsistent resulting rulings can be.

If regular or special education classroom teachers use motor, physical, or recreational activities as methods to reach certain students, has the physical education requirement been satisfied (AAHPER, November 1977)?

By the very wording of PL 94–142 which includes "... instruction in physical education, ..." as a defined part of special education and defines physical education as "... development of (1) physical and motor fitness, (2) fundamental motor skills and patterns, and (3) skills in aquatics, dance, and individual and group games and sports (including intramural and lifetime sports), ..." the answer to this should be an emphatic NO. While these uses of motor, physical, and recreational activities are to be encouraged and supported, this emphasis needs to be in addition to, not in place of, programs and activities that focus on attaining motor and physical objectives that are important to good physical and mental health.

When would a regular physical education program not be appropriate for a student receiving special education and related services (AAHPER, November 1977)?

Because a student meets the definition of a handicapped child and is receiving special education does not in and of itself mean that this child cannot and should not take part in a regular physical education program. As for any specially designed program, special physical education must be prescribed in the child's individualized education program. This must be done when the child's needs cannot be met through the regular program. In these instances the education agency is expected to provide appropriate supportive services to enable the child to participate in the regular program. Only when this cannot be accomplished is removal from the regular physical education program justified and permissible.

What are the implications for and applications of PL 94–142 and Section 504 in states where physical education is not required at all or not at certain grade levels (AAHPER, January 1978)?

As in all aspects of programming for children receiving special education, provisions contained in the individualized education program are key determinants. If specially designed physical education is contained in the individualized education program, then these services must be provided regardless of the general state mandate for physical education. This is consistent with provisions of both PL94–142 and Section 504 that require full educational services based on individualized needs of handicapped children regardless of whether services are currently available or not. However, if recommendation of the individualized planning committee calls for the child to take part in regular physical education programs and activities, no physical education is then required when it is not required for nonhandicapped students at the same grade level.

Must a child be placed in regular classes if his/her needs can be more effectively met in a separated setting such as adapted or remedial physical education classes (AAHPER, January 1978)?

Several factors must be taken into consideration in these situations. First, least restrictive environment and most normal setting appropriate both connote various alternatives that must be available to meet the needs of each child. In addition, rules and regulations of PL 94–142 contain sections that deal specifically with a continuum of alternative placements including instruction in regular classes, special classes, special schools, home instruction, and instruction in hospitals and institutions. Provisions for supplementary services such as resource room or itinerant instruction must be provided in conjunction with regular class placement. Duration of placement must also be considered. For some, short term placement in separate classes or segregated settings for intensive attention can be less restrictive than longer periods in which the child is placed part time in both regular and special classes. Therefore, both the setting itself and length of time in that setting must be considered when applying the least restrictive alternative mandate.

We have several children with orthopedic conditions, including some in wheelchairs, who participate fully in all academic classes but need specially designed physical education programs. Are they eligible for these services and do individualized education programs have to be developed for them (AAHPER, January 1978)?

Since these students are not now currently receiving special education services they are not eligible to be counted under PL 94–142 and therefore no individualized education programs have to be developed for them. However, since physical education is a defined part of special education under PL 94–142 their eligibility can be gained through the following process: (1) identification as a handicapped child meeting one of the categorical conditions delineated in the law (obviously this condition has been satisfied); (2) referral as a handicapped child not receiving full educational services; (3) assessment in terms of educational, psychological, medical, sociological, and adaptive behavior factors; and (4) determination of eligibility as an individual in need of specially designed education (in this case physical education) based on results of the assessment. When need for specially designed instruction has been established, then the individualized education program process begins by convening the individualized planning committee.

Do these same provisions apply to children who are obese, are malnourished, possess low levels of physical fitness, or have a poor level of motor development (AAHPER, January 1978)?

It is possible for children with conditions such as those listed to qualify for special education services under the category of other health impaired conditions. Conditions listed in the rules and regulations do not represent all possible conditions covered by this category. However, these conditions must limit strength, vitality, or alertness in ways that adversely affect a child's educational performance.

Suppose a child in need of a specially designed physical education program brings a note from a physician requesting that the child be excused from taking part in all physical education activities (AAHPER, January 1978)?

PL 94–142 requires that physical education be made available to every handicapped child receiving special education; Section 504 does not permit an individual to be discriminated against because of a handicapping condition. Therefore, such excuses as this are technically and legally not permissible under the law. In many instances such excuses are sent at the request of, or because of, pressures brought to bear on the physician by parents. In addition, many physicians are not aware of new directions in physical education, much less what can, and is, being done through adapted or individualized programs. Since many physicians undoubtedly base their excuses on their perceptions of what goes on in physical education—roll out the ball, steady diets of team sports, formal calisthentics and exercises, mass bedlam—it is vital that they understand the type of program, activities, methods and approaches, and other aspects of individualizing programs according to each child's needs. If, after making such presentations to the physician so that representatives of the local education agency can document their efforts and feel certain that the physician understands individualized physical education programs, the physician still insists that the child be excused, the excuse should at that point be honored.

Must physical education be in every handicapped child's individualized education program (AAHPER January 1978)?

Since only specially designed instruction must be included in individualized education programs, physical education must be only in individualized education programs of students needing specially designed physical education. However, elements of physical education as defined in the rules and regulations of PL 94–142 must be dealt with by individualized planning committees in deliberations about each child. For children able to take part fully in regular programs and activities, no further treatment of or inclusion of physical education is necessary in their individualized education programs.

What if a state does not include or mention physical education in its state plan (AAHPER, January 1978)?

Nothing in rules and regulations for PL 94–142 require that physical education be dealt with in state plans. However, this does not change responsibility for, and need of, requirements for physical education being made available to every handicapped child receiving special education. Physical education must be discussed by every individualized planning committee for each child and these services made available to them.

Does a hearing-impaired child who is in an academic setting where both manual and oral communication are used and who is mainstreamed into a class of hearing children for physical education have to be supplied with an interpreter to sign for him or her (AAHPER, April 1978)?

As in all decisions the key to programming for any individual child is his or her individualized education program which includes teaching strategies and approaches. Even though interpreters must be provided for deaf students (reasonable accommodation required by Section 504), this does not mean every deaf child must have an interpreter in every situation and setting. These decisions are made as part of individualized planning meetings. Many factors must be considered in making these decisions—ability of a child to benefit from instruction without an interpreter, ramifications of forcing a child to focus on both signing by an interpreter and demonstrations by a physical education teacher, and possibilities of communicating in other ways with a child during physical education classes. If a physical education teacher is able to communicate adequately with a child and an interpreter calls unnecessary additional attention to the hearing deficiency so that it adversely affects effective mainstreaming, use of an interpreter in that situation would be neither required nor appropriate.

Students in special schools do not attend any program of a physical education nature. Many infants and older students within the 3- to 21-year range are provided physical therapy or recreation as substitutes for physical education. Please comment (AAHPER, April 1978).

It appears that PL 94–142 is not being fulfilled in this situation. Physical education is specified as part of the definition of special education which includes "... instruction in physical education ..." as part of the free appropriate education guaranteed every handicapped child. Neither physical therapy nor recreation are physical education.

Transportation and bus schedules make it impossible for our special education students to stay after school and take part in either intramural or interscholastic programs. Please comment (AAHPER, April 1978).

If a local education agency provides late or special buses so that nonhandicapped students can take part in intramural or interscholastic programs, similar services must be provided for handicapped students. When participation in these programs is included in a student's individualized education program, transportation supported through PL 94–142 funds can be justified as a related service necessary so that the child can participate in and benefit from the program.

We have difficulty getting funds to purchase equipment, uniforms, and other necessary supplies for intramural and interscholastic programs in a special school (AAHPER, April 1978).

If a local education agency or school board provides financial support for intramural and interscholastic programs in its regular junior and senior high schools, similar support must be provided for comparable programs in special schools.

What criteria can be used to transfer a child from special education to regular classes (AAHPER, April 1978)?

Little definitive information is included in rules and regulations about this process. However, several possibilities exist. When a child attains goals specified in the individualized education program and no further specialized instruction is deemed necessary, he or she automatically returns to regular programs. The same basic assessment and evaluation processes used to determine a child's eligibility for special programs can be used to determine appropriateness of return to regular programs. Many state and local education agencies have established admission, review, and dismissal procedures as part of the process designed to assure free appropriate education programs for every handicapped child.

What steps must be followed for a handicapped child to be assured a free appropriate education (AAHPER, April 1978)?

These steps must be followed in this process—(1) identify the child on the basis of a defined handicapping condition and according to priorities specified by the law—i.e., children not receiving any educational services or those not benefiting from full services; (2) refer the child according to state procedures for assessment and evaluation; (3) assess the child to determine levels of function in educational, psychological, medical, sociological, and adaptive behavior areas; (4) determine eligibility of the child for special education services by an eligibility committee and, once a child's eligibility has been determined, an individualized planning meeting must be convened within thirty days; and (5) convene the individualized planning meeting and initiate the process for developing and implementing an individualized education program for the child.

If parents object to a specific program or placement against judgment and recommendation of professional personnel involved in the individualized planning meeting, what can be done (AAHPER, April 1978)?

When a parent objects, or is unwilling to agree to, a specific program or placement, the process ends at that point and the child remains in his or her present placement and program. However, a local education agency is guaranteed the same rights of appeal and due process as parents.

Even though rules and regulations specifically state that an agency, teacher, or other person not be held accountable if a child does not achieve growth projected in annual goals and short term instructional objectives, what can teachers be held accountable for regarding individualized education programs (AAHPER, April 1978)?

While no individual can be held accountable if a child does not attain annual goals or short term instructional objectives contained in an individualized education program, he or she is accountable for the process and procedures specified in that program. If outlined procedures are not followed an individual could be held accountable for not implementing an individualized education program as agreed to in the planning meeting.

Must activities offered through school based elective physical education programs be available and accessible to students with handicapping conditions (AAHPERD, June 1979)?

Yes. The prime consideration throughout application and implementation of Section 504 to all programs and activities is program accessibility. Since elective physical education activities are part of the overall physical education program, they must be available and accessible to individuals with handicapping conditions. To keep these populations from such activities would deny them benefits of, exclude them from, and discriminate against them because of their handicapping conditions. Section 504 rules and regulations state explicitly that no otherwise qualified individual can be denied opportunities to participate in such programs. Sections dealing specifically with physical education state that no qualified handicapped student can be denied the opportunity to compete for teams or participate in courses that are not separate or different. If an individual student does not meet certain basic prerequisites or entry level criteria for taking part in an activity, he or she can be denied admission into that activity in the same ways that students without handicapping conditions can be denied admission.

In our senior high school there is only one student in a wheelchair; he wants to play wheelchair basketball. What are our responsibilities in providing for this student (AAHPERD, June 1979)?

Responsibility for providing a free appropriate education, including extracurricular activities, is actually that of the local education agency, not individual schools. Several courses of action can be pursued to provide opportunities in wheelchair basketball for this student such as having this student along with others in wheelchairs in other schools throughout the local education agency combine into a system-wide wheelchair basketball team, or investigating opportunities in wheelchair basketball available to the community through teams taking part independently as part of the community recreation department's programs or in National Wheelchair Basketball Association play. If such opportunities are not available, then other sports activities must be pursued and provided for this student.

Although I am legally blind I do have sufficient functional vision to play volleyball if the ball is some color other than white—e.g., yellow, orange, or even dark blue. The Director of Intramural Sports at the university I attend will not hear of making such a modification in the official volleyball rules. What are his responsibilities and my rights (AAHPERD, June 1979)?

This is an excellent example of a type of accommodation that is both expected and required by Section 504 to enable an individual with a handicapping condition equality of opportunity to participate in this activity. It further shows that treatment can in and of itself be discriminatory and therefore in conflict with requirements of Section 504. This type of accommodation in no way places participants with greater vision at any disadvantage. The first step to attain the student's guaranteed rights and opportunity to participate in this intramural volleyball program is to discuss the matter thoroughly with the Director of Intramural Sports emphasizing his responsibilities and the student's rights; these can be fulfilled by painting a regulation volleyball a different color. If such discussion results in no action or resolution of the discriminatory action, the Director of Athletics or individual to whom the Director of Intramural Sports is responsible should then be contacted. If action and resolution of the problems are still unresolved, the specifics of the situation should be called to the attention of the Section 504 Enforcement Officer at the college or university and/or the case entered for civil court action. Situations of this type should be resolved in informal stages before formal actions are necessary. These same responsibilities and rights apply to higher levels of competition—i.e., extramural and intercollegiate—as well as to high school, junior high school, and elementary school levels.

> *A severely physically involved child in our school could benefit from swimming. However, there is no pool in any of the schools so swimming is not currently available to any students in our system. How can swimming be made available to meet the specific and special needs of this student* (AAHPERD, June 1979)?

As is continually emphasized, current availability of an activity to students without handicapping conditions and/or through a local education agency is not the criterion to be used in determining this inclusion in a student's individualized education program. If members of an individualized planning program committee agree that swimming is an appropriate activity to meet specific needs of a student, then it is the responsibility of the local education agency to see that swimming is made available to the student.

> *Our school is a traditional elementary school—i.e., grades one to six—and contains a wing of children in special education. Our principal will not schedule and does not allow members of the physical education staff to work with and teach children in special education since provisions in their individualized education programs are being carried out by their classroom special education teachers. Is this a valid and acceptable procedure* (AAHPERD, June 1979)?

This is a Section 504 violation. Children in special education are being discriminated against and not being provided equal opportunities in physical education since they are not receiving services of personnel trained and certificated in physical education to the same degree as their nonspecial education age and grade equivalents. Regardless of specific physical and motor needs of children in special education they, too, must have access to services of physical education specialists to the same degree or more as nonspecial education students.

> *What are examples of accommodations, adaptations, and adjustments expected so that individuals with handicapping conditions can take part in regular physical education programs and activities* (AAHPERD, June 1979)?

No hard and fast provisions for accommodations in physical education can be made since these are to be made in terms of individual needs and situations. Rules and regulations of Section 504 provide some representative examples of ways in which recipients of federal funds are required to make adjustments and adaptations in programs and activities so that no individual is denied opportunities to take part solely because of a handicapping condition. Trends in physical education itself provide directions to assist in accommodating children with handicapping conditions in activities: (1) problem-solving, exploratory, movement education, and station or circuit approaches at elementary school levels; (2) flexible or optional unit scheduling especially at middle, intermediate, and junior high school levels; and (3) elective or selective program patterns emphasizing lifetime, recreational, or leisure time activities, especially at senior high school and college or university levels.

Various other approaches can be introduced so that students with special needs can be accommodated in regular physical education programs: (1) a buddy system which pairs a child with a handicapping condition with an able-bodied partner for specific activities, (2) peer tutoring, (3) students as squad leaders, (4) circuit or station organizational patterns, (5) contract techniques, (6) team teaching involving regular physical education teachers and adapted physical education teachers or resource teachers, (7) preteaching certain activities to select students with special needs, and (8) additional physical education classes to supplement, not replace, regular physical education classes.

Within individual classes types of accommodations that can be considered include (1) letting blind or partially sighted students hit a beeper ball, bat off a tee, or hit out of their hands in softball, (2) letting physically involved students serve in volleyball or take foul shots for both teams in basketball, (3) having students in wheelchairs on the sideline in soccer (4) organizing locomotor activities, fleeing-chasing games, and similar activities involving running so that everyone takes part on scooter boards or gym scooters, (5) using individuals on crutches as goalies in activities such as soccer, line soccer, speedball, or related activities, (6) organizing relays in ways to compensate for individuals in wheelchairs, with braces, or on crutches when situations do not permit the same number of these students on each team or squad, (7) giving some individuals more than three strikes in games such as softball or kickball, (8) applying decathlon scoring approaches so individuals are competing for points against records applicable to their conditions and then devising ways in which points attained are compared for all individuals, and (9) developing and using appropriate assistive and/or adaptive devices.

Who is responsible for enforcing PL 94–142 in a school district (AAHPER, October 1978)?

The local education agency (LEA) is responsible for enforcing PL 94–142 and for abiding by educational provisions of Section 504 throughout its district and in individual school buildings. The LEA is also responsible for monitoring programs and activities of its students who receive services on a contractual basis from other agencies and organizations, including private schools from whom such services are purchased.

Is the secondary student in special education entitled to a four-year physical education program provided by the physical education department (our state only requires and provides one year of secondary physical education) (AAHPER, October 1973)?

Provisions of PL 94–142 included "... instruction in physical education ..." as a defined part of special education. Therefore, physical and motor needs of every child for whom an individualized planning meeting is convened must deal with these areas. When valid assessment and evaluation procedures indicate that a child does have special physical and motor needs, annual goals, short-term instructional objectives, instructional strategies, and other provisions and requirements regarding individualized education programs must deal with his or her physical and motor needs. This process must be followed whether or not a state requires physical education for nonhandicapped students at grade levels in which a handicapped student is enrolled (the case in question). The key consideration is that when individuals have special physical and motor needs, they must be met whether the state education agency requires physical education for that grade level or not and whether the local education agency has offerings in this area or not.

Physical education is defined in PL 94–142 as "... the development of (a) physical and motor fitness, (b) fundamental motor skills and patterns, and (c) skills in aquatics, dance, individual and group games, and sports (including intramural and lifetime sports) . . ." The law states further that ". . . physical education services, specially designed if necessary, must be made available to every handicapped child receiving a free appropriate education." Does this mean each handicapped child will receive instruction in each of the defined areas? What if the child is placed in a regular physical education class which does not cover an area, e.g., aquatics (AAHPER, October 1978)?

The PL 94–142 definition of physical education includes areas or elements considered to be physical education under the law. Several important points need emphasis—(1) to be considered physical education under the law, focus must be upon instruction and development of skills in one or more of the define areas, (2) valid assessments in these delineated areas provide basis for determining whether specific physical and motor needs exist, (3) children with no special physical and motor needs are placed in regular physical education programs and activities, and (4) children with special physical and motor needs are provided appropriate programs, activities, and placement according to their particular needs. Therefore, a child for whom an individualized planning committee deems aquatic activities necessary can not be placed in a physical education program if that program does not provide opportunities in the prescribed area—aquatics in this instance.

Will the regular classroom teacher be responsible for the handicapped child's physical education if there is no physical education program in the school district (AAHPER, October, 1978)?

Children with special physical and motor needs must be programmed in ways that ensure these needs are met. If a school district has no physical education program for nonhandicapped children, meeting special physical and motor needs of handicapped children is still the responsibility of the local education agency. As such the classroom teacher can be the individual responsible for implementing this program and appropriate physical education activities. However, these services can also be contracted for from some other community agency such as parks and recreation departments, community agencies such as YM/YWCA, or private contractors.

We are building a new physical education building that is to be connected to the existing physical education building. The new building will be totally accessible. To what extent must the existing building be made accessible (AAHPER, December 1978)?

Even though the new physical education building will be connected to the existing one so that one functional building results, several factors must be considered. Obviously the new building must be totally accessible under Section 504 provisions governing new construction, PL 90–480 (Architectural Barriers Act of 1968), and state requirements governing use of state funds in new construction. Any parts of the old building renovated must also be made accessible. If the only way in which construction affects the old building is to connect it to the new building, accessibility does not have to be considered in the existing structure. However, all programs sponsored or conducted by the department must be accessible.

We have a competency-based physical education major program. Some students with handicapping conditions desire to enter this program knowing they cannot fulfill certain required competencies. What is our responsibility as a department in these situations (AAHPER, December 1978)?

Section 504 indicates that no otherwise qualified individual can be denied opportunities in, excluded from, or discriminated against solely because of a handicapping condition. Rules and regulations are explicit in types of modifications and adaptations expected within various curricular areas so that individuals are not excluded from these programs and activities because of their handicapping conditions. For example, if an individual's condition is such that a given activity must be changed, then this would be appropriate and expected. Moderate modifications in more than one area might also be appropriate and expected. However, whole or dramatic changes in requirements that drastically weaken or reduce standards of quality would indicate that an individual is not otherwise qualified.

Does a college or university with a specific scholarship program for intercollegiate sports have to grant scholarships to athletes participating in activities such as wheelchair track and field (AAHPERD, November 1979)?

No. Section 504 specifies that scholarship programs when viewed as a whole cannot discriminate against individuals with handicapping conditions. However, Section 504 neither intends nor implies that scholarships must be given in specific sports. Therefore, athletic scholarships do not have to be provided for wheelchair sports just as they do not have to be provided for any other officially recognized intercollegiate sport. If scholarships are given for specific sports, individuals cannot be denied such scholarships because of their handicapping conditions. An individual with a handicapping condition can be denied an athletic scholarship in such sports when decisions are based on comparative skills and abilities in those sports.

If a student with a handicapping condition has only *physical and motor needs and is being considered for specialized physical education, does he or she need to be assessed* only *in appropriate and necessary physical, motor and related areas (AAHPERD, November 1979)?*

Review of PL 94–142 rules and regulations [121a.532(f)] indicates that "the child is assessed in all areas related to the suspected disability, including, *where appropriate* [emphasis added], health, vision, hearing, social and emotional status, general intelligence, academic performance, communicative status, and motor abilities." Children with speech impairments as their primary handicapping conditions may not need a complete battery of assessments—e.g., psychological, physical, or adaptive behavior. Evaluations of these children should emphasize procedures appropriate for diagnosis and appraisal of speech and language disorders. Assessment and evaluation need only include procedures appropriate for diagnosis and appraisal of physical and motor deficits.

Does a special education program in excess of the normal one hundred eighty school days have to be provided any child with a handicapping condition requiring such a program (AAHPERD, November 1979)?

A United States District Court judge has ruled that the state of Pennsylvania must provide such special education. The judge held that state and local school district policies of refusing to provide or fund provisions of special education programs in excess of one hundred eighty school days "deprived plaintiffs and the class they represent of an 'appropriate education' and violates PL 94–142."

This case, *Armstrong v. Kline,* was brought as a class action suit on behalf of children with severe handicapping conditions who, according to their attorneys, require schooling in excess of one hundred eighty days to prevent regression which might occur as a result of interrupting their special education programs for the summer months and/or weekends.

Does parental consent apply to college or university students who wish to participate in contact sports (AAHPERD, November 1979)?

No. Parental consent may be required for students who have not reached majority ages. For individuals who have reached majority age, personal rather than parental consent is intended.

Are physical maintenance goals and objectives valid in establishing physical education programs and activities for students with specific handicapping conditions (AAHPERD, November 1979)?

By definition development of physical and motor fitness is an accepted focus of physical education programs and activities for students with specific physical and motor needs. As such, approaches designed to maintain appropriate levels of physical and motor fitness are legitimate concerns and considerations in physical education for students with handicapping conditions. Recent research reports from the Paralyzed Veterans of America show that individuals confined to wheelchairs because of paraplegia, quadriplegia, or leg amputations have significantly higher incidences of fatal cardiac, cardiorespiratory, and cardiovascular dysfunctions than age comparisons of individuals not confined to wheelchairs. Other studies and reports have shown that when special attention is given to these functions through hand-operated bicycle ergometry, cardiac, cardiorespiratory, and cardiovascular functions of these populations improve significantly. Similar findings have been found with mentally retarded participants in various combinations of vigorous and regular physical activity focusing on aerobic approaches. Conversely, overweight and low levels of physical fitness, including poor cardiorespiratory, low function in mentally retarded individuals, have been associated with overeating and sedentary life styles. With current emphasis on regular participation in vigorous physical activity as an important means of maintaining high levels of cardiac, cardiorespiratory, cardiovascular functions, for health purposes, physical maintenance for individuals with handicapping conditions would not only be valid but is to be encouraged as an important inclusion in these programs.

For a child entering special education for the first time, when must the IEP be written—before or after placement (AAHPERD, March 1980)?

Since the IEP sets our specific special education services to be provided, including placement, it is not appropriate to place a child first and then develop an IEP. At state and local options, teachers may *expand* an IEP by writing more specific instructional objectives after placement.

Who is a representative of the public agency, a teacher or administrator (AAHPERD, March 1980)?

The public agency representative can be a teacher, principal, supervisor, or any other administrator as long as the individual serving in this capacity has authority to commit agency resources. A first level criterion in selecting an agency representative is that whatever services are agreed upon at the IEP meeting will actually be provided and the IEP will not be vetoed at higher administrative levels within the agency.

When must IEP objectives be written—before or after placement (AAHPERD, March 1980)?

An IEP must be in effect and short-term instructional objectives written *before* special education and related services are provided to a child with a handicapping condition. However, this applies only to initial placement. State and/or local authorities have options which result in additional details being developed by receiving teachers for inclusion in a child's IEP following placement.

Does the IEP list services needed or those to be provided based on availability (AAHPERD, March 1980)?

Each child with a handicapping condition must be provided all services necessary to meet his or her special education and related needs whether these services are currently available in the agency or not.

Must the IEP specify the extent or amount of services or simply list services to be provided (AAHPERD, March 1980)?

Extent and duration of services must be stated in the IEP so the resource commitment can be clear to parents and other IEP team members. Some general standard of time must be indicated which is both appropriate to the specific service to be provided and clear to all IEP participants.

Is it permissible for an agency to have the IEP completed when the meeting begins (AAHPERD, March 1980)?

It is not appropriate for an agency to present a completed IEP to parents for their signatures. The statute defines the IEP as a written statement developed in a meeting with the agency representative, teacher, and parent. IEP provisions apply to any area in which a student with a handicapping condition has needs requiring special education. Individuals possessing special physical and motor needs identified through appropriate assessment procedures must have these needs addressed in their IEPs. All basic requirements of IEP meetings, contents, development, implementation, and evaluation apply to physical and motor areas when special needs in these areas are identified. Individuals with no special physical and motor needs or for whom only accommodations are needed do not require IEPs for these areas. However, these decisions must be based on appropriate and adequate assessment information about physical and motor functions and abilities of each individual.

What are some of the unanswered questions and issues regarding interpretations of PL 94–142 (AAHPERD, November 1979)?

Various issues surfaced about individualized education programs—whether the IEP is a contract and if so what kind of a contract; whether or not legal suits can be brought against a school district for nondelivery of services; clarification of nature and extent of parental involvement with individualized education programs; problems with IEPs that call for providing available services rather than services needed by a child with a handicapping condition; definitions of short-term instructional objectives; who is entitled to copies of the individualized education plan under confidentiality rules; whether computer generated or other pre-prepared IEPs are acceptable; situations where all children in a special class have the same mimeographed IEPs; IEPs written *before-the-fact* which parents are simply asked to sign at IEP meetings; if IEPs should contain only services above and beyond regular education of the child, services needed by the child but not available from the school district, or activities the child receives in the mainstream; if specific staff assignments should be listed in the IEP; whether a limitation on pupil/teacher ratio should be specifically listed for the child; and whether the length of the child's school day should be specified on the IEP since some children who are bused to school lose instruction time at the beginning and/or end of the school day.

Other topics include least-restrictive environment; inconsistencies in administering and implementing special educational programs within the same local education agency in the same school and even in the same class; what is the official BEH policy dissemination mechanism; who has authority to make policy statements regarding PL 94–142; where to appeal when mixed signals are received; increasing both minimum and maximum ages so that individuals under 3 and over 21 can be legally counted and eligible for special education services guaranteeing a free appropriate education.

REFERENCES

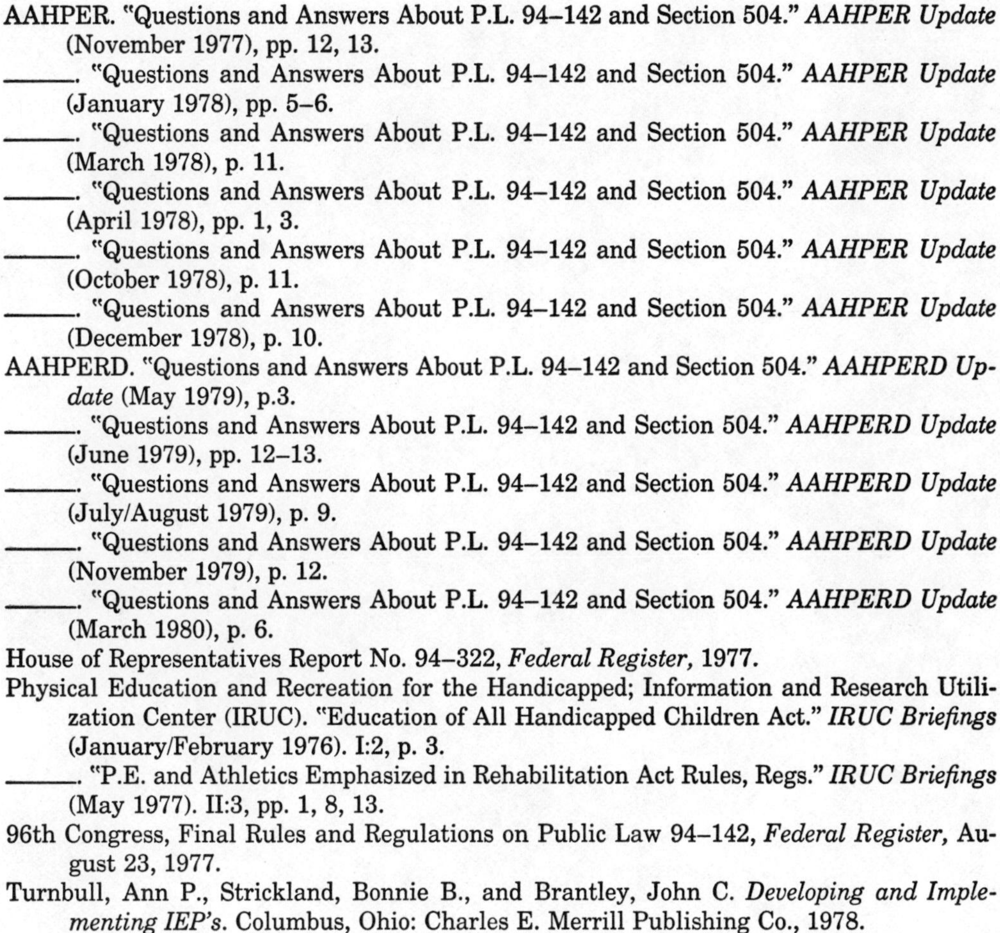

AAHPER. "Questions and Answers About P.L. 94–142 and Section 504." *AAHPER Update* (November 1977), pp. 12, 13.

———. "Questions and Answers About P.L. 94–142 and Section 504." *AAHPER Update* (January 1978), pp. 5–6.

———. "Questions and Answers About P.L. 94–142 and Section 504." *AAHPER Update* (March 1978), p. 11.

———. "Questions and Answers About P.L. 94–142 and Section 504." *AAHPER Update* (April 1978), pp. 1, 3.

———. "Questions and Answers About P.L. 94–142 and Section 504." *AAHPER Update* (October 1978), p. 11.

———. "Questions and Answers About P.L. 94–142 and Section 504." *AAHPER Update* (December 1978), p. 10.

AAHPERD. "Questions and Answers About P.L. 94–142 and Section 504." *AAHPERD Update* (May 1979), p.3.

———. "Questions and Answers About P.L. 94–142 and Section 504." *AAHPERD Update* (June 1979), pp. 12–13.

———. "Questions and Answers About P.L. 94–142 and Section 504." *AAHPERD Update* (July/August 1979), p. 9.

———. "Questions and Answers About P.L. 94–142 and Section 504." *AAHPERD Update* (November 1979), p. 12.

———. "Questions and Answers About P.L. 94–142 and Section 504." *AAHPERD Update* (March 1980), p. 6.

House of Representatives Report No. 94–322, *Federal Register,* 1977.

Physical Education and Recreation for the Handicapped; Information and Research Utilization Center (IRUC). "Education of All Handicapped Children Act." *IRUC Briefings* (January/February 1976). I:2, p. 3.

———. "P.E. and Athletics Emphasized in Rehabilitation Act Rules, Regs." *IRUC Briefings* (May 1977). II:3, pp. 1, 8, 13.

96th Congress, Final Rules and Regulations on Public Law 94–142, *Federal Register,* August 23, 1977.

Turnbull, Ann P., Strickland, Bonnie B., and Brantley, John C. *Developing and Implementing IEP's.* Columbus, Ohio: Charles E. Merrill Publishing Co., 1978.

3

THE PSYCHOMOTOR COMPONENT OF THE INDIVIDUALIZED EDUCATIONAL PROGRAM (IEP)

Public Law (PL) 94–142 requires for each handicapped student who needs specially-designed instruction a written *Individualized Educational Program (IEP).* The IEP is based upon a determination of the handicapped student's present levels of educational performance. A total statement of educational performance includes academic achievement, social adaptation, prevocational and vocational skills, self-help skills, and psychomotor performance levels. The focus of this book is upon the psychomotor component of the IEP, developed in accordance with the stipulations and requirements of PL 94–142.

This chapter describes general procedures and specific steps to follow in order to develop the psychomotor component of the IEP in terms of evaluation and programming. Samples of completed forms are provided. A blank IEP form is to be found at the end of this chapter.

The psychomotor IEP form will provide foundational information to the teacher who, as a member of the IEP team, participates in the writing of the comprehensive IEP for an individual student during the IEP conference with the parent.

GENERAL PROCEDURES

1. Administer the long form or the short form of appropriate age-level section of the *Geddes Psychomotor Inventory (GPI) Part I: Normal Psychomotor Development.*
2. Administer the appropriate checklist(s) of the *Geddes Psychomotor Inventory (GPI) Part II: Checklists for Specific Deviations from Normal Development.*
3. If appropriate, administer additional assessment items or batteries selected from appendix A to this book. Enter a summary of findings on the *GPI Profile.*
4. Enter information gained from part I, part II, and (optional) additional

tests on the *GPI Profile* located at the beginning of each part I age-range section.

5. Using the completed *GPI Profile,* complete the *Psychomotor Individualized Educational Program (IEP)* form (located at the end of this chapter).
6. Implement the *Geddes Psychomotor Development Program (GPDP).*
7. Reassess psychomotor performance levels and revise the IEP form and GPDP accordingly.

To complete the *Psychomotor Individualized Educational Program (IEP)* form,[1] follow these steps:

GPI Part I

1. Select either the long form of the *Geddes Psychomotor Inventory (GPI) Part I: Normal Psychomotor Development* or the subsequent short form that is appropriate for the functional age level of the individual (Infant, Early Childhood, Primary, Intermediate, or Young Adult Level).
2. Arrange the testing situation and materials as indicated.
3. Use *test administration instructions* if indicated for a test item (located at the end of part I).
4. Assess performance levels on the selected part I section and record, using code, in the *pretest* column.[2] Enter date(s) of assessment under "date" in pretest column.
5. If the person is unsuccessful at the selected functional age level for a performance competency, go to a lower (younger) age level and then progress to the highest (oldest) level possible.
6. Enter the information from the pretest column onto the *GPI Profile* provided at the beginning of the selected age-level section.[3]

GPI Part II

7. Select the appropriate checklist(s) of the *Geddes Psychomotor Inventory (GPI) Part II: Checklists for Specific Deviations from Normal Psychomotor Development* according to the particular type(s) of handicapping condition manifested by the individual (mild to moderate subaverage intellectual function, severe to profound subaverage intellectual function, specific learning disabilities, behavior disabilities, and autistic-like conditions).
8. Describe the observed behaviors in the "behavior observed" column. Summarize important findings, especially deviations noted, on the selected profile following Checklist(s) Summary.

---

1. An example of a completed IEP form is on page 29–30.

2. Record the score in the pretest column opposite the selected age level. This score, however, will be entered on the Profile in accordance with actual functional age level. The example on page 32 shows that a teacher should enter the score of 4 steps for "walks (on balance beam)" opposite the Primary level of part I for a 7-year-old child. However, enter the symbol meaning "functions within this age range" at the bottom of the 6–7 years age range on the Profile, since the level of function is below-age.

3. If a child scores in several age range levels of a part I competency, enter the best estimate of age range level on the Profile.

General performance competency levels for the entire age range and not yearly increments have been described from Primary through Young Adult Levels. On the Profile, record beginning or minimal performances at the bottom of the age range, average or satisfactory performances in the middle of the age range, and highly refined or superior performances at the top of the age range.

Additional Assessment Items and Batteries

9. Select, obtain, and administer additional assessment items and batter-ized Educational Program (IEP) form.[5] Identify performance areas, marize the information gained on the selected profile following Other Assessment Items or Batteries—Summary.

Psychomotor Individualized Educational Program (IEP) Form

10. Using the completed *GPI Profile,* complete the Psychomotor Individualized Educational Program (IEP) form.[5] Identify performance areas, goals, and competencies (objectives) to be improved or maintained by the *Geddes Psychomotor Development Program (GPDP).*

Geddes Psychomotor Development Program (GPDP)

11. Implement the Geddes Psychomotor Development Program (GPDP).

Reassess Psychomotor Performance Levels

12. Periodically retest selected performance levels in the appropriate age range section. Record scores in the interim and posttest columns of the GPI part I, long or short forms. Add the information to the previously completed profile. Revise the previously completed IEP form, which would then indicate any necessary changes to be made in the *Geddes Psychomotor Development Program (GPDP).*

PARTIAL SAMPLE OF COMPLETED PSYCHOMOTOR INDIVIDUALIZED EDUCATIONAL PROGRAM (IEP)

Name of student: *Smith, John William* Birthdate: *8* / *1* / *73* C.A.: *7* yr. *1* mo.
mo. day yr.

Class/group: *Special Class* Teacher: *Mrs. Jones* School: *Brown Special Elementary*

Height: *45"* Weight: *60* lbs. Sex: *X* Male ___ Female Primary language: *English*

Handicapping condition(s): *Moderate subaverage intellectual function–Reason for placements: Sep, LRE*

Present Levels of Psychomotor Performance (see attached GPI Profile)

4. Additional evaluative procedures include information and data derived from sources such as student cumulative files, medical referral forms, conferences with student, parents, other educational, medical, or clinical personnel, and teacher observation.

5. The IEP form is located on pages 34–36.

SAMPLE OF GEDDES COMPLETED PSYCHOMOTOR INVENTORY (GPI) PROFILE (1)

ANNUAL GOALS to be achieved by the end of the school year

The student will improve (I) or maintain (M) present levels of psychomotor performance in:

Performance area	*I or M**	*Responsible personnel†*	*Educational service(s)‡*	*Begin mo/yr*	*End mo/yr*
Balance and postural maintenance	*I*	*APE*	*APE 100%*	*9/80*	*6/81*
Locomotion and basic movement	*I*	*APE*	*APE 100%*	*9/80*	*6/81*
Body awareness	*I*	*APE*	*APE 100%*	*9/80*	*6/81*
Perceptual abilities	*I*	*APE, Sp Ed T*	*APE 50%, Sp Ed Cl 50%*	*10/80*	*6/81*
Eye-body coordination	*M*	*Sp Ed T*	*Sp Ed Cl 100%*	*9/80*	*6/81*
Manipulation	*I*	*OT Sp Ed T*	*OT 50% Sp Ed Cl 50%*	*9/80*	*6/81*
Performs on apparatus	*I*	*APE*	*APE 100%*	*2/81*	*3/81*
Aquatics	*N.A.*				
Ball handling	*I*	*APE*	*APE 100%*	*11/80*	*4/81*
Other:‖ Physical Fitness	*I*	*PT, APE*	*PT 50% APE 50%*	*9/80*	*6/81*
Other:‖					

SHORT-TERM INSTRUCTIONAL OBJECTIVES to be fulfilled as intermediary steps to meet goals.

The student will improve (I) or maintain (M) the following performance competencies as measured by the GPI Performance Level indicated for chronological age (C.A.).

Performance Competency	*I or M #*	*Programming§§ Date*	*Infant GPI p. #***	*Early Child GPI p. #***	*Primary GPI p. #***	*Primary GPDP p. #††*	*Intermediate GPI p. #***	*Intermediate GPDP p. #††*	*Young Adult GPI p. #***	*Young Adult GPDP p. #††*
Has head control			42, 45							
Rolls over			42, 45							
Sits			42, 45							
Stands			42, 45							
Specific balance				48, 57						
Crawls			43, 46							
Creeps			43, 46							
Walks			43, 46	48, 57	64, 70	144				
Runs			43, 46	49, 57	64, 70	145	74, 78	184	81, 85	206
Climbs			43, 46	49, 58	64, 70	146	74, 78	184		
Body mechanics			43, 46	49, 58	64, 70	146				
Jumps			43, 46	50, 58	65, 70	147	74, 78	185	81, 85	206
Hops				50, 58	65, 70	148				
Gallops				50, 58	65, 70	149				
Skips				51, 58	65, 70	150				
Total body control							75, 78	186		
Drown-proofing skills							75, 78	187		
Floats and glides							75, 78	187		
Arm and leg strokes							75, 78	187		
Styles of swimming							76, 79	187	82, 85	207
Dives									82, 85	207
Stunts									82, 85	207
Spatial orientation				51, 58	65, 70	151				
Identify body parts				51, 59	66, 71	155				
Laterality					65, 71	151				

SAMPLE OF GEDDES COMPLETED PSYCHOMOTOR INVENTORY (GPI) PROFILE (2)

GEDDES PSYCHOMOTOR INVENTORY (GPI) PROFILE
Section appropriate for Primary Level
(approximately 6-9 years)

	LOCOMOTION AND BASIC MOVEMENT								BODY AWARENESS						PERCEPTUAL ABILITIES			EYE-BODY COORDINATION			MANIPULATION		PERFORMS ON APPARATUS		BALL HANDLING			
AGE RANGE	Walks	Runs	Climbs	Body Mechanics	Jumps	Hops	Gallops	Skips	Spatial Orientation	Laterality	Verticality	Body Image	Midline of Body	Identify Body Parts	Response - Aud. Perception	Response - Vis. Perception	Response - Tact. Perception	Hand Preference	Eye Preference	Foot Preference	Writing and Drawing	Manipulates Objects	Rides Bicycle	Moves Along Horizontal Ladder	Throws	Catches	Kicks	Strikes
8–9																												
7–8			•	X			•	X	•	•			•					?	•	•		•		X				
6–7											•			•	•	•	•								•	•	•	•
	•	•			•	•						•									•		•					

Directions: Enter scores (using code) that best represent the performance levels identified on the Geddes Psychomotor Inventory (GPI). Use different colors to record the following on the chart:

9/1/80 Pretest ____ Interim ____ Posttest
(date) (date) (date)

Code: [•] Functions within this age range [X] Not testable/no performance

[?] Assumed level of function

Name: Smith John William Birthdate: 8 / 1 / 73
(Last) (First) (Middle) mo. day yr.

C.A.: 7, 1 Pretest ______ Interim ______ Posttest Class/Group: Mrs. Jones

Type of Handicapping Condition: subaverage intellectual function - moderate impairment

Checklist(s) Summary: uncoordinated, poor balance, poor arm and abdominal strength, poor leg power, poor spine flexibility, hamstring tightness

Other Assessment Items or Batteries - Summary: ~~AAHPERD Motor Fitness Testing~~ Manual for the Moderately Mentally Retarded (modified for younger age): Sit-ups - below age.

Other: Specific Balance items from Early Childhood Level (GPI): 5-6 yrs level

SAMPLE OF ONE COMPLETED PAGE OF SHORT FORM†

Name of individual: *Smith* (Last) *John* (First) *William* (Middle)

Birthdate: *8* / *1* / *73* (mo. day yr.)

Chronologic Age (C.A.) at: *7* yrs. *1* mo. Pretest ___yrs. ___mo. Interim ___yrs. ___mo. Posttest

GEDDES PSYCHOMOTOR INVENTORY (GPI)
SECTION APPROPRIATE FOR *PRIMARY LEVEL* (approximately 6–9 years)

Assess performance levels according to chronological age. If a child is unsuccessful, go to younger age level and progress to highest (oldest) level possible.

Record scores:

X — Not testable/no performance
?— Assumed level/ inconsistent
Yes— Successful Performance
No — Unsuccessful performance
___"— Number of inches
___#— Number
___'— Number of feet

Enter other pertinent information as indicated or appropriate

Performance levels *LOCOMOTION AND BASIC MOVEMENT*	*Pretest* *Date Score*	*Interim* *Date Score*	*Posttest* *Date Score*
Walks (GPDP p. 144): Alternates (heel-to-toe) 10 steps forward on 2" balance beam‡	*9/1/80* *4* #	#	#
Runs (GPDP p. 145): Runs skillfully around obstacles a distance of 20' (Record *?* well cordinated, *?* arm and leg opposition, *No* dodging, *No* change of direction, *Yes* stopping, and *Yes* starting)	*Yes?*		
Climbs (GPDP p. 146): Climbs on apparatus such as a Lind Climber or playground gym	*Yes*		
Body Mechanics (GPDP p. 146–147): Lifts (by bending at knees) moderately heavy box and carries it close to chest	*X*		
Jumps (GPDP p. 147–148): Does standing broad jump a distance of 35–58"	*34*		
Hops (GPDP p. 148): Hops skillfully 10 or more hops forward (Record *Yes* one foot take-off, *Yes* lands on same foot as takeoff foot, *?* well coordinated)	*8* #	#	#

SAMPLE OF COMPLETED CHECKLIST FOR INDIVIDUALS WITH MILD TO MODERATE SUBAVERAGE INTELLECTUAL FUNCTION

Name: *Smith, John*

*Behavior**	*Behavior Observed†*
Locomotion and Basic Movement	
Moves in an uncoordinated or jerky pattern	*Yes—especially in precise skills*
Frequently stumbles or loses balance	*Yes—especially when changing directions quickly*
Does not swing arms in cross pattern (alternation of arms and legs) while walking or running	*Yes?*
Physical Proficiency	
Unable to maintain grasp while hanging from overhead bar (after age 6)	*Yes (Unable)*
Unable to perform bent-knee sit-ups according to age (after age 7)	*Yes*
Unable to jump vertically off floor so that both feet leave floor simultaneously (after age 4)	*No*
Unable to touch head to knees while in straight-knee sitting position (after age 7)	*Yes*
Becomes overly fatigued, takes excessive rest breaks, and/or breathes too hard in proportion to physical activity performed	*No*

PSYCHOMOTOR INDIVIDUALIZED EDUCATIONAL PROGRAM (IEP) (1)

Name of student: ______________________ Birthdate: ___/___/___ C.A.: ___ yr. ___ mo.

Class/group: ____________ Teacher: ____________ School: ____________

Height: ___" Weight: ___lbs. Sex: Male___ Female___ Primary language: ____________

Handicapping condition(s): ____________. Reason for placement:§ ____________

Present Levels of Psychomotor Performance—see attached GPI Profile

ANNUAL GOALS to be achieved by the end of the school year.
The student will improve (I) or maintain (M) psychomotor performance levels in:

Performance area	*I or M**	*Responsible personnel†*	*Educational service(s)‡*	*Begin mo/yr*	*End mo/yr*
Balance and postural maintenance					
Locomotion and basic movement					
Body awareness					
Perceptual abilities					
Eye-body coordination					
Manipulation					
Performs on apparatus					
Aquatics					
Ball handling					
Other:‖					

§Enter the reason(s) for the type of education placement: LRE—least restrictive environment, Sep—child is enrolled in separate special facility.

*In the I or M column, enter I (Improve) opposite the performance areas that have been identified on the GPI Profile as below age. Enter M (Maintain) opposite the at-age or above-age areas. If an area is not applicable, enter N. A.

†Enter the personnel responsible for attaining this annual goal: APE—adapted physical education teacher, T—regular classroom teacher, SP Ed T—special education teacher, OT—occupational therapist, PT—physical therapist, ST—speech therapist, N—nurse, Cons—consultant, P—parent or legal guardian, A—aide, Ad—administrator or supervisor, Psy—psychologist, Com—community agency personnel.

‡Enter the educational service(s) that will be provided the student: APE—adapted physical education, PE—regular physical education, PT—physical therapy, OT—occupational therapy, ST—speech therapy, Sp Ed Cl—special education class, Reg Ed Cl—regular education class.

After each code, enter the percentage of time for each service. Example: APE 90%, PT 10%. Teachers may wish also to add the average number of minutes per week for this service (i.e. 50 min./week).

‖Add other teacher-selected performance areas.

PSYCHOMOTOR INDIVIDUALIZED EDUCATIONAL PROGRAM (IEP) (2)

SHORT-TERM INSTRUCTIONAL OBJECTIVES to be fulfilled as intermediary steps to meet goals.
The student will improve (I) or maintain (M) the following performance competencies as measured by the GPI Performance Level indicated for chronological age (C.A.).

		Program-	Infant	Early Child	Primary		Intermediate		Young Adult	
Performance Competency	*I or M #*	*ming§§ Date*	*GPI p. #***	*GPI p. #***	*GPI p. #***	*GPDP p. #††*	*GPI p. #***	*GPDP p. #††*	*GPI p. #***	*GPDP p. #††*
Has head control			42, 45							
Rolls over			42, 45							
Sits			42, 45							
Stands			42, 45							
Specific balance				48, 57						
Crawls			43, 46							
Creeps			43, 46							
Walks			43, 46	48, 57	64, 70	144				
Runs			43, 46	49, 57	64, 70	145	74, 78	184	81, 85	206
Climbs			43, 46	49, 58	64, 70	146	74, 78	184		
Body mechanics			43, 46	49, 58	64, 70	146				
Jumps			43, 46	50, 58	65, 70	147	74, 78	185	81, 85	206
Hops				50, 58	65, 70	148				
Gallops				50, 58	65, 70	149				
Skips				51, 58	65, 70	150				
Total body control							75, 78	186		
Drown-proofing skills							75, 78	187		
Floats and glides							75, 78	187		
Arm and leg strokes							75, 78	187		
Styles of swimming							76, 79	187	82, 85	207
Dives									82, 85	207
Stunts									82, 85	207
Spatial orientation				51, 58	65, 70	151				
Identify body parts				51, 59	66, 71	155				
Laterality					65, 71	151				
Verticality					66, 71	152				
Body image					66, 71	153				
Midline of body					66, 71	154				
Psychomotor response to:										
Auditory perception					66, 71	156				
Visual perception					66, 71	157				
Tactile perception					67, 71	158				
Hand preference				51, 59	67, 71	159				
Eye preference				51, 59	67, 71	159				
Foot preference				51, 59	67, 71	159				
Grasp and release			43, 46	52, 59						
Builds tower			44, 46	52, 59						
Writing and drawing			44, 46	52, 59	67, 71	160				
Places cubes			44, 46	53, 60						

#Enter I (Improve), M (Maintain) or N. A. (Not applicable) based upon interpretation of the GPI Profile.

§§Enter date programming started for performance competency. Circle date when objective accomplished.

**Page number(s) of the Geddes Psychomotor Inventory (GPI), Part I, on which the competency is described.

††Page number(s) of the Geddes Psychomotor Development Program (GPDP) on which activities are described to develop this performance competency.

PSYCHOMOTOR INDIVIDUALIZED EDUCATIONAL PROGRAM (IEP) (2)

SHORT-TERM INSTRUCTIONAL OBJECTIVES to be fulfilled as intermediary steps to meet goals
The student will improve (I) or maintain (M) the following performance competencies.

Performance Competency	*I or M*	*Programming Date§*	*Infant GPI p. #***	*Early Child GPI p. #***	*Primary GPI p. #***	*Primary GPDP p. #††*	*Intermediate GPI p. #***	*Intermediate GPDP p. #††*	*Young Adult GPI p. #***	*Young Adult GPDP p. #††*
Places forms			44, 46	53, 60						
Manipulates objects				53, 59	67, 71	160				
Rides tricycle				53, 60						
Rides bicycle					67, 71	161				
Moves along horizontal ladder					68, 71	161				
Uses horizontal bar							75, 78	185		
Uses vaulting box							75, 78	186		
Throws			44, 46	53, 60	68, 71	162	76, 79	188	82, 85	207
Catches				54, 61	68, 71	163	76, 79	189	83, 86	208
Kicks				55, 61	68, 71	164	77, 79	189	83, 86	208
Strikes				56, 61	69, 71	165	77, 79	190	83, 86	209
Other:‡‡										

Projected Date for Annual Review of IEP: ________ Reevaluation (every 3 years): ________________

Evaluator________________________________ Title________________________________

‡‡Add other teacher-selected performance competencies.

II

GEDDES PSYCHOMOTOR INVENTORY (GPI)
An Assessment Model for Formulating Individualized Educational Programs

4

GPI PART I
Normal Psychomotor Development

Part I of the Geddes Psychomotor Inventory (GPI) describes psychomotor skill performances that have been reported in such sources as observational studies, empirical and case history evidence, cross-sectional and longitudinal studies, experimental studies, and other related literature. Since the inventories on developmental milestones describe motor performance intermingled with other developmental areas (such as adaptive behavior) and since existing developmental scales are narrow in age range, evaluation of psychomotor skills from beginning to later, more refined levels is difficult. Therefore the GPI emphasizes a different perspective in that it is concerned only with psychomotor development and from a much wider age range (infancy through young adulthood).

Competency statements are presented in accordance with the available literature:

- Chronologic age ranges for performances have been widened to include the majority of specified ages indicated by the literature.
- The age ranges include both boys' and girls' performance (skill analyses provide information regarding expected superior performance of either boys or girls for that skill).
- If necessary, terminology has been changed if several sources used different wording to mean the same thing.
- When appropriate, several competencies have been combined in one age range with the understanding that later performances will be more skillful than earlier attempts.
- If criteria specifying time, distance, length, numbers, or form are available, they are described for a skill.
- There is often disagreement in the literature regarding ages for appearance of skills, especially after the infancy level. In addition, no developmental scales were available for portions of the older age ranges.

- The total GPI long form compilation describes both qualitative and quantitative criteria determined from existing literature and from the author's previous research investigations.

In part I, basic skills such as walking, running, jumping, throwing, and catching are viewed as sequences on a continuum from infancy or early childhood through young adulthood.[1] These performance competencies are developed following acquisition of necessary foundational prerequisites during earlier developmental periods. Representative competencies have been described in age range standards in the GPI from Infant through Young Adulthood levels.[2] The teacher should assess each individual on an appropriate age range standard section so that comparison to normal psychomotor development might be made. If necessary because of a handicapping condition, competencies should be modified and special methods should be used to obtain performance, and/or reference to a younger age range should be made.

A short form is provided following the GPI long form at each age level. Teachers may use the short form as a screening technique since it shortens the testing time. Students who have difficulties on the short form should be tested on the GPI long form, especially in sections where delayed or impaired performance has been demonstrated.

Teachers should use part I of the GPI to complete the *GPI Profile* presented at the beginning of each age range section.[3] A common-sense approach should be employed. If a student performs at or near an age range standard, this is probably normal progression. Obviously abnormalities such as obesity or a muscular impairment will affect motor performance. Teachers should consider the entire person in analyzing the developmental profile to determine if extreme delays or quite erratic performances in several areas are demonstrated. For example, if a child scores low in only one or two areas, it might mean only that he or she has not had such training or experience in this skill.

Part I reflects the available literature regarding psychomotor development. At the infant level, specific information for representative performance has been described in the literature for narrow time spans such as for 0 to 6 or 6 to 12 months of age. At the early childhood level, specific information has been reported for many of the performance areas in these age ranges. For example, competencies have been stated for 2 to 3 years or 5 to 6 years. This facilitates the charting of functional levels on the *GPI Profiles* for Infant and Early Childhood levels. However, from Primary Level through Young Adult Level, less specific data have been revealed. Therefore general performance competency levels for each age range (not yearly increments) are described from Primary through Young Adult Levels.

1. Aquatic and apparatus skills were added at some of the older age levels since these skills were considered too important not to be identified.

2. The term *level* is used intentionally instead of *stage* to avoid indicating that skills are observed in abrupt, rigid, hierarchical, and qualitative changes that are very different from preceding stages.

3. Additional instructions are given in the "Steps to Follow" part on page 28.

GEDDES PSYCHOMOTOR INVENTORY (GPI) PROFILE
Section appropriate for Infant Level
(approximately neonatal period to 2 years)

	BALANCE AND POSTURAL MAINTENANCE				LOCOMOTION AND BASIC MOVEMENT							MANIPULATION					BALL HANDLING
AGE RANGE	Has Head Control	Rolls Over	Sits	Stands	Crawls	Creeps	Walks	Runs	Climbs	Body Mechanics	Jumps	Grasp & Release	Builds Tower	Writing & Drawing	Places Cubes	Places Forms	Throws
1-2 yrs																	
6-12 mo																	
0-6 mo																	

Directions: Enter scores (using code) that best represent the performance levels identified on the Geddes Psychomotor Inventory (GPI). Use different colors to record the following on the chart:

_____Pretest _____Interim _____Posttest
(date) (date) (date)

Code: [•] Functions within this age range [X] Not testable/no performance

[?] Assumed level of function

Name: ______________________________ Birthdate: ___/___/___
(Last) (First) (Middle) mo. day yr.

C.A.: ______Pretest ______Interim ______Posttest Class/Group: __________

Type of Handicapping Condition: ______________________________

Checklist(s) Summary: ______________________________

Other Assessment Items or Batteries - Summary: ______________________________

____

GEDDES PSYCHOMOTOR INVENTORY (GPI)

LONG FORM—INFANT LEVEL (1)

Name of individual: ____
(Last) (First) (Middle)

Birthdate: ___/___/___ Chronologic ___yrs. ___mo. Pretest ___yrs. ___mo. Interim
mo. day yr. Age (C. A.) at: ___yrs. ___mo. Posttest

GEDDES PSYCHOMOTOR INVENTORY (GPI)
SECTION APPROPRIATE FOR *INFANT LEVEL* (approximately neonatal period to 2 years)

Assess performance levels according to chronologic age. If a child is unsuccessful, go to younger age level and progress to highest (oldest) level possible.

Record scores: X— Not testable/no performance ?— Assumed level/ inconsistent
Yes— Successful performance No— Unsuccessful
___#— Number

Enter other pertinent information as indicated or appropriate

Performance levels		*Pretest* *Date Score*	*Interim* *Date Score*	*Posttest* *Date Score*
BALANCE AND POSTURAL MAINTENANCE				
Has Head Control Materials: Tumbling mat				
0–6 mo.	*Lifts head up and upper chest off mat while in prone lying position (4–6 mo.)	______	______	______
	Holds head up when pulled to sitting (4–5 mo.)	______	______	______
Rolls Over Materials: Mat				
0–6 mo.	Immature attempts to roll over	______	______	______
6–12 mo.	*Rolls from prone to supine and from supine to prone lying (6–7 mo.)	______	______	______
Sits Materials: Tumbling mat, small chair				
0–6 mo.	*Grasps fingers of examiner and pulls self upright to sitting position (4–7 mo.)	______	______	______
	Holds self upright and head erect with support (4–7 mo.)	______	______	______
6–12 mo.	*Sits without support in various positions (7–9 mo.)	______	______	______
	Regains sitting position after leaning forward (9 mo.)	______	______	______
1–2 yrs.	*Sits on small chair (14–18 mo.)	______	______	______
Stands Materials: Table				
6–12 mo.	*Supports part of weight in standing position while holding onto table (6–10 mo.)	______	______	______
	Supports full weight in standing position while held by examiner (6–10 mo.)	______	______	______

LONG FORM—INFANT LEVEL (2)

	Pulls self to standing position without support (9–10 mo.)			
	Stands independently (11–13 mo.)			
1–2 yrs.	*Stands independently (11–13 mo.)			

LOCOMOTION AND BASIC MOVEMENT

Crawls (Sometimes not observed)
Materials: Tumbling mat
Skill analysis: Propels self forward with abdomen on floor

6–12 mo.	*Crawls forward in effective fashion (7–10 mo.)			

Creeps (Sometimes not observed)
Materials: Tumbling mat
Skill analysis: Propels self forward on hands and knees with abdomen off floor

6–12 mo.	*Creeps forward in effective fashion (9–11 mo.)			

Walks
Materials: None

1–2 yrs.	Walks with support (12–13 mo.)			
	*Walks without support (13–15 mo.)			

Runs

1–2 yrs.	*Runs with poor coordination and incomplete balance (improves later) (18 mo.–2 yrs.)			

Climbs
Materials: Stairs (protect against falling)

1–2 yrs.	*Climbs *up* stairs one at a time with hand(s) held (18–23 mo.)			
	Climbs *down* stairs one at a time with support (18–30 mo.)§			
	Climbs up on small chair and sits down (14–24 mo.) or stands up (19–24 mo.)			

Body Mechanics
Materials: Push/pull toy

1–2 yrs.	*Pushes and pulls toy around floor (18–30 mo.)			

Jumps
Materials: Low (about 6″ high) platform

1–2 yrs.	*Steps off low platform (18 mo.)			
	Jumps in place with both feet together (18–30 mo.)			

MANIPULATION

Grasp and Release
Materials: Rattle, small object, cube

0–6 mo.	*Grasps rattle (2–4 mo.)			
	Reaches for small object (2–5 mo.)			
	Transfers cube from one hand to other hand (5–7 mo.)			
6–12 mo.	*Uses pincer grasp on small objects (7–12 mo.)			

LONG FORM—INFANT LEVEL (3)

Builds Tower
Materials: 6 cubes

1–2 yrs.	*Builds tower of 6 cubes (18–30 mo.)	#	#	#

Writing and Drawing
Materials: 8½ × 11" paper, pencils, crayons

1–2 yrs.	*Makes spontaneous scribbles with crayon or pencil (18–24 mo.)			
	Imitates vertical strokes (18 mo.–3 yrs.)			

Places Cubes in a Cup or Box
Materials: 16 cubes, cup or box

1–2 yrs.	*Places 10–16 cubes in a cup or box (18–30 mo.)	#	#	#

Places Forms in Formboard or Pegboard
Materials: Formboard, pegboard

1–2 yrs.	*Places triangle, square, and circle in formboard (18 mo.–3 yrs.)			
	Places 2 round and 2 square blocks in formboard (18–24 mo.)			
	Places 6 round pegs in pegboard (18–24 mo.)			

BALL HANDLING

Throws
Materials: Small cube, small rubber ball

6–12 mo.	Releases small cube in crude throwing fashion without aim (6–12 mo.)			
	*Throws object with some aim by use of arms only (12 mo.)			
1–2 yrs.	*Throws small rubber ball (18–24 mo.)			

*If several items are described, select this representative item and omit others in order to shorten testing time. Use the short form provided following the long form.

§Demonstrate with verbal instruction to "go down one step at a time."

SHORT FORM†—INFANT LEVEL (1)

Name of individual: ____
(Last) (First) (Middle)

Birthdate: __/__/__ Chronologic __yrs. __mo. Pretest __yrs. __mo. Interim
mo. day yr. Age (C. A.) at: __yrs. __mo. Posttest

GEDDES PSYCHOMOTOR INVENTORY (GPI)
SECTION APPROPRIATE FOR *INFANT LEVEL* (approximately neonatal period to 2 years)

Assess performance levels according to chronologic age. If a child is unsuccessful, go to younger age level and progress to highest (oldest) level possible.

Record scores: X—Not testable/no performance ? —Assumed level/inconsistent
Yes—Successful performance No —Unsuccessful
__# —Number

Enter other pertinent information as indicated or appropriate.

Performance Levels	*Pretest Date Score*	*Interim Date Score*	*Posttest Date Score*
BALANCE AND POSTURAL MAINTENANCE			
Has Head Control			
0–6 mo. Lifts head up and upper chest off mat while in prone lying position (4–6 mo.)			
Rolls Over			
6–12 mo. Rolls from prone to supine and from supine to prone lying (6–7 mo.)			
Sits			
0–6 mo. Grasps fingers of examiner and pulls self upright to sitting position (4–7 mo).			
6–12 mo. Sits without support in various positions (7–9) mo.			
1–2 yrs. Sits on a small chair (14–18 mo.)			
Stands			
6–12 mo. Supports part of weight in standing position while holding onto table (6–10 mo.)			
1–2 yrs. Stands independently (11–13 mo.)			

†See GPI long form for details on assessing performance levels and recording scores. This short form contains only representative items in abbreviated format.

GEDDES PSYCHOMOTOR INVENTORY (GPI)

SHORT FORM—INFANT LEVEL (2)

LOCOMOTION AND BASIC MOVEMENT

Crawls

6–12 mo. Crawls forward in effective fashion (7–10 mo.) ____ ____ ____

Creeps

6–12 mo. Creeps forward in effective fashion (9–11 mo.) ____ ____ ____

Walks

1–2 yrs. Walks without support (13–15 mo.) ____ ____ ____

Runs

1–2 yrs. Runs with poor coordination and incomplete balance (improves later) (18 mo.–2 yrs.) ____ ____ ____

Climbs

1–2 yrs. Climbs *up* stairs one at a time with hand(s) held (18–23 mo.) ____ ____ ____

Body Mechanics

1–2 yrs. Pushes and pulls toy around floor (18–30 mo.) ____ ____ ____

Jumps

1–2 yrs. Steps off low platform (18 mo.) ____ ____ ____

MANIPULATION

Grasp and Release

0–6 mo. Grasps rattle (2–4 mo.) ____ ____ ____

6–12 mo. Uses pincer grasp on small objects (7–12 mo.) ____ ____ ____

Builds Tower

1–2 yrs. Builds tower of 6 cubes (18–30 mo.) ____# ____# ____#

Writing and Drawing

1–2 yrs. Makes spontaneous scribbles with crayon or pencil (18–24 mo.) ____ ____ ____

Places Cubes in a Cup or Box

1–2 yrs. Places 10–16 cubes in a cup or box (18–30 mo.) ____# ____# ____#

Places Forms in Formboard or Pegboard

1–2 yrs. Places triangle, square, and circle in formboard (18 mo.–3 yrs.) ____ ____ ____

BALL HANDLING

Throws

6–12 mo. Throws object with some aim by use of arms only (12 mo.) ____ ____ ____

1–2 yrs. Throws small rubber ball (18–24 mo.) ____ ____ ____

GEDDES PSYCHOMOTOR INVENTORY (GPI) PROFILE
Section appropriate for Early Childhood Level (approximately 2-6 years)

	BALANCE & POSTURAL MAINTENANCE	LOCOMOTION & BASIC MOVEMENT								BODY AWARENESS		EYE-BODY COORDINATION	MANIPULATION						PERFORMS ON APPARATUS	BALL HANDLING			
AGE RANGE	Specific Balance	Walks	Runs	Climbs	Body Mechanics	Jumps	Hops	Gallops	Skips	Spatial Orientation	Identify Body Parts	Hand, Eye, Foot Preference	Grasp and Release	Builds Tower	Writing and Drawing	Manipulates Objects	Places Cubes in Cup	Places Forms	Rides Tricycle, Bicycle	Throws	Catches	Kicks	Strikes
5-6																							
4-5																							
3-4																							
2-3																							

Directions: Enter scores (using code) that best represent the performance levels identified on the Geddes Psychomotor Inventory (GPI). Use different colors to record the following on the chart:

_____Pretest _____Interim _____Posttest
(date) (date) (date)

Code: [•] Functions within this age range [X] Not testable/no performance

[?] Assumed level of function

Name: ______________________________ Birthdate: ___/___/___
(Last) (First) (Middle) mo. day yr.

C.A.: _____Pretest _____Interim _____Posttest Class/Group: __________

Type of Handicapping Condition: ______________________

Checklist(s) Summary: ______________________

Other Assessment Items or Batteries - Summary: ______________________

____

LONG FORM—EARLY CHILDHOOD LEVEL (1)

Name of individual: ______________________________
(Last) (First) (Middle)

Birthdate: ___/___/___ Chronologic __yrs. __mo. Pretest __yrs. __mo. Interim
mo. day yr. Age (C.A.) at: __yrs. __mo. Posttest

GEDDES PSYCHOMOTOR INVENTORY (GPI)
SECTION APPROPRIATE FOR *EARLY CHILDHOOD LEVEL* (approximately 2–6 years)

Assess performance levels according to chronologic age. If a child is unsuccessful, go to younger age level and progress to highest (oldest) level possible.

Record scores:

X— Not testable/no performance	?— Assumed level/inconsistent
Yes—Successful performance	No— Unsuccessful performance
___"—Number of inches	___#— Number
___'—Number of feet	___min— Number of minutes
___sec—Number of seconds	

Enter other pertinent information as indicated or appropriate

Performance levels	*Pretest* *Date Score*	*Interim* *Date Score*	*Posttest* *Date Score*
BALANCE AND POSTURAL MAINTENANCE (If indicated, select additional items from Infant Level)			
Specific Balance Materials: Stopwatch			
2–3 yrs. *Stands on preferred foot, eyes open, for 1–5 sec.‡ (Record____R,____L foot)	sec	sec	sec
3–4 yrs. *Stands on preferred foot, eyes open, for 2–10 sec.‡ (Record____R,____L foot)	sec	sec	sec
4–5 yrs. *Stands on preferred foot, eyes open, for 4–15 sec.‡ (Record____R,____L foot)	sec	sec	sec
Stands on nonpreferred foot, eyes open, for 2–5 sec.‡ (Record____R,____L foot)	sec	sec	sec
5–6 yrs. *Stands on preferred foot, eyes open, for 5–20 sec.‡ (Record____R,____L foot)	sec	sec	sec
Stands on nonpreferred foot, eyes open, for 5–20 sec.‡ (Record____R,____L foot)	sec	sec	sec
LOCOMOTION AND BASIC MOVEMENT			
Walks Materials: 2", 4", 6", 8" wide balance beams (4" high), chalk			
2–3 yrs. *Alternates 10 steps (heel-to-toe) forward on 8" balance beam‡	#	#	#
Alternates 6–10 steps (heel-to-toe) forward on 6" balance beam‡	#	#	#

LONG FORM—EARLY CHILDHOOD LEVEL (2)

3–4 yrs.	*Alternates 10 steps (heel-to-toe) forward on 6″ balance beam‡	#	#	#
	Slides (no alternation) feet along 4″ balance beam‡			
4–5 yrs.	*Alternates 10 steps (heel-to-toe) forward on 4″ balance beam (4–6 yrs.)‡	#	#	#
	Walks on a circle 21″ in diameter, 1″ wide on floor (allow one step-off)			
5–6 yrs.	*Alternates 2–6 steps (heel-to-toe) forward on 2″ balance beam‡	#	#	#
	Alternates 10 steps (heel-to-toe) forward on 4″ balance beam (4–6 yrs)‡	#	#	#

Runs
Materials: Obstacles

2–3 yrs.	*Runs in basic pattern of coordinated arm and leg opposition with adequate balance			
3–4 yrs.	*Runs with improved coordination. Arm and leg opposition combined with stopping and starting skills is seen.			
4–5 & 5–6 yrs	*Runs in well-coordinated pattern that combines arm and leg opposition, stopping and starting skills, and dodging and change of direction skills around obstacles (record)			

Climbs
Materials: Stairs, ladder, playground gym (protect against falling)

2–3 yrs.	*Climbs *up* stairs alternating feet, holding stair rail			
	Climb *down* stairs, one step at a time, holding stair rail (18–30 mo.)			
3–4 yrs.	*Climbs *up* stairs alternating feet, without support			
	Climbs *down* stairs, one step at a time, without support (3–5 yrs)§			
	Climbs playground gym apparatus			
4–5 yrs.	*Climbs *down* stairs, one step at a time, without support (3–5 yrs.)			
	Climbs *up* ladder one rung at a time			
5–6 yrs.	*Climbs *down* stairs, alternating feet without support			
	Climbs *up* and *down* ladder alternating feet			

Body Mechanics
Materials: Push/pull toy, obstacle, large box with medium-weight objects in it

2–3 yrs.	*Pushes and pulls toy around floor (18–30 mo.)			
3–4 yrs.	*Runs around obstacles while pulling a pull toy			
4-5 & 5–6 yrs.	*Lifts (without much bending at knees) moderately heavy box and carries it close to chest			

GEDDES PSYCHOMOTOR INVENTORY (GPI) PROFILE

LONG FORM—EARLY CHILDHOOD LEVEL (3)

	Pushes moderately heavy large box (using leg muscles) with both hands at top of box and feet together on floor			

Jumps

Materials: String, tape, tape measure, short jump rope, 12″ and 18″ high platform

Skill analysis: Jumping usually progresses from one foot stepping down to floor onto other foot, subsequently followed by a jump on one foot from a height to a landing on the other foot. Next, a takeoff with two feet from a height to a landing on two feet is seen. Later, a child will do running broad jumps followed by standing broad jumps. Child must develop the concept of pushing off with both feet before he or she is able to do a standing broad jump or a vertical jump.

2–3 yrs.	*Does standing broad jump a distance of 4–16″‡ǁ	″	″	″
	Jumps from 12″ height with one foot step-off to either ____ one or ____ both feet landing (Record)			
	Jumps (two foot takeoff) over string extended horizontally at a 2–8″ height	″ height	″ height	″ height
3–4 yrs.	*Does standing broad jump a distance of 14–32″‡	″	″	″
	Jumps from 18″ height with two foot step-off to a two feet landing			
	Does vertical jump at height of 1–6″ (Record____″ stretch height, ____R, ____L hand)	″	″	″
	Does running broad jump a distance of 24–34″‡	″	″	″
4–5 yrs.	*Does standing broad jump a distance of 20–38″‡	″	″	″
	Does vertical jump a height of 2–7″‡ (record ____″ stretch height, ____R, ____L hand)	″	″	″
5–6 yrs.	*Does standing broad jump a distance of 24–45″‡	″	″	″
	Does vertical jump a height of 3–9″‡ (Record ____″ stretch height, ____R, ____L hand)	″	″	″
	Does running broad jump a distance of 28–35″	″	″	″
	Starts to jump short rope			

Hops

Materials: None

Skill analysis: Body is lifted off the ground by action of takeoff on one foot and landing on the same foot. Hopping on one foot usually follows jumping skills. Previous literature indicates that girls often excel in hopping. This may be because of hopping experience in games traditionally played by girls. Recent cultural changes in sex role-playing might alter this.

2–3 yrs.	Hopping is not usually seen			
3–4 yrs.	*Hops skillfully (see skill analysis above) 1–7 hops forward	#	#	#
4–5 yrs.	*Hops skillfully (see skill analysis above) 3–10 hops forward	#	#	#
5–6 yrs.	Hops skillfully (see skill analysis above) 7–10 hops forward	#	#	#

Gallops

Materials: None

Skill analysis: Uneven leap and walk-step combination with one foot always leading. Galloping appears sooner than skipping. Form is more important than number of repetitions. Skillful galloping may not be achieved until 5–6 years of age.

2–3 yrs. Galloping is not often observed although it might appear at about 3 yrs.				
3–4 yrs. *Gallops in basic pattern (see skill analysis above) with stiff and inconsistent movements				
4–5 years *Gallops skillfully (see skill analysis above) 1–3 gallops		#	#	#
5–6 years. *Gallops skillfully (see skill analysis above) 10 or more gallops forward		#	#	#

Skips
Materials: None
Skill analysis: Combination of a walk-step followed by a hop ("step-hop") by alternating feet. Skipping initially is confused with galloping by the children. Skipping appears after hopping. Girls often are more skillful which is probably due to skipping experience.

2–3 yrs. Skipping is not often observed			
3–4 yrs. *Skipping may not be observed although it might appear at about 4 yrs. of age.			
4–5 yrs. *Starts to skip in basic pattern (see skill analysis above) 1–3 skips	#	#	#
5–6 yrs. *Skips skillfully (see skill analysis above) 10 or more skips foward	#	#	#

BODY AWARENESS

Spatial Orientation
Materials: 2 chairs, obstacles
Skill analysis: Awareness of space around oneself in terms of distance, form, direction, and position.

2–3 yrs. *Moves quickly between two chairs (about 3′ apart) without touching			
3–4, 4–5, & 5–6 yrs. *Negotiates obstacles in obstacle course (runs between, forward, backward, and slides sideways) without touching			

Identify Body Parts
Materials: None
Skill analysis: Concept and awareness of parts of one's own body.

*Touches body parts without confusion (say "touch your ____") (Record below)

2–3 yrs. ____eyes, ____ears, ____nose			
3–4, 4–5, & 5–6 yrs. ____eyes, ____ears, ____nose, ____feet, ____mouth, ____hips (more often at 5–6 yrs.)			

EYE-BODY COORDINATION

Hand, Eye, and Foot Preference
Materials: 9½″ playground ball, cube, kaleidoscope

LONG FORM—EARLY CHILDHOOD LEVEL (5)

2–3 yrs. Hand, eye, and foot preferences may or may not be present ____ ____ ____

3–4,
4–5, &
5–6 yrs. *Shows some hand preference to pick up a cube with one hand (definite preference 4–6 yrs.) (Record ____R, ____L hand) ____ ____ ____

*Shows increasing eye preference in looking through kaleidoscope (Record ____R, ____L eye) ____ ____ ____

*Shows increasing foot preference in kicking stationary ball (Record ____R, ____L foot) ____ ____ ____

MANIPULATION

Grasp and Release
Materials: Pencils, crayons

2–3 yrs. *Closes fist and moves thumb ____ ____ ____

3–4 yrs. *Touches thumb to two fingers on same hand ____ ____ ____

4–5 &
5–6 yrs. *Grasps and releases pencils and crayons ____ ____ ____

Builds Tower
Materials: 10 or more cubes

2–3 yrs. *Builds tower of 6 cubes ____# ____# ____#

3–4 yrs. *Builds tower of 7–10 cubes ____# ____# ____#

4–5 yrs. *Builds tower of 10 cubes ____# ____# ____#

5–6 yrs. *Builds tower of 10 or more cubes ____# ____# ____#

Writing and Drawing
Materials: 8½ × 11″ paper, pencils, crayons

2–3 yrs. *Imitates vertical strokes on paper ____ ____ ____

Imitates horizontal strokes on paper ____ ____ ____

Imitates the form of a cross with 2 or more crude strokes on paper ____ ____ ____

3–4 yrs. *Draws head of person on paper with one major body part (say "draw a person") ____ ____ ____

Copies the letters__V, __H, __T on paper ____ ____ ____

4–5 yrs. *Draws a person with 2 to 6 major parts (say "draw a person") on paper ____ ____ ____

Copies the forms ____cross and ____square on paper ____ ____ ____

Copies __V, __H, __T and __O on paper ____ ____ ____

5–6 yrs. *Draws recognizable person on paper (say "draw a person"). (Record ____head, ____trunk, ____legs, ____arms) ____ ____ ____

Copies the forms ____square, ____triangle, and ____ rectangle on paper ____ ____ ____

Prints letters, numerals, and simple words on paper ____ ____ ____

LONG FORM—EARLY CHILDHOOD LEVEL (6)

Manipulates Objects
Materials: Book, 8½ × 11″ paper, scissors

2–3 yrs.	*Turns pages of book one at a time			
	Begins to cut with scissors			
3–4 yrs.	*Cuts paper into long lengths			
	Folds piece of paper lengthwise			
4–5 & 5–6 yrs.	*Cuts triangles out of paper by use of scissors			

Places Cubes in Cup
Materials: 16 or more cubes, cup

2–3 yrs.	*Places 10–16 cubes in a cup	#	#	#
3–4, 4–5, & 5–6 yrs.	*Places 16 or more cubes in a cup	#	#	#

Places Forms
Materials: Forms, formboard

2–3 & 3–4 yrs.	*Places the forms ____triangle, ____square, and ____ circle in formboard			
4–5 & 5–6 yrs.	*Places 4–10 forms in formboard	#	#	#

PERFORMS ON APPARATUS

Rides Tricycle, Bicycle
Materials: Tricycle, bicycle, obstacles

2–3 yrs.	*Starts to ride tricycle			
3–4 & 4–5 yrs.	*Rides tricycle in small circles and around obstacles			
5–6 yrs.	*Starts to ride bicycle			

BALL HANDLING

Throws
Materials: 9½″ and 16¼″ rubber playground balls, small softball, tape, tape measure
Skill analysis: Throwing progression usually is observed from a crude release of an object by an infant to a basically mature throwing pattern at about 5–6 years. Evidently cultural opportunities and training experiences affect ball-throwing skill development. Poorer throwing performance by girls may be due to lack of experience rather than because of sex differences. Yearly improvement is observed in measures of velocity, form, accuracy, and distance.

2–3 yrs.	*SKILL FORM—Softball Throw			
	The *hand* is brought *backward* until *ball over shoulder.*			
	The *arm* is brought *forward and downward* during ball release.			
	There is *no body rotation,*			

LONG FORM—EARLY CHILDHOOD LEVEL (7)

no shifting of weight, and
no opposition of feet.
Throws 9½" ball 30–70"‡ " " "
Throws 16¼" ball 24–60"‡ " " "
Throws softball 50–80"‡ " " "

3–4 yrs. *SKILL FORM—Softball Throw
The *arm* is brought *backward and sideward* until *ball is over shoulder.*
The *arm* is brought *forward and downward* during ball release.
There may be *slight body rotation* but
no shifting of weight and
no opposition of feet.
Throws 9½" ball 35–100"‡ " " "
Throws 16¼" ball 30–80"‡ " " "
Throws softball 55–150"‡ " " "

4–5 yrs. *SKILL FORM—Softball Throw: Inconsistent combination of patterns of 3–4 and 5–6 yrs. Evaluate at those levels:
Primarily *3–4 yrs.* pattern
Primarily *5–6 yrs.* pattern
Inconsistent combination of 3–4 and 5–6 yrs. patterns
Throws 9½" ball 45–130"‡ " " "
Throws 16¼" ball 45–90"‡ " " "
Throws softball 75–230"‡ " " "

5–6 yrs. *SKILL FORM—Softball Throw
The *arm* is *swung backward* and *sideward* until *hand over shoulder.*
The *arm is brought forward* and *downward* while
weight is *shifted* to forward foot on *same side* as throwing arm.
Some *body rotation* is present.
Later, *arm and leg opposition* is seen.
Throws 9½" ball 75–180"‡ " " "
Throws 16¼" ball 55–140"‡ " " "
Throws softball 100–245"‡ " " "

Catches
Materials: 9½" and 16¼" rubber playground balls
Skill analysis: Catching progression is observed from stopping a rolling ball to catching an aerial ball with a hand catch. Catching appears later than throwing. Larger balls are caught more easily than are smaller balls. Poorer performance by girls probably is a reflection of lack of training and catching experience.

2–3 yrs. *SKILL FORM—Catch 16¼" Ball
Initially, *unsuccessful* attempts are made to catch a large ball tossed chest high.
Fear reaction causes child to *turn head* to side, *close eyes,* and *bat ball away.*
Later, child *spread arms out stiffly* in front of body with *fingers pointing forward.*

	Ball may *bounce out of arms.* Finally, *arms* are *relaxed* and child *clutches ball to chest.*	___ ___ ___ ___ ___ ___ ___ ___ ___		
3–4 yrs.	*SKILL FORM—Catch 9½" Ball: Child starts to *watch ball* with *fingers pointing forward.* Child *progresses from clutching* ball to chest, to an *arm catch,* to ultimately a *hand catch.* *Little elbow flexion* is seen to absorb impact.	___ ___ ___ ___ ___ ___ ___ ___ ___ ___ ___ ___		
4–5 yrs.	*SKILL FORM—Catch Ball: Inconsistent combination of patterns of 3–4 and 5–6 yrs. Evaluate at those levels: Primarily *3–4 yrs.* pattern Primarily *5–6 yrs.* pattern *Inconsistent* combination of 3–4 and 5–6 yrs. patterns	___ ___ ___ ___ ___ ___ ___ ___ ___		
5–6 yrs.	*SKILL FORM—Catch 9½" Ball Beginning of a basically mature pattern that is *well coordinated.* Child *watches ball* closely, stands with *arms stretched out,* *elbows flexed,* and *hands cupped* (fingers pointing downward). A *hand catch* is made with *elbow flexion* to absorb impact. Child consistently *maintains grasp of ball*	___ ___		

Kicks

Materials: 9½" rubber playground ball

Skill analysis: Initial attempts consist of drawing one leg back to kick "at" the ball positioned in front of child. Later, the child will run up to a stationary ball and kick with forward shifting of weight. Poorer performance by girls probably is due to inexperience. Kicking patterns have not been investigated to a great extent.

2–3 yrs.	*SKILL FORM—Kicks Stationary Ball: Child *kicks "at"* ball with little or *no body lean,* *poor contact* of ball, *poor coordination,* and *little follow-through.*	___ ___ ___ ___ ___ ___ ___ ___ ___ ___ ___ ___ ___ ___ ___		
3–4 yrs.	*SKILL FORM—Kicks Stationary Ball: Child *runs up* to ball and kicks with *slight body lean* (either forward or backward), *good contact* of ball, *good coordination,* and *slight follow-through.*	___ ___ ___ ___ ___ ___ ___ ___ ___ ___ ___ ___ ___ ___ ___		
4–5 & 5–6 yrs.	*SKILL FORM—Kicks Stationary Ball: Child takes a *full leg backswing,* *leans forward,* and *holds arms out* for balance. Has *good contact* of ball, *good coordination,* and *definite follow-through.*	___ ___ ___ ___ ___ ___ ___ ___ ___ ___ ___ ___ ___ ___ ___ ___ ___ ___		

LONG FORM—EARLY CHILDHOOD LEVEL (9)

Strikes
Materials: Plastic bat, whiffle softball, batting tee
Skill analysis: Striking progresses from immature overarm striking attempts with the hand or an implement at a stationary ball. Later, a sidearm pattern is observed in addition to the ability to strike a tossed ball. Striking patterns have not been studied to a great extent in children.

2–3 yrs.	*SKILL FORM—Strikes Ball on Batting Tee:			
	Child holds *bat in front* of self	____	____	____
	with *inconsistent hand position*.			
	The *bat is swung* in overarm pattern that is a "chopping" motion	____	____	____
	with *poor contact* with the ball.	____	____	____
	There is *no weight shift* and	____	____	____
	no body rotation. There is	____	____	____
	poor coordination and	____	____	____
	no arm and leg opposition.	____	____	____
3–4 yrs.	*SKILL FORM—Strikes Ball on Batting Tee:			
	Child *holds bat to the side*	____	____	____
	with *improved hand position*.	____	____	____
	The *bat is swung* in a stiff *sidearm* pattern	____	____	____
	with *good contact* with the ball.	____	____	____
	There is *slight weight shift* and	____	____	____
	slight body rotation. There is	____	____	____
	good coordination and	____	____	____
	some arm and leg opposition.	____	____	____
4–5 & 5–6 yrs.	SKILL FORM—Strikes Ball on Batting Tee:			
	Bat is held over shoulder with	____	____	____
	dominant hand above other hand in a *good hand placement* on bat.			
	The bat is swung in a *sidearm striking* pattern accompanied by	____	____	____
	definite *hip and trunk rotation* and	____	____	____
	forward *shifting of weight*. There is	____	____	____
	definite *arm and leg opposition*.	____	____	____
	Later, *wrists uncock* before ball contact.	____	____	____

*If several items are described, select this representative item and omit others in order to shorten testing time. Use the short form provided following the long form.

‡See test administration instructions on pages 87–88.

§Demonstrate with verbal instruction to "go down one step at a time."

‖Demonstrate with verbal instruction to "push off in one long jump."

SHORT FORM[†]—EARLY CHILDHOOD LEVEL (1)

Name of individual:____
(Last) (First) (Middle)

Birthdate: ___/___/___ Chronologic Age (C.A.) at: __yrs. __mo. Pretest __yrs. __mo. Interim
mo. day yr. __yrs. __mo. Posttest

GEDDES PSYCHOMOTOR INVENTORY (GPI)
SECTION APPROPRIATE FOR *EARLY CHILDHOOD LEVEL* (approximately 2–6 years)

Assess performance levels according to chronologic age. If a child is unsuccessful, go to younger age level and progress to highest (oldest) level possible.

Record scores

X—Not testable/no performance	?—Assumed level/inconsistent
Yes—Successful performance	No—Unsuccessful performance
___"—Number of inches	___#—Number
___'—Number of feet	___min—Number of minutes
___sec—Number of seconds	

Enter other pertinent information as indicated or appropriate.

Performance levels	*Pretest* *Date Score*	*Interim* *Date Score*	*Posttest* *Date Score*
BALANCE AND POSTURAL MAINTENANCE			
Specific Balance Stands on preferred foot, eyes open:			
2–3 yrs. For 1–5 sec‡ (Record ____R, ____L foot)	sec	sec	sec
3–4 yrs. For 2–10 sec‡ (Record ____R ____L foot)	sec	sec	sec
4–5 yrs. For 4–15 sec‡ (Record ____R, ____L foot)	sec	sec	sec
5–6 yrs. For 5–20 sec‡ (Record ____R, ____L foot)	sec	sec	sec
LOCOMOTION AND BASIC MOVEMENT			
Walks			
2–3 yrs. Alternates 10 steps (heel-to-toe) forward on 8" balance beam‡	#	#	#
3–4 yrs. Alternates 10 steps (heel-to-toe) forward on 6" balance beam‡	#	#	#
4–5 yrs. Alternates 10 steps (heel-to-toe) forward on 4" balance beam‡ (4–6 yrs.)	#	#	#
5–6 yrs. Alternates 2–6 steps (heel-to-toe) forward on 2" balance beam‡	#	#	#
Runs			
2–3 yrs. Runs in basic pattern of coordinated arm and leg opposition with adequate balance			
3–4 yrs. Runs with improved coordination. Arm and leg opposition combined with stopping and starting skills is seen.			

GEDDES PSYCHOMOTOR INVENTORY (GPI)

SHORT FORM—EARLY CHILDHOOD LEVEL (2)

4–5 & 5–6 yrs.	Runs in well-coordinated pattern that combines ____arm and leg opposition, ____stopping and starting skills, and ____dodging and change of direction skills around obstacles. (Record)			
Climbs				
2–3 yrs.	Climbs *up* stairs alternating feet, holding stair rail			
3–4 yrs.	Climbs *up* stairs alternating feet, without support			
4–5 yrs.	Climbs *down* stairs, one step at a time, without support (3–5 yrs.)			
5–6 yrs.	Climbs *down* stairs, alternating feet without support			
Body Mechanics				
2–3 yrs.	Pushes and pulls toy around floor (18–30 mo.)			
3–4 yrs.	Runs around obstacles while pulling a pull toy			
4–5 & 5–6 yrs.	Lifts (without much bending at knees) moderately heavy box and carries it close to chest			
Jumps				
	Does standing broad jump a distance:			
2–3 yrs.	Of 4–16″‡#ǁ	″	″	″
3–4 yrs.	Of 14–32″‡	″	″	″
4–5 yrs.	Of 20–38″‡	″	″	″
5–6 yrs.	Of 24–45″‡	″	″	″
Hops				
	Hops skillfully (see skill analysis on p. 50)			
3–4 years.	1–7 hops forward	#	#	#
4–5 yrs.	3–10 hops forward	#	#	#
5–6 yrs.	7–10 hops forward	#	#	#
Gallops				
	Gallops in a skillful pattern (see skill analysis on p. 50–51).			
3–4 yrs.	Basic pattern with stiff movements			
4–5 yrs.	Skillful pattern			
5–6 yrs.	Skillful pattern of 10 or more gallops forward			
Skips				
	Skips in a skillful pattern (see skill analysis on p. 51).			
3–4 yrs.	Basic pattern, if observed			
4–5 yrs.	Basic pattern			
5–6 yrs.	Skillful pattern of 10 or more skips forward			
BODY AWARENESS				
Spatial Orientation				
2–3 yrs.	Moves quickly between two chairs (about 3′ apart) without touching			

SHORT FORM—EARLY CHILDHOOD LEVEL (3)

3–4,
4–5, & 5–6 yrs. Negotiates obstacles in obstacle course (runs between, forward, backward, and slides sideways) without touching

Identify Body Parts
Touches body parts without confusion (say "touch your ____") (Record below)

2–3 yrs. ____eyes, ____ears, ____nose

3–4,
4–5, &
5–6 yrs. ____eyes, ____ears, ____nose, ____feet, ____mouth, ____hips (more often at 5–6 yrs.)

EYE-BODY COORDINATION

Hand, Eye, and Foot Preference

3–4,
4–5, &
5–6 yrs. Shows some hand preference to pick up a cube with one hand (definite preference 4–6 yrs.) (Record ____R, ____L hand)

Shows increasing eye preference in looking through kaleidoscope (Record ____R, ____L eye)

Shows increasing foot preference in kicking stationary ball (Record ____R, ____L foot)

MANIPULATION

Grasp and Release

2–3 yrs. Closes fist and moves thumb

3–4 yrs. Touches thumb to two fingers on same hand

4–5 &
5–6 yrs. Grasps and releases pencils and crayons

Builds Tower
Builds tower of:

2–3 yrs. 6 cubes ____# ____# ____#

3–4 yrs. 7–10 cubes ____# ____# ____#

4–5 yrs. 10 cubes ____# ____# ____#

5–6 yrs. 10 or more cubes ____# ____# ____#

Writing and Drawing

2–3 yrs. Imitates vertical strokes on paper

3–4 yrs. Draws head of person with one major body part on paper (say "draw a person")

4–5 yrs. Draws a person with 2 to 6 major parts on paper (say "draw a person")

5–6 yrs. Draws recognizable person on paper (say "draw a person"). (Record ____head, ____trunk, ____legs, ____arms)

Manipulates Objects

2–3 yrs. Turns pages of book one at a time

GEDDES PSYCHOMOTOR INVENTORY (GPI)

SHORT FORM—EARLY CHILDHOOD LEVEL (4)

3–4 yrs. Cuts paper into long lengths ______ ______ ______

4–5 &
5–6 yrs. Cuts triangles out of paper by use of scissors ______ ______ ______

Places Cubes in Cup
Places cubes in a cup in the amount of:

2–3 yrs. 10–16 cubes ______# ______# ______#

3–4,
4–5, &
5–6 yrs. 16 or more cubes ______# ______# ______#

Places Forms
2–3 & Places the forms ____triangle, ____square, and ____circle
3–4 yrs. in formboard (Record) ______ ______ ______

4–5 &
5–6 yrs. Places 4–10 forms in formboard ______# ______# ______#

PERFORMS ON APPARATUS

Rides Tricycle, Bicycle

2–3 yrs. Starts to ride tricycle ______ ______ ______

3–4 &
4–5 yrs. Rides tricycle in small circles and around obstacles ______ ______ ______

5–6 yrs. Starts to ride bicycle ______ ______ ______

BALL HANDLING

SKILL FORM—Softball Throw

2–3 yrs. The *hand* is *brought backward* until *ball over shoulder.* ______ ______ ______
The *arm* is brought *forward and downward* during ball release. ______ ______ ______
There is *no body rotation,* ______ ______ ______
no shifting of weight, and ______ ______ ______
no opposition of feet. ______ ______ ______

3–4 yrs. The *arm* is brought *backward and sideward* until *ball is over shoulder.* ______ ______ ______
The *arm* is brought *forward and downward* during ball release. ______ ______ ______
There may be *slight body rotation* but ______ ______ ______
no shifting of weight and ______ ______ ______
no opposition of feet. ______ ______ ______

4–5 yrs. Inconsistent combination of patterns 3–4 and 5–6 yrs. Evaluate at those levels.
Primarily *3–4 yrs.* pattern ______ ______ ______
Primarily *5–6 yrs.* pattern ______ ______ ______
Inconsistent combination of 3–4 and 5–6 yrs. patterns ______ ______ ______

5–6 yrs. The *arm* is *swung backward* and *sideward* until *hand is over shoulder.* ______ ______ ______
The *arm* is brought *forward and downward* while ______ ______ ______
weight is shifted to forward foot on *same side* as throwing arm. ______ ______ ______
Some body rotation is present. ______ ______ ______
Later, *arm and leg opposition* is seen. ______ ______ ______

SHORT FORM—EARLY CHILDHOOD LEVEL (5)

SKILL FORM—Catch Ball

2–3 yrs. Initially, *unsuccessful* attempts to catch a large ball tossed chest high are seen.
Fear reaction causes child to *turn head* to side, *close eyes,* and *bat ball away.*
Later, child *spreads arms out stiffly* in front of body with *fingers pointing forward.*
Ball may *bounce out of arms.*
Finally, *arms* are *relaxed* and
child *clutches ball to chest.*

3–4 yrs. Child starts to *watch ball* with fingers pointing forward.
Child *progresses from clutching* ball to chest, to an
arm catch and
ultimately to a *hand catch.*
Little elbow flexion is seen to absorb impact.

4–5 yrs. Inconsistent combination of patterns of 3–4 and 5–6 yrs.
Evaluate at those levels:
Primarily *3–4 yrs.* pattern
Primarily *5–6 yrs.* pattern
Inconsistent combination of 3–4 and 5–6 yrs. patterns

5–6 yrs. Beginning of a basically mature pattern that is *well coordinated.*
Child *watches ball* closely,
stands with *arms stretched out,*
elbows flexed, and
hands cupped (fingers pointing *downward).*
A *hand catch* is made with
elbow flexion to absorb impact.
Child consistently *maintains grasp* of ball.

SKILL FORM—Kicks Stationary Ball

2–3 yrs. Child *kicks "at"* ball with
little or *no body lean,*
poor contact of ball,
poor coordination, and
little follow-through.

3–4 yrs. Child *runs up* to ball and kicks
with *slight body lean* (either forward or backward),
good contact of ball,
good coordination, and
slight follow-through.

4–5 & 5–6 yrs. Child takes a *full leg backswing,*
leans forward, and
holds arms out for balance. Child has
good contact of ball,
good coordination, and
definite follow-through.

SKILL FORM—Strikes Ball on Batting Tee

2–3 yrs. Child holds *bat in front* of self
with *inconsistent hand position.*

GEDDES PSYCHOMOTOR INVENTORY (GPI)

SHORT FORM—EARLY CHILDHOOD LEVEL (6)

	The *bat* is *swung* in overarm pattern that is a *"chopping" motion* with *poor contact* with the ball. There is *no weight shift* and *no body rotation*. There is *poor coordination* and *no* arm and leg *opposition*.			
3–4 yrs.	Child *holds bat to the side* with *improved hand position*. The *bat is swung* in a stiff *sidearm* pattern with *good contact* with the ball. There is *slight weight shift* and *slight body rotation*. There is *good coordination* and *some arm and leg opposition*.			
4–5 & 5–6 yrs.	*Bat is held over shoulder* with dominant hand above other hand in a *good hand placement* on bat. The bat is swung in a *sidearm striking* pattern accompanied by definite *hip and trunk rotation* and forward *shifting of weight*. There is definite *arm and leg opposition*. Later, *wrists uncock* before ball contact.			

†See GPI long form for details on assessing performance levels and recording scores. This short form contains only representative items in abbreviated format.

‡See test administration instructions on pages 87–88.

‖Demonstrate with verbal instruction to "push off in one long jump."

GEDDES PSYCHOMOTOR INVENTORY (GPI) PROFILE
Section appropriate for Primary Level
(approximately 6-9 years)

	LOCOMOTION AND BASIC MOVEMENT								BODY AWARENESS						PERCEPTUAL ABILITIES			EYE-BODY COORDINATION			MANIPULATION		PERFORMS ON APPARATUS		BALL HANDLING			
AGE RANGE	Walks	Runs	Climbs	Body Mechanics	Jumps	Hops	Gallops	Skips	Spatial Orientation	Laterality	Verticality	Body Image	Midline of Body	Identify Body Parts	Response - Aud. Perception	Response - Vis. Perception	Response - Tact. Perception	Hand Preference	Eye Preference	Foot Preference	Writing and Drawing	Manipulates Objects	Rides Bicycle	Moves Along Horizontal Ladder	Throws	Catches	Kicks	Strikes
8–9																												
7–8																												
6–7																												

Directions: Enter scores (using code) that best represent the performance levels identified on the Geddes Psychomotor Inventory (GPI). Use different colors to record the following on the chart:

_____ Pretest _____ Interim _____ Posttest
(date) (date) (date)

Code: [•] Functions within this age range [X] Not testable/no performance

[?] Assumed level of function

Name: ______________________________ Birthdate: ___/___/___
(Last) (First) (Middle) mo. day yr.

C.A.: _______ Pretest _______ Interim _______ Posttest Class/Group: ________

Type of Handicapping Condition: ______________________________

Checklist(s) Summary: ______________________________

Other Assessment Items or Batteries - Summary: ______________________________

____

GEDDES PSYCHOMOTOR INVENTORY (GPI)

LONG FORM—PRIMARY LEVEL (1)

Name of individual:____
(Last) (First) (Middle)

Birthdate: ___/___/___ Chronologic ___yrs. ___mo. Pretest ___yrs. ___mo. Interim
mo. day yr. Age (C.A.) at: ___yrs. ___mo. Posttest

GEDDES PSYCHOMOTOR INVENTORY (GPI)
SECTION APPROPRIATE FOR *PRIMARY LEVEL* (approximately 6–9 years)

Assess performance levels according to chronologic age. If a child is unsuccessful, go to younger age level and progress to highest (oldest) level possible.

Record scores:
- X— Not testable/no performance
- Yes— Successful performance
- ___"— Number of inches
- ___'— Number of feet
- ?— Assumed level/inconsistent
- No— Unsuccessful performance
- ___#— Number

Enter other pertinent information as indicated or appropriate

Performance levels#	*Pretest Date Score*	*Interim Date Score*	*Posttest Date Score*
LOCOMOTION AND BASIC MOVEMENT (If indicated, select additional items from Early Childhood Level)			
Walks (on balance beam) (GPDP p. 144) Materials: 2" wide balance beam (4" high)			
*Alternates 10 steps (heel-to-toe) forward on 2" balance beam‡	#	#	#
Runs (GPDP p. 145) Materials: Game equipment Skill analysis: Well-coordinated pattern: arm and leg opposition combined with dodging, change of direction, stopping, and starting skills.			
*Runs skillfully (see skill analysis above) in physical activities			
Climbs (GPDP p. 146) Materials: Lind Climber, playground gym, ladder			
Climbs on apparatus such as a Lind Climber or playground gym			
Climbs up and down ladder, alternating feet, on 4 or more rungs	#	#	#
Body Mechanics (GPDP pp. 146–147) Materials: Box with medium-weight objects in it			
*Lifts (by bending at knees) moderately heavy box and carries it close to chest			
Pushes moderately heavy large box (using leg muscles) with both hands at center of box and feet spread apart			

LONG FORM—PRIMARY LEVEL (2)

Jumps (GPDP pp. 147–148)
Materials: Tape, tape measure, short rope
Skill analysis: Well-coordinated basic jumping patterns are observed. Toward end of Primary Level, boys perform better than girls in standing broad jump and in vertical jump. Efficient combinations of jumping and hopping tasks are seen, with better performance by girls in this more complex pattern.

*Does standing broad jump a distance of 35–58"‡	"	"	"
Does vertical jump a height of 4–10"‡ (Record ____" stretch height, ____R, ____L hand)	"	"	"
Jumps short rope 10 or more repetitions	#	#	#

Hops (GPDP p. 148)
Materials: None
Skill analysis: Body is lifted off ground by action of takeoff on one foot and landing on same foot. Hopping on one foot usually follows jumping skills. Girls often excel in hopping, which is probably because of hopping experience. Basic hopping skills are combined with other locomotor skills in activities such as relays and tag games.

*Hops skillfully (see skill analysis above) 10 or more hops forward	#	#	#

Gallops (GPDP p. 149)
Materials: Phonograph, records
Skill analysis: Uneven leap and walk-step combination with one foot always leading.

*Gallops skillfully (see skill analysis above) 10 or more gallops forward	#	#	#
Gallops in rhythm to phonograph records designed for galloping			

Skips (GPDP p. 150)
Materials: Phonograph, records
Skill analysis: Combination of a walk-step followed by a hop ("step-hop") by alternating feet.

*Skips well (see skill analysis above) 10 or more skips forward	#	#	#
Skips in rhythm to phonograph records designed for skipping			

BODY AWARENESS

Spatial Orientation (GPDP p. 151)
Materials: Obstacles, tumbling mat
Skill analysis: Awareness of space around the child in terms of distance, direction, and position.

*Negotiates obstacles in obstacle course (between, over, and under) without touching			
Is aware of body position while performing forward roll with eyes closed (ask: "are you upside down now?")			

Laterality (GPDP pp. 151–152)
Materials: Ball, poster with word "left" and poster with word "right" printed on it.
Skill analysis: Knowledge of left or right sides of body.

*Raises left or right hand appropriately on verbal command ["raise your left (right) hand"]			

LONG FORM—PRIMARY LEVEL (3)

Raises left or right hand appropriately after reading word "left" or "right" on poster _____ _____ _____

Kicks stationary ball with left or right foot on verbal command ["kick ball with your left (right) foot"] _____ _____ _____

Verticality (GPDP pp. 152–153
Materials: Poster with words "go up" and poster with words "go down" printed on it.
Skill analysis: Concepts of upward and downward directions of own body

*Moves body upward from crouching position to upright position on verbal command ["go up"]. Or moves body downward from crouching or upright position on verbal command ["go down"]. _____ _____ _____

Moves body upward from crouching position to upright position after reading "go up." Or moves body downward from crouching or upright position after reading words "go down" on poster. _____ _____ _____

Body Image (GPDP p. 153)
Materials: 8½ × 11″ paper, pencils
Skill analysis: Concept and awareness of body.

*Draws well-formed person with major body parts (Record _____nose, _____ears, _____fingers, _____eyes, _____elbows, _____mouth, _____feet, _____legs, _____arms) _____ _____ _____

**Midline of Body* (GPDP p. 154)
Materials: Chalk, chalkboard
Skill analysis: Concept of vertical midline of body.

*Draws line on chalkboard without hesitation from right to left (and vice versa) while crossing midline of body _____ _____ _____

Identify Body Parts (GPDP p. 155)
Materials: None
Skill analysis: Concept and awareness of parts of one's own body.

*Touches body parts without confusion (say "touch your _____"). Record _____eyes, _____ears, _____nose, _____mouth, _____knees, _____feet, _____elbows, _____shoulders, _____hips) _____ _____ _____

PERCEPTUAL ABILITIES

Psychomotor Response to Auditory Perception (GPDP p. 156)
Materials: None
Skill analysis: Psychomotor response is made by child based on auditory perceptual abilities such as auditory discrimination, closure, figure-ground, localization and attention (defined on page 114; see also page 114 for potential problems child might be having).

*Responds appropriately when words "talk" and "walk" (similar sounds with different meanings) are spoken (say "I want you to _____") _____ _____ _____

Psychomotor Response to Visual Perception (GPDP pp. 157–158)
Materials: Poster with word "go" and poster with word "stop" printed on it, white whiffle ball
Skill analysis: Psychomotor response is made by child based on visual perceptual abilities such as visual closure, discrimination, form

discrimination, figure-ground relationship, size perception, depth and distance perception, and object recognition (defined on pages 114–115; see also page 115 for potential problems child might be having).

*Moves appropriately when reads poster with words "go" or "stop" ______ ______ ______

Distinguishes and catches whiffle ball against white or light background (sky) ______ ______ ______

Psychomotor Response to Tactile Perception (GPDP p. 158)
Materials: None
Skill analysis: Psychomotor response is made by child based upon tactile discrimination ability (defined on page 115)

*Identifies, without vision, the finger touched by examiner (child raises finger) ______ ______ ______

EYE-BODY COORDINATION

Hand Preference (GPDP p. 159)
Materials: 8½ × 11" paper, pencils, scissors

*Shows definite hand preference during drawing, cutting with scissors and manipulation of objects (Record ____R, ____L hand) ______ ______ ______

Eye Preference (GPDP p. 159)
Materials: Kaleidoscope

*Shows definite eye preference in looking through kaleidoscope (Record ____R, ____L eye) ______ ______ ______

Foot Preference (GPDP p. 159)
Materials: Ball

*Shows definite foot preference in kicking stationary ball (Record ____R, ____L foot) ______ ______ ______

MANIPULATION

Writing and Drawing (GPDP p. 160)
Materials: 8½ × 11" paper, pencils, cards with forms, words, or letters illustrated on them (see below)

*Copies accurately forms displayed on cards (Record ____square, ____triangle, ____diamond, ____circle, ____cross, ____rectangle) ______ ______ ______

Copies simple words or letters without confusion or any letter reversals, for example, "top is not written as "pot" (Record ____"top," ____"big," ____"pet," ____"h," ____"n") ______ ______ ______

Manipulates Objects (GPDP pp. 160–161)
Materials: Scissors, construction paper

*Cuts circles and triangles out of construction paper by use of scissors ______ ______ ______

PERFORMS ON APPARATUS

Rides Bicycle (GPDP p. 161)
Materials: Bicycle, obstacles

*Rides bicycle appropriate for size around street corners or obstacles ______ ______ ______

LONG FORM—PRIMARY LEVEL (5)

Moves along Horizontal Ladder (GPDP p. 161)
Materials: Horizontal Ladder

*Does single rung traveling for 3–6 rungs (task more appropriate for 8–9 yrs.) ______ ______ ______

BALL HANDLING

Throws (GPDP p. 162)
Materials: 9½" and 16¼" playground balls, softball
Skill analysis: Beginning of a basically mature throwing pattern with greatly improved performance toward end of Primary Level. Boys usually perform better than girls in terms of form, distance, and accuracy. This is probably because of differences in training experiences, play opportunities, strength development and body build.

*SKILL FORM—Softball Throw
The *arm* is *brought backward and upward* until hand is over shoulder. ______ ______ ______
The *trunk rotates* as ______ ______ ______
weight shifts to back foot on that side. ______ ______ ______
A *forward step* is taken on the *opposite foot* as ______ ______ ______
the *body rotates* in that direction. The ______ ______ ______
elbow leads during forward throwing motion of the arm. ______ ______ ______
The *wrist snaps* forward as the ball is released. ______ ______ ______

Throws softball 15–75'‡ ______ ______ ______

Throws: Two-hand underhand pass of large ball ______ ______ ______

Throws: Two-hand overhand pass of small ball ______ ______ ______

Catches (GPDP p. 163)
Materials: Small whiffle ball, 9½" playground ball, bean bag
Skill Analysis: Catching progression is slower than throwing because more complex skill factors are involved. These factors include intercepting aerial balls, adjusting to different sizes and shapes of balls, and reacting to different forces received in catching. The beginning of a basically mature pattern is seen. Little or no difference between performance of boys and girls is observed.

*SKILL FORM—Two-hand Catch of Aerial Whiffle Ball Chest High
The child stands with arms *extended forward,* ______ ______ ______
spreads fingers toward ball, and ______ ______ ______
flexes slightly at the *elbows.* ______ ______ ______
A *hand catch* is made with additional ______ ______ ______
elbow flexion and *"giving"* at the *shoulder joints.* ______ ______ ______

Catches: Two-hand overhand catch of 9½" ball ______ ______ ______

Catches: Two-hand underhand catch of bean bag ______ ______ ______

Kicks (GPDP p. 164)
Materials: Soccer ball
Skill analysis: Kicking progression depends upon the complexity of the skill. Stationary balls usually are kicked with a mature form; however, rolling, dropped (punted), or aerial balls are kicked less efficiently. Boys perform better in terms of accuracy and distance probably because of training experiences, cultural expectations, and play opportunities.

LONG FORM—PRIMARY LEVEL (6)

*SKILL FORM—Kicks Stationary Ball

Child *steps forward* onto support foot while *extending kicking thigh.*
The kicking thigh is brought forward by *flexion at the hip* accompanied by
flexion at the knee. The
foot contacts the *ball.*
Arms are *held out* for balance as
child *follows through* onto kicking foot.

Kicks: Runs up to rolling ball and kicks it

Kicks: Dribbles a soccer ball

Strikes (GPDP p. 165)
Materials: Small whiffle ball, plastic batting tee
Skill analysis: Sidearm patterns are observed in striking progression with an implement. Basically mature forms are seen in batting on a batting tee. Striking at aerial balls is more complex, and performance is not as advanced on this type of striking. Little information is available on striking patterns.

*SKILL FORM—Strikes Ball on Batting Tee:

Bat is held over shoulder with
dominant hand above other hand in a *good hand placement* on bat.
The bat is swung in a *sidearm striking* pattern accompanied by
definite *hip and trunk rotation* and
forward shifting of weight. There is
definite *arm and leg opposition.*
Wrists uncock before ball contact.

Strikes: Bats underhand tossed whiffle ball

*Performance levels in competencies described below are developed by activities in the Geddes Psychomotor Development Program (GPDP). A reference to the page number(s) in the GPDP that describes these activities is given following each competency.

*If several items are described, select this representative item and omit others in order to shorten testing time. Use the short form provided following the long form.

‡See test administration instructions on pages 87–88.

GEDDES PSYCHOMOTOR INVENTORY (GPI)

SHORT FORM†—PRIMARY LEVEL (1)

Name of individual: ____________________
(Last) (First) (Middle)

Birthdate: ___/___/___
mo. day yr.

Chronologic ___yrs. ___mo.
Age (C.A.) at: ___yrs. ___mo.

Pretest ___yrs. ___mo. Interim
Posttest

GEDDES PSYCHOMOTOR INVENTORY (GPI)
SECTION APPROPRIATE FOR *PRIMARY LEVEL* (approximately 6–9 years)

Assess performance levels according to chronologic age. If a child is unsuccessful, go to younger age level and progress to highest (oldest) level possible.

Record scores: X— Not testable/no performance
Yes— Successful performance
___″— Number of inches
___′— Number of feet
?— Assumed level/inconsistent
No— Unsuccessful performance
___#— Number

Enter other pertinent information as indicated or appropriate

*Performance levels**	*Pretest* *Date Score*	*Interim* *Date Score*	*Posttest* *Date Score*
LOCOMOTION AND BASIC MOVEMENT			
Walks (GPDP p. 144): (Alternates (heel-to-toe) 10 steps forward on 2″ balance beam‡	#	#	#
Runs (GPDP p. 145): Runs skillfully around obstacles a distance of 20′ (Record ____well coordinated, ____arm and leg opposition, ____ dodging, ____change of direction, ____stopping, and ____starting)			
Climbs (GPDP p. 146): Climbs on apparatus such as a Lind Climber or playground gym			
Body Mechanics (GPDP pp. 146–147): Lifts (by bending at knees) moderately heavy box and carries it close to chest			
Jumps (GPDP pp. 147–148): Does standing broad jump a distance of 35–58″‡	″	″	″
Hops (GPDP pp. 148): Hops skillfully 10 or more hops forward (Record ____one foot takeoff, ____lands on same foot as takeoff foot, ____well coordinated)	#	#	#
Gallops (GPDP p. 149): Gallops skillfully 10 or more *gallops* forward (Record ____uneven leap and walk-step combination, one foot always leading)	#	#	#
Skips (GPDP p. 150): Skips well 10 or more skips forward (Record ____walk-step combined with a hop ["step-hop"], ____alternates feet in a "step-hop")	#	#	#
BODY AWARENESS			
Spatial Orientation (GPDP p. 151): Negotiates obstacles in obstacle course (between, over, and under) without touching			

GPI PART I

SHORT FORM—PRIMARY LEVEL (2)

Laterality (GPDP pp. 151–152): Raises left or right hand appropriately on verbal command ["raise your left (right) hand"]

Verticality (GPDP pp. 152–153): Moves body upward from crouching position to upright position on verbal command ["go up"]. Or moves body downward from crouching or upright position on verbal command ["go down"].

Body Image (GPDP p. 153): Draws well-formed person with major body parts (Record _____nose, _____ears, _____fingers, _____eyes, _____elbows, _____mouth, _____feet, _____legs, _____arms)

Midline of Body (GPDP p. 154): Draws line on chalkboard without hesitation from right to left (and vice-versa) while crossing midline of body

Identify Body Parts (GPDP p. 155): Touches body parts without confusion (say "touch your _____"). (Record _____eyes, _____ears, _____nose, _____mouth, _____knees, _____feet, _____elbows, _____shoulders, _____hips)

PERCEPTUAL ABILITIES

Psychomotor Response to Auditory Perception (GPDP p. 156): Responds appropriately when words "talk" and "walk" (similar sounds with different meanings) are spoken (say "I want you to _____")

Psychomotor Response to Tactile Perception (GPDP pp. 157–159): Identifies, appropriately when reading posters with either word "go" or "stop" on it

Psychomotor Response to Tactile Perception (GPDP p. 158): Moves appropriately when reading posters with either word "go" or "stop" on it

EYE-BODY COORDINATION

Hand Preference (GPDP p. 159): Shows definite hand preference during drawing, cutting with scissors, and manipulating objects (Record _____R, _____L hand)

Eye Preference (GPDP p. 159): Shows definite eye preference in looking through kaleidoscope (Record _____R, _____L eye)

Foot Preference (GPDP p. 159): Shows definite foot preference in kicking stationary ball (Record _____R, _____L foot)

MANIPULATION

Writing and Drawing (GPDP p. 160): Copies accurately forms displayed on cards (Record _____square, _____triangle, _____diamond, _____circle, _____cross, _____rectangle)

Manipulates Objects (GPDP pp. 160–161): Cuts circles and triangles out of construction paper by use of scissors

PERFORMS ON APPARATUS

Rides Bicycle (GPDP p. 161): Rides bicycle appropriate for size around street corners or obstacles

Moves Along Horizontal Ladder (GPDP p. 161): Does single rung traveling for 3–6 rungs (task more appropriate for 8–9 yrs.)

BALL HANDLING

Throws (GPDP p. 162): SKILL FORM—Softball Throw:

The *arm* is *brought backward and upward* until hand is over shoulder.

The *trunk rotates* as

SHORT FORM—PRIMARY LEVEL (3)

weights shifts to back foot on that side.
A forward step is taken on the *opposite foot* as the *body rotates* in that direction. The *elbow leads* during forward throwing motion of the arm.
The *wrist snaps* forward as the ball is released.

Catches (GPDP p. 163): SKILL FORM—Two-hand Catch of Aerial Whiffle Ball Chest High:
The child stands with arms *extended forward, spreads fingers toward ball,* and *flexes slightly* at the *elbows.*
A *hand catch* is made with additional *elbow flexion* and *"giving"* at the *shoulder joints.*

Kicks (GPDP p. 164): SKILL FORM—Kicks Stationary Ball:
Child *steps forward* onto support foot while *extending kicking thigh.*
The kicking thigh is brought forward by *flexion at the hip* accompanied by *flexion at the knee.* The *knee extends* forcefully as the *foot contacts the ball.*
Arms are *held out* for balance as child *follows through* onto kicking foot.

Strikes (GPDP p. 165): SKILL FORM—Strikes Ball on Batting Tee:
Bat is held over shoulder with dominant hand above other hand in a *good hand placement* on bat.
The bat is swung in a *sidearm striking* pattern accompanied by definite *hip and trunk rotation* and *forward shifting of weight.* There is definite *arm and leg opposition.*
Wrists uncock before ball contact.

†See GPI long form for details on assessing performance levels and recording scores. This short form contains only representative items in abbreviated format.

*Performance levels in competencies described below are developed by activities in the Geddes Psychomotor Development Program (GPDP). A reference to the page number(s) in the GPDP that describes these activities is given following each competency.

‡See test administration instructions on pages 87–88.

GEDDES PSYCHOMOTOR INVENTORY (GPI) PROFILE
Section appropriate for Intermediate Level
(approximately 9-13 years)

AGE RANGE	LOCOMOTION AND BASIC MOVEMENT				PERFORMS ON APPARATUS		AQUATICS				BALL HANDLING			
	Runs	Climbs	Jumps	Total Body Control	Uses Horizontal Bar	Uses Vaulting Box	Drown-proofing Skills	Floats and Glides	Arm & Leg Strokes	Styles of Swimming	Throws	Catches	Kicks	Strikes
12-13														
11-12														
10-11														
9-10														

Directions: Enter scores (using code) that best represent the performance levels identified on the Geddes Psychomotor Inventory (GPI). Use different colors to record the following on the chart:

_____ Pretest _____ Interim _____ Posttest
(date) (date) (date)

Code: [•] Functions within this age range [X] Not testable/no performance

[?] Assumed level of function

Name: ______________________________ Birthdate: ___/___/___
(Last) (First) (Middle) mo. day yr.

C.A.: _______ Pretest _______ Interim _______ Posttest Class/Group: _______

Type of Handicapping Condition: ______________________________

Checklist(s) Summary: ______________________________

Other Assessment Items or Batteries - Summary: ______________________________

____

GEDDES PSYCHOMOTOR INVENTORY (GPI)

LONG FORM—INTERMEDIATE LEVEL (1)

Name of individual: ____
(Last) (First) (Middle)

Birthdate: ___/___/___
mo. day yr.

Chronologic Age (C.A.) at: __yrs. __mo. Pretest __yrs. __mo. Interim __yrs. __mo. Posttest

GEDDES PSYCHOMOTOR INVENTORY (GPI)
SECTION APPROPRIATE FOR *INTERMEDIATE LEVEL* (approximately 9–13 years)

Assess performance levels according to chronologic age. If a child is unsuccessful, go to younger age level and progress to highest (oldest) level possible.

Record scores:

X— Not testable/no performance
Yes— Successful performance
___"— Number of inches
___'— Number of feet
___sec— Number of seconds
?—Assumed level/inconsistent
No— Unsuccessful performance
___#— Number
___min— Number of minutes

Enter other pertinent information as indicated or appropriate.

*Performance levels**	*Pretest* *Date Score*	*Interim* *Date Score*	*Posttest* *Date Score*
LOCOMOTION AND BASIC MOVEMENT (If indicated, select additional items from Primary Level)			
Runs (GPDP p. 184) Materials: Stopwatch, lead-up game equipment			
*Runs 50-yd dash in 9.2–7.5 sec‡	sec	sec	sec
Completes 600-yd. run-walk in 3 min, 13 sec–2 min, 11 sec‡	min sec	min sec	min sec
Runs bases in lead-up games to softball, displaying well-coordinated pattern			
Runs skillfully around obstacles in basketball dribble relays			
Runs skillfully while dribbling soccer ball in soccer ball lead-up games			
Climbs (GPDP p. 184) Materials: Suspended climbing ropes			
*Climbs ropes suspended from ceiling a minimum distance of 4′	′	′	′
Jumps (GPDP p. 185) Materials: Short jump rope, tape, tape measure Skill analysis: Basic jumping patterns are observed with refinement of those skills for use in lead-up games and jumping activities			

LONG FORM—INTERMEDIATE LEVEL (2)

*Does standing broad jump a distance of 38–77"‡	______"	______"	______"
Does vertical jump a height of 9–12"‡ (Record ______" stretch height, ______R, ______L hand)	______"	______"	______"
Jumps short jump rope fast and slow in both forward and backward directions	______	______	______
Has Total Body Control (GPDP p. 186) Materials: Tumbling Mat			
*Does simple cartwheel	______	______	______
Does headstand	______	______	______
PERFORMS ON APPARATUS			
Uses Horizontal Bar (GPDP pp. 185–186) Materials: Horizontal bar, shock-absorbing mat			
*Does pull-over: Jumps up, grasps bar with palms forward and rolls over bar with leg swing	______	______	______
Does bird's nest: Jumps up, grasps bar with palms forward, raises legs over bar, hangs by back of heels and extended arms. Abdomen faces floor.	______	______	______
Uses Vaulting Box (GPDP p. 186) Materials: Vaulting Box, shock-absorbing mat			
*Does squat vault: Legs between arms with knees to chest as vaults over box	______	______	______
Does flank vault: Boths hands on box initially, swings legs to side then over box	______	______	______
AQUATICS			
Does Drown-proofing skills (GPDP p. 187) Materials: Swimming pool			
*Does survival floating: Take in deep breath, put head in water while floating vertically. Intermittently scissor kick (modified) to raise head above surface to exhale and then inhale. Return to original resting/floating position.	______	______	______
Treads water: While in vertical position, tread water by using modified scissors kick (or breaststroke kick) and broad sculling (figure 8) movements of the arms.	______	______	______
Does Floats and Glides (GPDP p. 187) Materials: Swimming pool			
*Does front (prone) float: Lie extended in a prone position at the water surface with head in water while floating. Return to vertical position by tucking legs under body, pushing down with arms.	______	______	______
Does front (prone) glide: Push off bottom of pool, assume front float position as body glides forward. Return to vertical position by tucking legs under body, pushing down with arms.	______	______	______
Does Arm and Leg Strokes (GPDP p. 187) Materials: Swimming pool.			

LONG FORM—INTERMEDIATE LEVEL (3)

*Does front crawl arm stroke: From prone position with arms extended, alternately draw hands beneath body and then return arm over the water to original extended position.

Does flutter kick: While in prone lying position with legs extended, alternately kick legs up and down.

Does Styles of Swimming (GPDP p. 187)
Materials: Swimming pool

Does front crawl (freestyle): Coordinate front crawl arm stroke and flutter kick with breathing cycle.*

Does back crawl: Coordinate back crawl arm stroke (arm sweeps sideward and downward) and flutter kick with breathing cycle.

BALL HANDLING

Throws (GPDP p. 188)
Materials: Softball, junior size basketball, junior size football
Skill analysis: Improvement of mature pattern that is modified for throwing skills observed in lead-up games. Boys perform better than girls in terms of form, distance, and accuracy. This is probably because of differences in training experiences, strength development, and body build.

*SKILL FORM—Softball Throw: For a right-handed person,
the right *throwing arm* is
brought backward and upward while
body rotates to the right and
weight is shifted to back (right) foot.
The left foot *steps forward* as
body rotates to the left during throwing action.
The right *elbow leads* during forward motion of arm.
The *wrist snaps* foward as ball is released with *follow-through* toward target.

Throws softball a distance of 40–157′‡

Throws: Chest pass with basketball

Throws: Forward pass with football

Throws: Bounce pass with basketball

Throws: Underhand pitch in softball

Catches (GPDP p. 189)
Materials: Softball, basketball, 9½″ playground ball
Skill analysis: Mature form is modified for use as specialized catching skills in lead-up games. Little or no differences are observed between performances of boys and girls.

*SKILL FORM—Two-hand Catch of Small Aerial Ball Chest High:
Child stands with *arms extended* forward,
spreads *fingers toward ball,* and
flexes slightly at the *elbows.*
A *hand catch* is made with additional
elbow flexion and "giving" at shoulder joints. Child
steps toward ball to receive it.

Catches: Overhead fly ball in softball

LONG FORM—INTERMEDIATE LEVEL (4)

Catches: Two-hand underhand catch of basketball

Kicks (GPDP pp. 189–190)
Materials: Soccer ball, junior size football
Skill analysis: Stationary, rolling, dropped, and aerial balls are kicked with basically mature form in lead-up game situations. Skill displayed is affected by intended trajectory of ball, height of ball when kicked, placement of support foot, and the complexity of the game skill. Boys perform better than girls in terms of accuracy and distance, probably because of training, cultural expectations, and play experiences.

*SKILL FORM—Kicks Stationary Ball
The child *steps forward* onto support foot while
extending kicking thigh. The
kicking *thigh* is *brought forward* by
flexion at the hip accompanied by
flexion at the knee. The
knee extends forcefully as the
foot contacts the ball.
Arms are *held out* for balance as child
follows through onto kicking foot.

Kicks: Dribbles soccer ball in soccer lead-up games

Kicks: Place kick in football lead-up games

Kicks: Punt in football lead-up games

Strikes (GPDP p. 190)
Materials: Bat, softball, volleyball, tennis ball and racket
Skill analysis: Overarm, sidearm, and underhand striking patterns are seen. Implements and the hands are used to strike objects in a variety of lead-up games. Few investigations are available that analyze striking patterns. Little difference is seen between boys' and girls' performances except that boys bat longer distances.

*SKILL FORM—Bats Pitched Softball:
Child holds *bat over shoulder*, while
side of body faces pitcher with
weight on *back foot*. The
bat is *swung* forward in a *sidearm pattern* as the
hips and spine rotate forward.
Weight is shifted to *forward* foot during swing.
Wrists are *uncocked* as ball is batted.

Strikes: Serves volleyball in underhand pattern

Strikes: Tennis forehand stroke

---

*Performance levels in competencies described below are developed by activities in the Geddes Psychomotor Development Program (GPDP). A reference to the page number(s) in the GPDP that describes these activities is given following each competency.

*If several items are described, select this representative item and omit others in order to shorten testing time. Use the short form provided following the long form.

‡See test administration instructions on pages 87–88.

GEDDES PSYCHOMOTOR INVENTORY (GPI)

SHORT FORM[†]—INTERMEDIATE LEVEL (1)

Name of individual: ____

(Last) (First) (Middle)

Birthdate: ___/___/___ Chronologic ___yrs. ___mo. Pretest ___yrs. ___mo. Interim
mo. day yr. Age (C.A.) at: ___yrs. ___mo. Posttest

GEDDES PSYCHOMOTOR INVENTORY (GPI)
SECTION APPROPRIATE FOR *PRIMARY LEVEL* (approximately 9–13 years)

Assess performance levels according to chronologic age. If a child is unsuccessful, go to younger age level and progress to highest (oldest) level possible.

Record scores
X— Not testable/no performance
Yes— Successful performance
___"— Number of inches
___'— Number of feet
___sec— Number of seconds
?— Assumed level/inconsistent
No— Unsuccessful performance
___#— Number
___min— Number of minutes

Enter other pertinent information as indicated or appropriate.

Performance Levels[#]	*Pretest Date Score*	*Interim Date Score*	*Posttest Date Score*
LOCOMOTION AND BASIC MOVEMENT			
Runs (GPDP p. 184). Runs 50-yard dash in 9.2–7.5 sec.‡	sec	sec	sec
Climbs (GPDP p. 184): Climbs ropes suspended from ceiling a minimum distance of 4'	'	'	'
Jumps (GPDP p. 185): Does standing broad jump a distance of 38–77"‡	"	"	"
Has Total Body Control (GPDP p. 186): Does simple cartwheel			
PERFORMS ON APPARATUS			
Uses Horizontal Bar (GPDP pp. 185–186): Does pull over: jumps up, grasps bar with palm forward, and rolls over bar with leg swing			
Uses Vaulting Box (GPDP p. 186): Does squat vault: Legs between arms with knees to chest as vaults over box			
AQUATICS			
Does Drown-proofing Skills (GPDP p. 187): Does survival floating: Take in deep breath, put head in water while floating vertically. Intermittently scissor kick (modified) to raise head above surface to exhale and then inhale. Return to original resting/floating position.			
Does Floats and Glides (GPDP p. 187): Does front (prone) float: Lie extended in a prone position at the water surface with head in water while floating. Return to vertical position by tucking legs under body, pushing down with arms.			
Does Arm and Leg Strokes (GPDP p. 187): Does front crawl arm stroke: From prone position with arms extended, alternately draw hands beneath body and then return arm over the water to original extended position.			

SHORT FORM INTERMEDIATE LEVEL (2)

Does Styles of Swimming (GPDP p. 187): Does front crawl (freestyle):
Coordinate front crawl arm stroke and flutter kick with breathing cycle ______ ______ ______

BALL HANDLING

Throws (GPDP p. 188): SKILL FORM—Softball Throw:
For a right-handed person,
the right throwing *arm* is *brought backward and upward* while ______ ______ ______
body rotates to the right and ______ ______ ______
weight is shifted to back (right) foot. ______ ______ ______
The left foot *steps forward* as ______ ______ ______
body rotates to the left during throwing action. ______ ______ ______
The right *elbow leads* during forward motion of arm. ______ ______ ______
The *wrist snaps* forward as ball is released with ______ ______ ______
follow-through toward target. ______ ______ ______

Catches (GPDP p. 189): SKILL FORM—Two-hand Catch of Small Aerial Ball Chest High:
Child stands with *arms extended* forward, ______ ______ ______
spreads *fingers toward ball,* and ______ ______ ______
flexes slightly at the *elbows.* ______ ______ ______
A *hand catch* is made with additional ______ ______ ______
elbow flexion and "giving" at shoulder joints. Child ______ ______ ______
steps toward ball to receive it. ______ ______ ______

Kicks (GPDP pp. 189–190): SKILL FORM—Stationary Ball:
Child *steps forward* onto support foot while ______ ______ ______
extending kicking thigh. The ______ ______ ______
kicking *thigh* is *brought forward* by ______ ______ ______
flexion at the hip accompanied by ______ ______ ______
flexion at the knee. The ______ ______ ______
knee extends forcefully as the ______ ______ ______
foot contacts the ball. ______ ______ ______
Arms are *held out* for balance as child ______ ______ ______
follows through onto kicking foot. ______ ______ ______

Strikes (GPDP p. 190): SKILL FORM—Bats Pitched Softball:
Child holds *bat over shoulder,* while ______ ______ ______
side of body faces pitcher with ______ ______ ______
weight on back foot. The ______ ______ ______
bat is *swung* forward in a *sidearm pattern* as the ______ ______ ______
hips and spine rotate forward. ______ ______ ______
Weight is shifted to *forward* foot during swing. ______ ______ ______
Wrists are uncocked as ball is batted. ______ ______ ______

---

†See GPI long form for details on assessing performance levels and recording scores. This short form contains only representative items in abbreviated format.

*Performance levels in competencies described below are developed by activities in the Geddes Psychomotor Development Program (GPDP). A reference to the page number(s) in the GPDP that describes these activities is given following each competency.

‡See test administration instructions on pages 87–88.

GEDDES PSYCHOMOTOR INVENTORY (GPI) PROFILE

GEDDES PSYCHOMOTOR INVENTORY (GPI) PROFILE
Section appropriate for Young Adult Level
(approximately 13-17 years)

AGE RANGE	LOCOMOTION AND BASIC MOVEMENT		AQUATICS			BALL HANDLING			
	Runs	Jumps	Styles of Swimming	Dives	Stunts	Throws	Catches	Kicks	Strikes
16-17									
15-16									
14-15									
13-14									

Directions: Enter scores (using code) that best represent the performance levels identified on the Geddes Psychomotor Inventory (GPI). Use different colors to record the following on the chart:

____Pretest ____Interim ____Posttest
(date) (date) (date)

Code: [•] Functions within this age range [X] Not testable/no performance

[?] Assumed level of function

Name: ______________________________ Birthdate: ___/___/___
(Last) (First) (Middle) mo. day yr.

C.A.: _______Pretest _______Interim _______Posttest Class/Group: ________

Type of Handicapping Condition: ______________________________

Checklist(s) Summary: ______________________________

Other Assessment Items or Batteries - Summary: ______________________________

____

LONG FORM—YOUNG ADULT LEVEL (1)

Name of individual: ____
(Last) (First) (Middle)

Birthdate: ___/___/___ mo. day yr.

Chronologic Age (C.A.) at: __yrs. __mo. Pretest __yrs. __mo. Interim __yrs. __mo. Posttest

GEDDES PSYCHOMOTOR INVENTORY (GPI)
SECTION APPROPRIATE FOR *YOUNG ADULT* LEVEL (approximately 13–17 years)

Assess performance levels according to chronologic age. If a person is unsuccessful, go to younger age level and progress to highest (oldest) level possible.

Record Scores:

X— Not testable/no performance
Yes— Successful performance
___"— Number of inches
___'— Number of feet
___sec— Number of seconds
?— Assumed level/inconsistent
No— Unsuccessful performance
___#— Number
___min— Number of minutes

Enter other pertinent information as indicated or appropriate

Performance Levels *	*Pretest* *Date Score*	*Interim* *Date Score*	*Posttest* *Date Score*
LOCOMOTION AND BASIC MOVEMENT (If indicated, select additional items from Intermediate Level)			
Runs (GPDP p. 206) Materials: Stopwatch, game equipment for softball, basketball, and soccer			
Runs 50-yd dash in 8.6–6.7 sec.‡	sec	sec	sec
Completes 600-yd run-walk in 3 min., 15 sec.–2 min.‡	min sec	min sec	min sec
Runs bases and slides into home plate in softball games			
Runs around opponents while dribbling in basketball games			
Runs while dribbling then kicking soccer ball to teammate in soccer games			
Jumps (GPDP p. 206) Materials: Tape, tape measure, equipment for volleyball, basketball, and track hurdles			
*Does standing broad jump a distance of 62–90"‡	"	"	"
Does vertical jump a height of 12–16"‡ (Record _____" stretch height, _____R, _____L hand)			
Jumps hurdles in track events			
Does lay-up shot in basketball games			
Jumps to block in volleyball games			

LONG FORM—YOUNG ADULT LEVEL (2)

AQUATICS

Does Styles of Swimming (GPDP p. 207)
Materials: Swimming pool

*Does Sidestroke: Coordinate sidestroke arm action and scissors kick with breathing cycle

Does Elementary Backstroke: Coordinate elementary backstroke arm and leg action with breathing cycle

Does Breaststroke: Coordinate breaststroke arm and leg action with breathing cycle

Dives (GPDP p. 207)
Materials: Swimming pool, springboard

*Does Running Front Dive: Coordinate running approach (accelerated walk), arm and leg action for hurdle and spring off board, with dive execution and entry

Does Front Jackknife Dive: Coordinate running approach, arm and leg action for hurdle and spring off board, with dive execution and entry

Does Stunts (GPDP p. 207)
Materials: Swimming pool

*Does the shark (synchronized swimming)

Does back somersault tuck (synchronized swimming)

BALL HANDLING

Throws (GPDP pp. 207–208)
Materials: Softball, basketball, football, javelin
Skill analysis: Mature throwing pattern is improved and refined in various throwing skills observed in games and sports. Boys perform better than girls in terms of form, distance, and accuracy. This is probably because of training experiences, play opportunities, strength development, and body build.

*SKILL FORM—Softball Throw: For a right-handed person,
the *right throwing arm* is
brought backward and upward while
body rotates to the right and
weight is shifted to back (right) foot. The
left foot *steps forward* as
body rotates to the left during throwing action.
The *wrist snaps* forward as the ball is released with
follow-through toward target.

Throws softball a distance of 70–185′‡

Throws: Overhand pitch in softball

Throws: Forward pass in football

Throws: Hook pass in basketball

Throws: Field goal in basketball

Throws: Javelin

LONG FORM—YOUNG ADULT LEVEL (3)

Catches (GPDP p. 208)
Materials: Softball, basketball, football, game equipment
Skill analysis: Mature form is further refined for use as specialized catching skills in games and sports. Little or no difference is seen between boys and girls in catching skills.

*SKILL FORM—Two-hand Catch of Softball Chest High:
Person stands with *arms extended* forward, ____ ____ ____
spreads *fingers toward ball,* and ____ ____ ____
flexes slightly at the *elbows.* A ____ ____ ____
hand catch is made with ____ ____ ____
elbow flexion and "giving" at the shoulder joints. ____ ____ ____
Person *steps toward* the *ball* to receive it. ____ ____ ____

Catches: Basketball in game situations and drills ____ ____ ____

Catches: Pitched balls in catcher's position in softball games and drills ____ ____ ____

Catches: Fields ground balls in softball games and drills ____ ____ ____

Catches: Forward pass in football games and drills ____ ____ ____

Kicks (GPDP pp. 208–209)
Materials: Football, soccer equipment
Skill analysis: Stationary, rolling, dropped, and aerial balls are kicked with mature form in games and sports. Boys perform better than girls in terms of accuracy and distance.

*SKILL FORM—Kicks Stationary Ball:
Person *steps forward* onto support foot while ____ ____ ____
extending kicking thigh. The ____ ____ ____
kicking *thigh* is *brought forward* by ____ ____ ____
flexion at the hip accompanied by ____ ____ ____
flexion at the knee. The ____ ____ ____
knee extends forcefully as the ____ ____ ____
foot contacts the ball. ____ ____ ____
Arms are *held out* for balance as person ____ ____ ____
follows through onto kicking foot. ____ ____ ____
Person *steps back* after kicking. ____ ____ ____

Kicks: Dribbles soccer ball in soccer games or drills ____ ____ ____

Kicks: Passes soccer ball in soccer games or drills ____ ____ ____

Kicks: Punts football in football games or drills ____ ____ ____

Kicks: Place kicks in football games or drills ____ ____ ____

Strikes (GPDP p. 209)
Materials: Softball, badminton, volleyball, tennis, and golf equipment
Skill analysis: Mature striking pattern is improved and refined as complex game skills. Implements and hands are used to strike a variety of objects. Little information is available about striking patterns. Little difference is seen between boys and girls except that boys bat longer distances.

*SKILL FORM—Bats Pitched Softball:
Person cocks *bat over shoulder,* ____ ____ ____
side of body is toward pitcher, and ____ ____ ____
weight is on *back foot.* A ____ ____ ____
forward step by the front foot is followed by ____ ____ ____

LONG FORM—YOUNG ADULT LEVEL (4)

hip, trunk, and arm rotation.	____	____	____
Forward movement of the trunk *slows* before contact of ball, but	____	____	____
whipping rotation is continued from shoulders and arm.	____	____	____
Wrists are *uncocked* as ball is batted with a	____	____	____
pushing motion of the arm.	____	____	____
Strikes: Tennis backhand stroke in tennis games and drills	____	____	____
Strikes: Badminton overhead clear in badminton games and drills	____	____	____
Strikes: Volleyball overhand serve in volleyball games and drills	____	____	____
Strikes: Tee shot in golf games and drills	____	____	____
Strikes: Overhand tennis serve in tennis games	____	____	____

*Performance levels in competencies described below are developed by activities in the Geddes Psychomotor Development Program (GPDP). A reference to the page number(s) in the GPDP that describes these activities is given following each competency.

*If several items are described, select this representative item and omit others in order to shorten testing time. Use the short form provided following the long form.

‡See test administration instructions on pages 87–88.

SHORT FORM[†]—YOUNG ADULT LEVEL (1)

Name of individual: ______________________________
(Last) (First) (Middle)

Birthdate: ___/___/___ mo. day yr.

Chronologic Age (C.A.) at: __yrs. __mo. Pretest __yrs. __mo. Interim __yrs. __mo. Posttest

GEDDES PSYCHOMOTOR INVENTORY (GPI)
SECTION APPROPRIATE FOR *YOUNG ADULT* LEVEL (approximately 13–17 years)

Assess performance levels according to chronologic age. If a person is unsuccessful, go to younger age level and progress to highest (oldest) level possible.

Record scores

X—Not testable/no performance	?—Assumed level/inconsistent
Yes—Successful performance	No—Unsuccessful performance
___"—Number of inches	___#—Number
___'—Number of feet	___min—Number of minutes
___sec—Number of seconds	

Enter other pertinent information as indicated or appropriate

*Performance Levels**	*Pretest* *Date Score*	*Interim* *Date Score*	*Posttest* *Date Score*
LOCOMOTION AND BASIC MOVEMENT			
Runs (GPDP p. 206): Runs 50-yd dash in 8.6–6.7 sec.‡	sec	sec	sec
Jumps (GPDP p. 206): Does standing broad jump a distance of 62–90"‡	"	"	"
AQUATICS			
Does Styles of Swimming (GPDP p. 207): Does sidestroke: Coordinate sidestroke arm action and scissors kick with breathing cycle			
Dives (GPDP p. 207): Does running front dive: Coordinate running approach (accelerated walk), arm and leg action for hurdle, and spring off board, with dive execution and entry			
Does Stunts (GPDP p. 207): Does the shark (synchronized swimming)			
BALL HANDLING			
Throws (GPDP pp. 207–208): SKILL FORM—Softball Throw: For a right-handed person,			
the right *throwing arm* is *brought backward and upward* while			
body rotates to the right and			
weight is shifted to back (right) foot. The			
left foot *steps forward* as			
body rotates to the left during throwing action.			
The *wrist snaps* forward as the ball is released with			
follow-through toward target.			

SHORT FORM—YOUNG ADULT LEVEL (2)

Catches (GPDP p. 208): SKILL FORM—Two-hand Catch of Softball Chest High:

Person stands with *arms extended* forward,	______	______	______
spreads *fingers toward ball,* and	______	______	______
flexes slightly at the *elbows.* A	______	______	______
hand catch is made with	______	______	______
elbow flexion and "giving" at the shoulder joints.	______	______	______
Person *steps toward* the ball to receive it.	______	______	______

Kicks (GPDP pp. 208–209): SKILL FORM—Kicks Stationary Ball:

Person *steps forward* onto support foot while	______	______	______
extending kicking thigh. The	______	______	______
kicking thigh is *brought forward* by	______	______	______
flexion at the hip accompanied by	______	______	______
flexion at the knee. The	______	______	______
knee extends forcefully as the	______	______	______
foot contacts the ball.	______	______	______
Arms are *held out* for balance as person	______	______	______
follows through onto kicking foot.	______	______	______
Person *steps back* after kicking.	______	______	______

Strikes (GPDP p. 209): SKILL FORM—Bats Pitched Softball:

Person cocks *bat over shoulder,*	______	______	______
side of body is toward the *pitcher,* and	______	______	______
weight is on *back foot.* A	______	______	______
forward step by the front foot is followed by	______	______	______
hip, trunk, and arm rotation.	______	______	______
Forward movement of the trunk *slows* before contact of ball, but	______	______	______
whipping rotation is continued from shoulders and arm.	______	______	______
Wrists are *uncocked* as ball is batted with a	______	______	______
pushing motion of the arm.	______	______	______

†See GPI long form for details on assessing performance levels and recording scores. This short form contains only representative items in abbreviated format.

*Performance levels in competencies described below are developed by activities in the Geddes Psychomotor Development Program (GPDP). A reference to the page number(s) in the GPDP that describes these activities is given following each competency.

‡See test administration instructions on page 87–88.

TEST ADMINISTRATION INSTRUCTION

Balances (Stands) on One Foot

Subject stands on preferred foot in unobstructed space. The preferred foot is identified by asking subject to stand on one foot.

Subject is told, "Stand on one foot as long as you can."

Tester demonstrates and repeats instructions if necessary.

Two practice trials are allowed.

Subject stands on one foot for four trials. Record the best time to the nearest second from time nonsupporting foot is raised clear of the floor or until any part of the body touches the floor.

Record R (right), L (left), or R/L (inconsistent) foot preference.

Walks Balance Beam

Subject walks beam that is specified for the selected age range and progresses to narrower widths (progression from 10″, 8″, 6″, 4″, 2″ beams) as long as is successful. If unsuccessful at own age range, test at younger age range (broader widths).

Subject walks balance beam in unobstructed space away from walls.

Subject is told, "Walk the balance beam heel-to-toe as far as you can. Try to walk to the end."

Tester demonstrates and repeats instructions if necessary.

One practice trial is allowed.

Subject walks balance beam in one trial. Allowing one stepoff, the test ends at the point of the second stepoff. Do not allow sliding or sideward steps.

Record the number of steps taken before the second step-off (maximum ten steps) in accordance with level of performance seen. For example, if a 5-year-old child cannot walk six to ten steps on 4″ beam, record the number, if any, performed and test/record number of steps performed at younger age ranges. Note: Length of balance beam may limit number of steps taken.

Standing Broad Jump

Subject stands with feet slightly apart and with toes just behind the takeoff line.

Subject is told, "Jump as far as you can along this red line" (one long jump).

Tester demonstrates and repeats instructions if necessary, using a takeoff with two feet and landing on both feet simultaneously.

Two practice trials are allowed.

Subject jumps four times. Record best distance to nearest inch on measuring strip where back of closest heel strikes. In case of mistrial (if, for example, the subject falls backward), repeat that trial.

Vertical Jump

Subject stands adjacent to wall with preferred side at right angle to wall. Feet are flat on floor. (Determine the preferred side by having subject first jump up to touch your hand while away from the wall.)

Determine stretch height by measuring maximum arm reach to tip of middle (longest) finger on measuring strip. Record stretch height and hand preference.

Subject is told, "Jump as high as you can up this red line. Try to touch my hand on the line."

Tester demonstrates and repeats instructions if necessary.

Allow two practice trials.

Subject jumps four times. Record best distance to nearest half-inch of height of jump (difference between stretch height and highest level reached with jump).

Throws

Subject stands behind restraining line with toe of closest foot just behind the line. No forward step over the line is allowed.

Subject is told, "Throw the ball as far as you can toward that red X on the wall."

Tester demonstrates an overhand throw. Repeat instructions, if necessary.

Allow two practice trials.

Subject throws ball four times. Record best distance to the nearest half-inch on measuring strip where ball first lands.

Use the above procedure for the 9½″ and 16¼″ balls and the softball.

Fifty-Yard Dash

Subject takes a position (preferably a sprinter's crouch) behind the starting line.

Tester demonstrates and repeats instructions, if necessary.

The starter gives the signal: "Ready? Go!" The word "go" is accompanied by the downward swing of the starter's arm to give a visual cue to the timer(s) who stands at the finish line. Subject runs as fast as possible across the finish line.

Two runners timed by two different timers may run together.

Subject runs one trial. Record elapsed time from start to crossing the finish line to the nearest tenth of a second.

Six-Hundred-Yard Run—Walk

Subject takes a standing position behind the starting line.

The starter gives the signal: "Ready? Go!" Subject runs (interspersed with walking if necessary) a marked distance of six hundred yards.

Two runners timed by two different timers may run together.

Record elapsed time from start to crossing the finish line in minutes and seconds.

REFERENCES

AAHPER, *Youth Fitness Test Manual.* Washington, D.C.: American Association for Health, Physical Education and Recreation, 1965.

Arnheim, Daniel D., and Pestolesi, Robert A. *Developing Motor Behavior in Children: A Balanced Approach to Elementary Physical Education.* St. Louis: C. V. Mosby Co., 1973.

Arnheim, Daniel D., and Sinclair, William A. *The Clumsy Child: A Program of Motor Therapy.* St. Louis: C. V. Mosby Co., 1975.

Bayley, Nancy. *The Bayley Scales of Infant Development.* New York: Psychological Corp., 1969.

———. *The Development of Motor Abilities During the First Three Years.* Monographs of the Society for Research in Child Development. Washington, D.C.: Society for Research in Child Development, National Research Council, 1935.

Bower, T. G. R. *Development in Infancy.* San Francisco: W. H. Freeman, 1974.

Brazelton, T. B. *Neonatal Behavioral Assessment Scale.* Clinics in Developmental Medicine, No. 50. London: National Spastic Society, 1973.

Brechenridge, Marian E., and Vincent, Lee E. *Child Development,* Philadelphia: W. B. Saunders Co., 1943.

Carmichael, L. "Ontogenetic Development." In *Handbook of Experimental Psychology,* edited by S. S. Stevens. New York: John Wiley, 1951.

Carpenter, Aileen. "Measurement of General Motor Capacity and General Motor Ability in the First Three Grades." *Research Quarterly* 13 (1942): 444–465.

Corbin, Charles B. *A Textbook of Motor Development.* Dubuque, Iowa: Wm. C. Brown Publishers, 1977.

Cratty, Bryant J. *Perceptual and Motor Development in Infants and Children.* Englewood Cliffs, N.J.: Prentice-Hall, 1979.

Egan, D. F.; Illingworth, R. S.; and MacKeith, R. C. *Developmental Screening 0–5 Years.* Clinics in Developmental Medicine, No. 30. London: National Spastic Society, 1969.

El Paso Rehabilitation Center. *Comprehensive Developmental Evaluation Chart.* El Paso, Tex.: El Paso Rehabilitation Center, 1975.

Espenschade, A. "Motor Development." In *Science and Medicine of Exercise and Sports,* edited by W. R. Johnson, pp. 419–439. New York: Harper and Brothers, 1960.

Espenschade, Anna S., and Eckert, Helen M. *Motor Development.* Columbus, Ohio: Charles E. Merrill Co., 1967.

Flinchum, Betty M. *Motor Development in Early Childhood: A Guide for Movement Education with Ages 2 to 6.* St. Louis: C. V. Mosby Co., 1975.

Frankenburg, W. K., and Dodds, J. B. "The Denver Developmental Screening Test." *Journal of Pediatrics* 71 (1967): 2.

Geddes, Dolores. "Motor Development of Autistic Monozygotic Twins: A Case Study." *Perceptual and Motor Skills* 45 (1977): 179–186.

———. "Motor Development Profiles of Preschool Deaf and Hard-of-Hearing Children." *Perceptual and Motor Skills* 46 (1978): 291–294.

———. "Motor Development of Preschool Children." Forthcoming.

Gessell, Arnold. *The First Five Years of Life.* New York: Harper and Brothers, 1940.

———. "The Ontogenesis of Infant Behavior." In *Manual of Child Psychology,* edited by L. Carmichael, pp. 335–373. 2d ed. New York: John Wiley, 1954.

Gessell, A., and Amatruda, C. S. *Developmental Diagnosis.* New York: Harper and Row, 1947.

Gessell, A., and Ilg, F. L. *The Child from Five to Ten.* New York: Harper and Brothers, 1946.

———. *Child Development.* New York: Harper and Brothers, 1949.

Glassow, R. N., and Kruse, P. "Motor Performance of Girls Age 6–14 Years." *Research Quarterly* 31 (1960): 426–433.

Goodenough, Frances L. *Measurement of Intelligence by Drawings.* Yonkers, N.Y.: Harcourt, Brace & World, 1926.

Gutteridge, M. "A Study of Motor Achievements of Young Children." *Archives of Psychology* 34 (1939): 1–178.

Hanson, Margie R. "Motor Performance Testing of Elementary School Age Children." Ph.D. dissertation, University of Washington, 1965.

Havighurst, Robert James. *Human Development and Education.* New York: Longmans, Green, 1953.

Hunsicker, P. A., and Reiff, G. G. "A Survey and Comparison of Youth Fitness 1958–1965." *Journal of Health, Physical Education and Recreation* 37 (1966): 23–25.

Hurlock, Elizabeth. *Child Development.* New York: McGraw-Hill, 1956.

Illingworth, R. S. *An Introduction to Developmental Assessment in the First Year.* Clinics in Developmental Medicine, No. 3. London: National Spastic Society, 1962.

———. *The Development of the Infant and Young Child.* London: E. and S. Livingstone, 1967.

———. *Basic Development Screening 0–2 Years.* Oxford: Blackwell Scientific Publications, 1973.

Keogh, J. F. *Motor Performance of Elementary School Children.* Los Angeles: University of California, Physical Education Department, 1965.

Koontz, Charles W. *Koontz Child Developmental Program: Training Activities for the First 48 Months.* Los Angeles: Western Psychological Services, 1974.

Latchaw, Marjorie. "Measuring Selected Motor Skills in Fourth, Fifth and Sixth Grades." *Research Quarterly* 25 (1954): 439–449.

McGraw, Myrtle B. *The Neuromuscular Maturation of the Human Infant.* 1945. Reprint: New York: Hafner Publishing Co., 1963.

Rarick, G. Lawrence. *Motor Development During Infancy and Childhood.* Madison, Wis.: College Printing and Typing Co., 1961.

Ridenour, Marcella, ed. *Motor Development, Issues and Applications.* Princeton, N.J.: Princeton Book Co., 1978.

Santa Cruz County Board of Education. *The Behavioral Characteristics Progression.* Palo Alto, Calif.: VORT Corp., 1973.

Shirley, M. M. *The First Two Years: A Study of Twenty-five Babies.* Vol. I: *Postural and Locomotor Development.* Minneapolis: University of Minnesota Press, 1931.

Sinclair, Caroline B. *Movement and Movement Patterns of Early Childhood.* Richmond, Va.: State Department of Education, Division of Research and Statistics, 1971.

Valett, R. E. *The Remediation of Learning Disabilities.* Palo Alto, Calif.: Fearon Publishers, 1967.

Wellman, B. L. "Motor Achievements of Preschool Children." *Child Education* 13 (1937): 311–316.

Whiting, H. T. A. *Acquiring Ball Skill: A Psychological Interpretation.* London: G. Bell and Sons, 1969.

Wickstrom, Ralph L. *Fundamental Motor Patterns.* 2d ed. Philadelphia: Lea and Febiger, 1979.

Wild, Monica R. "The Behavior Pattern of Throwing and Some Observations Concerning Its Course of Development in Children." *Research Quarterly* 9 (1938): 20–24.

5

GPI PART II: Checklists for Specific Deviations from Normal Psychomotor Development

Part II of the Geddes Psychomotor Inventory (GPI) describes specific deviations from normal psychomotor development that are often exhibited by individuals with a certain handicapping condition.[1] These individual differences have been observed in clinical situations or reported in related literature. Typical deviations are described in the following checklists so that each individual might be evaluated for manifestation of these deviations: (1) "Individuals with Mild to Moderate Subaverage Intellectual Function"; (2) "Individuals with Severe to Profound Subaverage Intellectual Function"; (3) "Individuals with Specific Learning Disabilities"; (4) "Individuals with Behavioral Disabilities"; and (5) "Individuals with Autistic-like Conditions." Any behavioral deviations that might be present are described on the selected checklist(s) and summarized in the Checklist(s) Summary portion of the selected GPI Profile.[2]

1. These specific deviations are presented as potential individual differences that might be observed in persons with various types of handicapping conditions. Generalizations should not be made that all persons with a particular handicapping condition will demonstrate these deficiencies. In other words, they may or may not be present.

2. Additional instructions are given in the "Steps to Follow" section on pages 28–29.

CHECKLIST FOR INDIVIDUALS WITH MILD TO MODERATE SUBAVERAGE INTELLECTUAL FUNCTION

Name:

*Behavior**	*Behavior Observed†*
Locomotion and Basic Movement	
Moves in an uncoordinated or jerky pattern	
Frequently stumbles or loses balance	
Does not swing arms in cross pattern (alternation of arms and legs) while walking or running	
Physical Proficiency	
Unable to maintain grasp while hanging from overhead bar (after age 6)	
Unable to perform bent knee sit-ups according to age (after age 7)	
Unable to jump vertically off floor so that both feet leave floor simultaneously (after age 4)	
Unable to touch head to knees while in straight-knee sitting position (after age 7)	
Becomes overly fatigued, takes excessive rest breaks, and/or breathes too hard in proportion to physical activity performed	

***Select other behaviors/characteristics described on pages 103–105.**

†Enter yes, no, or questionable. If appropriate, describe behavior. If person is too young for task, enter N.A. (not applicable).

CHECKLIST FOR INDIVIDUALS WITH SEVERE TO PROFOUND SUBAVERAGE INTELLECTUAL FUNCTION

Name:

*Behavior**	*Behavior Observed†*
Locomotion and Basic Movement	
If ambulatory, moves in an extremely uncoordinated or jerky pattern when walking	
Frequently stumbles or loses balance	
Uses a wheelchair or walking apparatus to move through environment	
Is confined to a bed	
Is extremely hypoactive	
Confuses or does not understand instructions to perform a complex motor task (such as independent performance through obstacle course or skipping) (after age 6)	
Reacts and moves slowly when told to put matchsticks in a box	
Physical Proficiency	
Unable to maintain grasp while hanging from overhead bar (after age 6)	
Unable to perform bent-knee sit-ups according to age (after age 7)	
If ambulatory, becomes overly fatigued, takes excessive rest breaks, and/or breathes too hard in proportion to physical activity performed	
Unable to jump vertically off floor so that both feet leave floor simultaneously (after age 4)	
Unable to touch head to knees while in straight-knee sitting position (after age 7)	
Physical Development	
Has smaller body size than normal for age	
Has visible physical defects or identifiable secondary physical handicapping conditions (such as speech or hearing impairment)	
Has a multiple handicapping condition (such as "retarded-blind")	

***Select other behaviors/characteristics described on page 105.**

†Enter yes, no, or questionable. If appropriate, describe behavior. If person is too young for task, enter N.A. (not applicable).

CHECKLIST FOR INDIVIDUALS WITH SPECIFIC LEARNING DISABILITIES

Name:

*Behavior**	*Behavior Observed†*
Locomotion and Basic Movement	
Stumbles or falls frequently	
Is clumsy or uncoordinated	
Exhibits poor performance in locomotor skills such as walking, running, galloping, and skipping	
Is extremely hyperactive (or hypoactive)	
Exhibits unusual movement patterns that are perseverated	
Unable to execute rapid and alternating movements	
Unable to motor plan the performance of a complex movement pattern (such as a series of motor tasks to skip or hop)	
Imitation of Movement	
Confuses up and down, back and front, right and left when copying movements of others	
Movements are stiff or awkward when copying other person's movements	
Fine-Motor Skills	
Demonstrates poor fine manual motor skills such as drawing, writing, or manipulating small objects	
Confuses shapes or forms to be copied with paper and pencil (forms are drawn poorly)	
Motor Output	
Does not express self well in speech, in writing, or in body gestures	
Confuses words or symbols used in linguistic patterns (for example, says "milk" instead of "water")	
Psychomotor Response to Specific Perceptual Abilities	
Does not respond appropriately when words "talk" and "walk" (similar sounds) are spoken as verbal commands	
Does not respond appropriately when words "go," "slow," "stop," and "hop" are read on a poster (words printed individually on four different posters)	
Is unable to bat a ball well	
Is unable to identify familiar objects by touch alone	
Body Awareness	
Has poor spatial orientation (for example, is unaware of body position when airborne on trampoline or is unable to move quickly between two chairs without bumping into them)	
Has poor identification of body parts (for example, confuses names of body parts such as eyes, ears, or knees)	
Confuses right and left sides of body	
Confuses up and down directions of body	
Has poor concept of body image	
Cannot cross midline of body when drawing line from left to right on chalkboard in front of self	

*Select other behaviors/characteristics described on pages 113–118.

†Enter yes, no, or questionable. If appropriate, describe behavior. If person is too young for task, enter N.A. (not applicable).

CHECKLIST FOR INDIVIDUALS WITH BEHAVIORAL DISABILITIES

Name:

*Behavior**	*Behavior Observed†*
Locomotion and Basic Movement	
Displays aggressive or "acting-out" behavior (such as disruptiveness, physically striking others, and/or hyperactivity)	
Is extremely hypoactive or withdrawn (manifested as thumb sucking, failure to talk, reluctance to socialize, playing alone and/or not responding when spoken to, and so forth)	
Extremely defensive (manifested as running away, reverting to infantile behavior, absenteeism, and/or stealing)	

*Select other behavioral characteristics described on pages 125–126.

†Enter yes, no, or questionable. If appropriate, describe behavior. If person is too young for task, enter N.A. (not applicable).

CHECKLIST FOR INDIVIDUALS WITH AUTISTIC-LIKE CONDITIONS

Name:

*Behavior**‡	*Behavior Observed*†
Locomotion and Basic Movement	
Is extremely hyperactive (or hypoactive)	
Walks in an uncoordinated manner	
Does not swing arms in cross pattern while walking	
Walks on tiptoe	
Runs in an uncoordinated or awkward manner	
Is more coordinated in quick movement than in slower, thought-out movement	
Assumes odd or awkward posture when standing, with strange positionings of hands and arms	
Jumps, claps hands, hits head, flaps arms, shakes hands, rocks body, makes facial grimaces (especially when stimulated)	
Exhibits unusual movement patterns, which are perseverated	
Imitation of Movement	
Confuses up and down, back and front, right and left when copying movement of others	
Plays pat-a-cake inappropriately or not at all	
Movements are stiff or awkward when copying other person's movement	
Fine-Motor Skills	
Superior performance in an isolated motor task (such as placing forms in a formboard) while doing poorly on other tasks	
Obsessive, unusual, repetitive manipulation of or attachment to toys or small objects	

***Select other behaviors/characteristics described on pages 136–137.**

†Enter yes, no, or questionable. If appropriate, describe behavior. If person is too young for task, enter N.A. (not applicable).

ANALYSIS OF HANDICAPPING CONDITIONS

The Basis for Determining Special Need and Functional Levels

6

SUBAVERAGE INTELLECTUAL FUNCTION

Participants in the physical activity program may demonstrate subaverage intellectual functioning associated with impairment in socioadaptive behavior. Many educational personnel will employ the term *mental retardation* in referring to this group although a term also currently in use is *developmentally disabled* (DD). Developmental disability refers to a group of handicapping conditions attributed to mental retardation, autism, epilepsy, and cerebral palsy that originated in the developmental period (from birth to about eighteen years of age). For the purposes of this book, however, the term *subaverage intellectual function* rather than *mental retardation* will be employed primarily.

In addition to the controversy of using the deficit label of *mental retardation,* other topics of dispute include the use of the intelligence quotient (IQ) as a criterion for measuring intelligence, the use of culturally biased intelligence tests to determine IQ, the inconsistencies in defining levels of mental retardation, and the identification of separate educational programs for those persons defined as mentally retarded.

SOCIOADAPTIVE BEHAVIOR

A person's reaction or adjustment to events or people that interact with him or her is considered to be socioadaptive behavior. Three aspects of socioadaptive behavior are:

- Rate of maturation: Rate of sequential development of self-help skills of infancy and early childhood such as sitting, crawling, standing, and interaction with age peers.
- Learning ability: Facility with which knowledge is acquired as a function of experience.
- Social adjustment: Degree to which the individual is able to maintain himself or herself independently in the community and in gainful em-

ployment, as well as the ability to meet and conform to other personal or social responsibilities and standards imposed by the community.

One of the greatest problems confronting the person with subaverage intellectual function is immature socioadaptive behavior. Indeed the value of mature social-emotional development in relation to chronologic age cannot be underestimated.[1] Therefore, it is important for teachers to realize the socialization that potentially is offered by physical activities. The social-emotional contributions of these activities include increased self-confidence, improved self-concept, increased patience, stability, and maturity, and desirable social-emotional abilities as an individual and member of a group (Geddes 1970).

Mature social relationships, peer acceptance, and improvement in other indicators of true group interaction do not always occur following participation in physical activity programs, however. Some studies have shown that intellectually impaired youngsters participating in both special and mainstreamed physical activity programs were less accepted and more rejected at the end of such programs (AAHPER 1975b).

There is support both for and against the suggestion that a relationship exists between participation in selected physical activities and increases in academic performance. Several studies revealed significant gains in the intellectual function of mentally retarded students following participation in certain physical activities (Oliver 1958; Corder 1965). This improvement should be interpreted as related to, rather than caused by, enhanced self-concept, improved self-confidence, and feelings of importance because of positive influences of successful experiences in physical activities. On the other hand, additional similar studies did not indicate significant improvement in intellectual function (Corder 1969; Robbins and Glass, 1968; and Buckland and Balow 1973).

PREVALENCE

Providers of physical activity programs often will encounter participants with subaverage intellectual function since this problem is one of the more prevalent handicapping conditions evidenced in the general population. According to the National Association for Retarded Citizens (NARC), approximately 3 percent of the population of the United States is considered to be mentally subnormal.

CAUSES

Mental retardation can be caused by any condition that hinders or interferes with development before birth, during birth, or in early childhood (NARC 1973). NARC has reported more than two hundred causes; some of them follow:

- Rubella (German measles): contracted by the mother during the first three months of pregnancy.
- Meningitis: Inflammation of the membranes of spinal cord or brain.
- Rh-factor incompatibility between mother and infant: Sensitization of the blood of a pregnant woman with Rh negative blood factor as the result of the fetus's blood being Rh positive. Rh antibodies are produced in the maternal blood because of this incompatibility. In subsequent pregnan-

1. A well-known instrument to measure social age is the Vineland Social Maturity Scale.

cies, if the fetus is Rh positive, Rh antibodies may cross the placenta and destroy fetal cells, causing erythroblastosis fetalis.

- Chromosome abnormalities: The most common type is Down's syndrome, which results from an abnormal number of chromosomes (one subtype has forty-seven instead of the normal forty-six). The archaic term *mongoloid* was used in the past to refer to persons with Down's syndrome since the child usually has features thought to be similar to those of a Mongol or Oriental person. Frequent complications are eye cataracts, crossed eyes, congenital heart defects, hernias, and marked susceptibility to respiratory infections. These persons range in intellectual function from mild to severe levels of impairment. Diagnosis usually can be made in early infancy on both physical appearance and behavior. In addition, chromosome studies either before or after birth can be made.
- Environmental deprivation: Delay in development caused by adverse effects of inadequate diet, inadequate prenatal and perinatal care, and lack of learning opportunities or sufficient environmental sensory stimulation.
- Toxoplasmosis: Disease caused by infection with *Toxoplasma gondii.*
- Brain damage: Damage to the brain as a result of an accident, inflammation, contagious disease, or a brain tumor. Destruction of brain tissue or interference with brain development in the infant or young child frequently produces mental retardation, as well as cerebral palsy, convulsive disorders, hyperactivity, or perceptual problems. Most biological causes of brain damage occur before, during, or soon after birth. Injury to the baby's brain during a difficult or complicated delivery or one that is exceptionally rapid or slow is a major cause. Anoxia (lack of oxygen) is a primary cause of brain damage that results in mental retardation.
- Lead poisoning: Damage to the brain as a result of ingesting lead by chewing on lead toys or objects covered with lead paints.
- Malnutrition: Lack of necessary food substances in the body or improper absorption and metabolism.
- Hydrocephalus: Blocking of ducts resulting in an accumulation of fluid in the brain.
- Metabolic errors: Some types of metabolic (body chemistry) errors are (1) cretinism, a deficiency or a complete lack of thyroid hormone; (2) myxedema, cretinism occurring during adulthood without dwarfism; (3) galactosemia, lack of an enzyme that is necessary for digestion of milk or lactose for proper metabolism; and (4) phenylketonuria (PKU), lack of or defective enzyme, phenylalanine hydroxylase, needed for metabolism.

USE OF INTELLIGENCE QUOTIENT

Currently, much less stress is placed upon IQ derived from individual psychometric testing since it is difficult to determine accurately specific levels of intellectual function and since many other factors affect performance on an individual intelligence test. One objection to the use of the IQ in educational programming is that it categorizes the person as to anticipated performance.[2] For example, a child may be tested on an individual intelligence test such as the Stanford-Binet Test of Intelligence or the Wechsler Intelligence Scale for Children and obtain an IQ of 70, which would be considered borderline mentally retarded. If the IQ is employed

2. Other objections include bias of a test relative to the language, culture and/or sex of the person tested.

as the only criterion measure of intelligence, then the child would be expected to function intellectually slightly lower than other children at that chronological age who obtain at-age IQ scores. However, this child might be experiencing socio-adaptive behavior problems causing him to function at a much lower intellectual level in everyday life. Conversely this child might be attaining optimal developmental levels and actually function similar to age peers with so-called normal IQ scores.

Although the IQ should not be overstressed, it does provide a point of reference for programming. A teacher would have a general idea of the range of abilities that have been exhibited by many children and youth with certain ranges of IQ scores. For example, specific deficits in motor or physical performance have been reported in the research literature (AAHPER 1975b) concerning groups of mentally retarded persons with IQs ranging approximately from 15 to 75. Therefore a teacher should evaluate motor performance to determine if any such deficits are manifested in program participants. Table 6–1 includes approximate IQ ranges with reported physical and motor performance levels and/or characteristics associated with each intellectual range. This information is presented to give a point of reference but should not be utilized as a rigid index for programming.

In addition to the IQ, psychometric testing provides a mental age (MA) score. MA scores are associated with chronologic age (CA) in the following formula: $\underline{MA/CA} \times 100 = IQ$. Since mental age is an indicator of level of mental development or a more accurate descriptor of what the child is like mentally or

TABLE 6–1
Psychomotor Development of Individuals with Subaverage Intellectual Function

Level of Subaverage Intellectual Function	*Psychomotor Development*
MILD level of impairment (approximately 50–70 IQ)*	Motor abilities and developmental curves are similar to general population. Persons range from highly skilled athletes to those with some deficits in physical fitness, motor ability, and/or movement patterns (see deficits described for moderate level)
MODERATE level of impairment (approximately 35–50 IQ*)	Higher levels than previously reported. Deficits in balance, coordination, physical fitness (muscular strength and endurance, cardiorespiratory endurance, hip and spine flexibility), reaction time, movement time, and locomotion. Delay of two to five years behind general population.
SEVERE level of impairment (approximately 20–35 IQ)*	Increased deficits in addition to secondary physical handicapping conditions (such as a speech problem) are observed.
PROFOUND level of impairment (below 20 IQ approximately)*	More profound deficits, additional physical handicapping conditions, and multiple handicapping conditions are seen. Deficiencies are observed in all developmental areas. Smaller than normal body size. Locomotor/mobility function ranges from ambulatory, to nonambulatory, to bed-confined.

*Exact IQ ranges such as those defined by the American Association on Mental Deficiency (for example, mildly retarded: IQ 52–68) are intentionally not included in this table since a general reference to IQ functioning levels is considered by the author to be more appropriate.

educationally, it should be considered in programming. For instance, a 12-year-old child with an MA of 6 years and an IQ of 50 probably would understand and might be interested in physical activities often offered to children in the 4 to 7 years (approximate) age range.[3] Of course, MA scores should be utilized as a general guide only since individual differences are present in all of the participants. A child functioning in the 35 to 50 IQ range could have a few or many physical or motor deficits to varying degrees of severity.

LEVELS OF SUBAVERAGE INTELLECTUAL FUNCTION

Levels of subaverage intellectual function range in progression of impairment from mild, to moderate, to severe, to profound. In general, as intellectual function is lowered, motor and physical development decrease. Although efforts should be made toward a noncategorical approach in programming, it is advantageous to understand characteristics generally demonstrated by persons who function in the different levels of severity of impairment. Caution should be taken so that an overemphasis is not made on the generalizations expressed.

Mild Degree of Impairment

Individuals with subaverage intellectual functioning at a mild level of severity are similar to persons who function in the normal range of intellectual function. However, some differences have been observed.

Academic Performance. Academic deficiencies that have been exhibited are deficits in cognition, intellectual association, memory, conceptualization, seriation (performing tasks in a series), transfer of learning from one situation to another, abstract thinking, judgment, and evaluation of situations. Specific difficulties relate to the comprehension, reproduction, and academic use of numerals, letters, and forms. Educational programs include development of reading, writing, spelling, arithmetic, and other academic skills; improved social adjustment for independent living in the community; and satisfactory job skills for independent vocational placement.

Social-emotional development. Some of the social-emotional skills emphasized in educational programs include:

1. Preschool: Emphasize basic social-emotional development skills.
2. Primary: Stress more complex social-emotional skills using increasingly larger groups to give confidence and desirable group attitudes.
3. Intermediate: Relate the child to her particular environment and the world, discussing people, customs, and the role of the child herself.
4. Secondary: Improve social-emotional skills relative to holding a job and being a member of society and the community.

Generally the following social-emotional problems have been observed: lack of stability, social maladjustment, impatience, low levels of self-confidence, immaturity, eagerness for approval, short-term goals, poor participation as an individual in a group, lowered leadership ability, and clannishness.

3. Caution should be taken not to provide lower-level activities that are considered by participants as "too baby-like."

Psychomotor Development. As table 6–1 indicates, persons with a mild degree of impairment range from highly skilled athletes to those with deficits in physical fitness factors, motor ability, and/or movement patterns. The research literature reports numerous delays or difficulties in groups of mildly mentally retarded persons such as in balance, physical fitness (cardiorespiratory endurance, muscular strength and endurance, and spine and hip flexibility), coordination, reaction time, movement time, and locomotor skills (AAHPER 1975a, 1975b). Generalizations regarding poor motor or physical skills should not be inferred, however, since these research investigations were primarily concerned with group performances only. Therefore, it remains the responsibility of teachers to evaluate the functional levels of each individual to ascertain if deficits are present. In addition, teachers should be cognizant of the fact that motor abilities and developmental curves of the mildly impaired are reported to be similar to the general population. Based upon the information gained from evaluative procedures and knowledge of general psychomotor performance of persons with mental retardation, appropriate, sequential, and progressive physical activity programs might be established. Indications from previous research investigations are that such programming will contribute to improvement of physical fitness, motor ability, and self-concept.

Moderate Degree of Impairment

More deviations in individual differences are noted in comparison of individuals with a moderate degree of impairment in subaverage intellectual function to persons with a mild degree of intellectual impairment. Although the person with a moderate level of impairment currently is considered to have higher levels of psychomotor performance than previously reported, considerable psychomotor deficits have been evidenced. In addition, secondary physical handicapping conditions and communication problems are observed.

Academic performance. Academic deficiencies described for the mild level of intellectual impairment are worsened at the moderate level of impairment. Such problems are considered in developing educational programs that include adjustment to life situations in the home and neighborhood, language skills, self-care skills or activities of daily living, job training for semi-independent employment situations, and other enrichment experiences to prepare the person to live essentially in semi-independent life situations.

Social-emotional development. Social-emotional skills emphasized are those that are needed for adapting to the home, neighborhood, and community social spheres in addition to work in sheltered or semi-independent work situations. Social-emotional problems may occur in getting along with others, taking and following directions, self-control, safety skills, group participation, and social-emotional skills relative to job situations.

Psychomotor development. The individual with a moderate level of intellectual impairment is considered to be two to five years behind the general population in growth and development (Wessel, Vogel, and Knowles, 1975). As table 6–1 indicates, the psychomotor function of this person is higher than previously expected; however, increased deficits are reported in balance, coordination, reaction time, movement time, physical fitness (cardiorespiratory endurance, muscular strength, muscular endurance, and spine and hip flexibility), and locomotor skills (Stein and Pangle 1966; Stein 1963; AAHPER 1975a, 1975b). In addition, evidence is available that motor abilities are organized similarly to those of normal children and that attainment of these abilities follows similar developmental curves. Finally, indications are that physical fitness, motor ability, and physical proficiency levels can be improved by appropriate psychomotor development programs based upon individual functional levels (AAHPER 1975a, 1975b).

Severe to Profound Degree of Impairment

Since there is an overlapping of functional levels and characteristics of individuals with severe and profound degrees of impairment, these levels are combined in this section. Extreme delays or deficits in all areas of social, emotional, mental, and physical development are observed in these participants. Secondary physical handicapping conditions become severe enough to be diagnosed as multiple handicapping conditions (in addition to subaverage intellectual function, deficits are seen in vision, hearing, speech, perception, and physical development).

Academic performance. Basic skills are stressed in the areas of self-help, independence, social interaction, activities of daily living, desirable responses to life experiences, optimum arousal levels, enhanced response to sensory stimuli, personal fulfillment, and enhanced amusement. Persons with severe impairment may perform supervised work activities and adapt to normal life routines.

Social-emotional development Semi-independent and dependent life situations are predominant at this level. Because of the person's extremely low intellectual function, the accompanying deficiencies in socioadaptive behavior create the need for emphasis upon social-emotional development for these participants. Observations of mental health characteristics include aggression and withdrawal, dependence upon others, autism, schizophrenia, and psychosis (Geddes 1976).

Psychomotor development. Little research has been accomplished with these participants, and there is a paucity of printed program materials. However, it appears that results of studies showing deficits in motor performance and physical proficiency of mild to moderately impaired persons also pertain to individuals with severe to profound degrees of impairment. In fact, these deficiencies are expected to be much more exacerbated.

The few investigations that have been done concerning the psychomotor development of these individuals have suggested that severe to profound impairment in intellectual function usually is accompanied by extremely poor performance on specific motor tasks, lack of abilities to perform complex motor tasks, small body size, poor physical development of body, and impairment in locomotor abilities (participants might be ambulatory, in a wheelchair, or confined to bed). Effects of physical activity programs have been revealed as improvement in the following: motor function, general awareness and arousal, simple job skills, movement activity, manipulation of objects, locomotion, attention to tasks at hand, and social maturity. Effective methodology includes behavior modification techniques and a well-organized and structured program setting. Unfortunately the overall motor performance of persons living in institutions is poorer than that of persons in other living environments (AAHPER 1975a, 1975b; Geddes 1974).

ADAPTATION OF PHYSICAL ACTIVITY PROGRAM

Physical activity programs offered for individuals with subaverage intellectual function can range from a slightly modified regular physical education program to a program that focuses upon basic skills. The type of program provided is dependent upon the student's level of intellectual, socioadaptive, and psychomotor function.

Teachers should select the appropriate age range section of part I of the Geddes Psychomotor Inventory (GPI) and the appropriate checklist(s) from part II for assessment of psychomotor performance levels. For example, a teacher might administer the Primary-Level age range of the GPI for a 12-year-old student with moderate intellectual impairment since persons at this intellectual level often function at about half the rate of normal development (see table 6–1). The checklist "Individuals with Mild to Moderate Subaverage Intellectual Function" should be utilized in addition to other pertinent assessment criteria. Information gained would then be used to complete the GPI Profile and the Psychomotor Individualized Educational Program (IEP) form. This will then indicate the activities to be selected from the Geddes Psychomotor Development Program (GPDP). Additional physical activity suggestions are provided below in accordance with general levels of intellectual impairment.

Subaverage Intellectual Functioning at a Mild Degree of Impairment

Since these individuals are similar to the general population in terms of psychomotor function, the physical activity program will be essentially the same as for nonhandicapped students. In addition, leisure-time activities and competitive sports should be offered to older students in accordance with individual functioning. However, for many of the participants, modifications may need to be made, such as these:

- Modify instructional directions for easy comprehension if the individual has difficulty understanding what is being said. For example, give short and simple instructions in presenting a skill or activity, using the language-understanding level of the participant.
- If a student has difficulty in team strategies or in understanding complex rules of play, simplify the strategies and rules for successful performance.
- Provide physical activities appropriate for the socioadaptive abilities of the participants. For example, progress from individual play, dual play, small group, semiteams (relays), and lead-up games to sports and games.
- Provide activities that reinforce academic concepts and performance: math—add and subtract persons physically from groups; art—draw themselves performing in physical activities; social studies—participate in dances or games from other countries; safety rules—act out crossing intersections governed by signal lights; language arts—write themes or compose posters on rules relative to physical activities; and intellectual function—perform activities in a series such as circuit training (seriation).
- Provide successful experiences for improvement of self-confidence and self-concept.
- Provide developmental activities if motor performance or physical proficiency deficits are identified.

Subaverage Intellectual Functioning at a Moderate Degree of Impairment

Physical activities will need to be provided in relation to the moderate level of subaverage intellectual function and existing psychomotor performance or physical proficiency levels. In addition, modifications should be made if additional physical problems or communication difficulties are manifested. Modifications of the physical activity program will include these:

- Provide activities in relation to mental age of the participant rather than chronologic age. Presumably this will cause the elimination of team games and sports and lower the level of the activities. For example, a 10-year-old child might be offered activities usually suitable for a 6- or 7-year-old child.
- Use simple and basic language to communicate instructions for the physical activities.
- Use simple to complex progression in teaching activities that proceed from gross- to fine-motor tasks.
- Employ multiple sensory stimulation in teaching skills; for example, physically guide the body through the skill performance, have the child obtain tactual input regarding the equipment to be used, use visual aids, and give verbal directions as child performs.
- Stress improvement in motor performance and physical proficiency if common psychomotor deficiencies are identified.
- Provide activities that will improve socioadaptive behavior in accordance with each person's needs.
- Provide activities that reinforce educational programs, such as using color-coded equipment for development of color concepts.
- Use motivational techniques and novelty activities to obtain participation.
- Provide experiences that lead to successful participation.
- Stress the part-whole method. For example, break down the skill of jumping a short rope into small parts and subsequently put the entire skill performance together.
- Know the methodology being employed in the classroom for the participant and use those methods in the physical education program.

Subaverage Intellectual Functioning at a Severe to Profound Degree of Impairment

Every individual, regardless of the severity of subaverage intellectual function, needs to move in and through the environment. Physical activities at this level can range from basic movement patterns and simple individual or dual games for the severely impaired to simple body positioning and sensory-motor activities for the profoundly impaired. Historically a custodial approach was employed with profoundly impaired persons, and many individuals simply vegetated in beds or wheelchairs or on the floors of state hospitals or schools. Fortunately this attitude is changing, although there still exist many situations in which warehouse conditions prevail. Activities should be provided based upon individual social-emotional, mental, and physical development in cooperation with members of medical, clinical, and therapeutic professions who also work with the same person. The teacher might assist in developing the following behaviors (Geddes 1974):

- Optimum arousal levels: Appropriate arousal or activation levels for motivation and participation in ongoing activities.
- Enhanced response to sensory stimuli: Reacting to and recognizing sensory stimulation input. Examples of sensory stimulation input include hot and cold temperatures, different textures and shapes, lights, colors, sounds, and kinesthetic feelings about body positions or movements.
- Efficient motor skills to learn about environment: Effective head and

trunk control, sitting, crawling, upright postural maintenance, and locomotion in addition to manipulation of objects.

- Increased independence: Improved self-direction, completion of tasks, making decisions, and independent play.
- More efficient self-help and activities of daily living skills: Improved fine manual motor skills for use in dressing, tying shoelaces, picking up items from floor, and brushing hair.
- Desirable responses to life experiences: Understanding cause-and-effect relationships of own actions and accepting other persons' reactions toward oneself.
- More mature social interaction: Increased social maturity in group situations and accepting responsibilities in play activities.
- Improved physical growth and development: Efficient basic movement patterns, improved gross motor and fine motor skills, and increased physical fitness levels.
- Creative fulfillment: Greater feelings of success and accomplishment.
- Enhanced amusement: Enjoyment of and appreciation for leisure-time activities.

REFERENCES

AAHPER. *Annotated Research Bibliography in Physical Education, Recreation, and Psychomotor Function of Mentally Retarded Persons.* Washington, D.C.: The Alliance, 1975a.

———. *Physical Education and Recreation for Impaired, Disabled, and Handicapped Individuals: Past, Present, Future.* Washington, D.C.: The Alliance, 1975b.

Buckland, P., and Balow, B. "Effect of Visual Perceptual Training on Reading Achievement." *Exceptional Children* 39 (1973): 299–304.

Chinn, Philip C.; Drew, Clifford; and Logan, Don R. *Mental Retardation: A Life Cycle Approach.* St. Louis: C. V. Mosby Co., 1975.

Corder, W. O. *Effect of Physical Education on the Intellectual, Physical, and Social Development of Educable Mentally Retarded Boys.* Education Specialist Project. Nashville, Tenn.: George Peabody College, 1965.

———. "Effects of Physical Education on the Psycho-physical Development of Educable Mentally Retarded Girls. Ph.D. dissertation, University of Virginia, 1969.

Gearheart, Bill R., and Litton, Freddie W. *The Trainable Retarded: A Foundation Approach.* St. Louis: C. V. Mosby Co., 1975.

Geddes, Dolores. "A Physical Educator's View of Social Aspects of Physical Activity for the Mentally Retarded." *Journal for Special Educators of the Mentally Retarded* 6 (1970).

———. "Physical Activity: A Necessity for Severely and Profoundly Mentally Retarded Individuals." *Journal of Health, Physical Education and Recreation* 45 (March 1974): 3.

———. "Physical Activity for Impaired, Disabled and Handicapped Individuals: What's Going On?" In *The Humanistic and Mental Health Aspects of Sports, Exercise and Recreation,* pp. 103–107. Chicago, Ill.: American Medical Association, 1976.

Kolstoe, Oliver P. *Teaching Educable Mentally Retarded Children.* New York: Holt, Rinehart and Winston, 1970.

National Association for Retarded Citizens. *Facts on Mental Retardation.* Dallas, Tex.: The Association, 1973.

Oliver, J. N. "The Effect of Physical Conditioning Exercises and Activities on the Mental Characteristics of Educationally Subnormal Boys." *British Journal of Educational Psychology* 28 (1958: 155–165).

Robbins, M. P. and Glass, G. V. "The Doman-Delacato Rationale: A Critical Analysis." In J. Hellmuth, ed., *Educational Therapy,* vol. 2. Seattle, Wash. Special Child Publications, B. Straub & J. Hellmuth Co., 1968.

Stein, Julian. "Motor Function and Physical Fitness of the Mentally Retarded." *Rehabilitation Literature* 24 (August 1963): 230.

Stein, Julian U., and Pangle, Roy. "What Research Says about Psychomotor Function of the Retarded." *Journal of Health, Physical Education and Recreation* 37 (April 1966): 36.

Wessel, Janet; Vogel, Paul A.; and Knowles, Claudia. "Studies Related to Moderately (Trainable) Persons." *Challenge* 10 (1975): 1–6.

7

SPECIFIC LEARNING DISABILITIES

A semantic problem exists in defining the term *learning disability* since different personnel perceive disorders that occur in the learning process in accordance with their own particular educational or clinical orientation. For example, a physician is likely to use the term *minimal cerebral dysfunction* or *brain injured* whereas an educator might employ terms such as *educationally handicapped* or *perceptually handicapped.* All of these terms are broad and indicate that a child is experiencing a deficit or delayed development in one or more of the areas of the learning process. Children with such learning disabilities usually have average or above intellectual function and are not classified with the mentally retarded label.

Use of the many different general terms to denote learning problems is very confusing and noninformative to teachers. The label *specific learning disability* (SLD) is used by many educators to indicate the specific problem that is manifested in the learning process. An example of a specific learning disability is a type of visual dyslexia: a visual discrimination disability that causes confusion in identifying similarly shaped letters such as "b" or "d."

Learning disabilities might occur in one or more of the basic processes involved in understanding or using spoken or written language. Examples include impairments in reading, writing, mathematics, spelling, listening, thinking, and memory. Deficiencies in perceptual skill, related motor skills, or in other aspects of learning might also be exhibited. According to the National Advisory Committee on Handicapped Children (1968), learning problems that arise primarily from visual, hearing, or motor handicaps, to mental retardation, emotional disturbance, or environmental disadvantage are not included in the learning disabilities category. Hallahan and Kauffman (1978) point out, however, that recent speculation recognizes environmental disadvantage as a possible contributing factor to learning disabilities.

Deficits might be experienced in one or more of the components of the learning process relative to psychomotor behavior (figure 7–1). A child learns by selectively receiving in the brain sensory input that give information regarding the world. In order to have meaning, this current sensory stimulation must be prop-

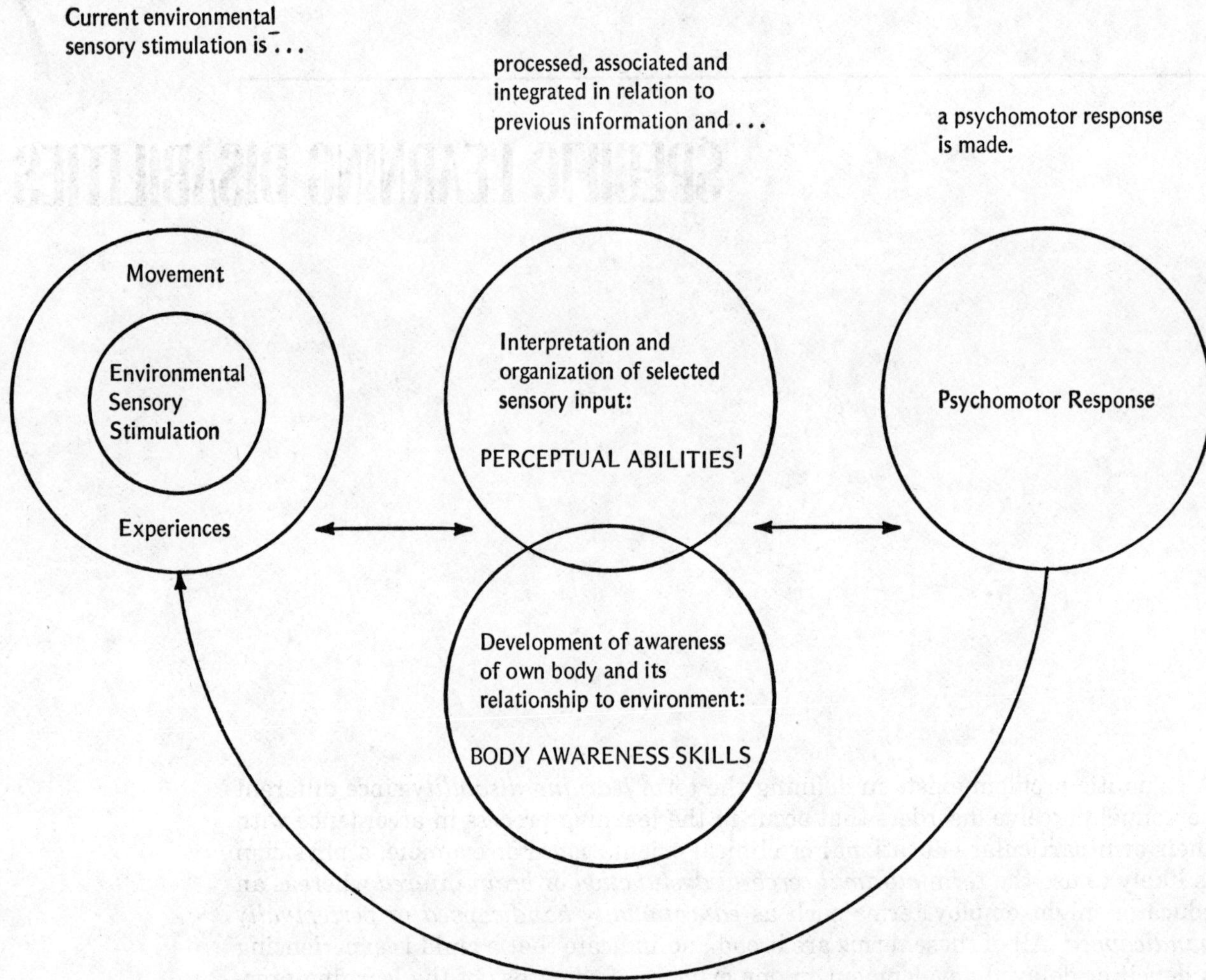

Figure 7–1 The Learning Process Related to Psychomotor Behavior

*Lowest level in the hierarchy of learning experiences for cognition.

erly processed, associated, and integrated in the cortex in relation to previous information obtained in the same manner. Information gained (perceptual abilities and body awareness skills) is stored in the brain for future use after the current response. If, after analysis, a decision is made to perform a task or to communicate an idea, a psychomotor response is demonstrated. Types of responses might be speech, writing, spelling, body gestures, facial expressions, movement patterns, or a specific psychomotor skill such as batting a ball.

The perceptual ability level is considered to be the lowest level in the hierarchy of learning experiences in cognition. Killen (1975) described the hierarchical progression as perception (attending to and decoding sensory information), imagery (recalling or having short-term memory and remembering of experiences), symbolism (inner, receptive, and expressive symbolization of experiences), and conceptualization (categorizing and classifying the experience).

PREVALENCE

Because of the semantic problems involved in defining the conditions, it is difficult to ascertain the level of incidence of learning disorders in children. Estimates range from 3 percent to 15 percent or higher (Kirk 1972). Educators who include mild or minimal learning difficulties in their estimates of prevalence will cite a higher percentage level.

CAUSES

Since a myriad of deficits might occur in the total complex learning process and since it often is impossible to identify the etiology for a specific disability, educational programs generally are established on the basis of symptomatology rather than exact cause. Organically and environmentally based etiologies are described as follows.

ORGANICALLY BASED ETIOLOGIES

1. Concept of minimal brain dysfunction: The brain operates in a suboptimal manner, not necessarily due to structural damage to cortex.
2. Pathologies from which brain dysfunction arises: Conditions such as cerebral hemorrhage, diseases, head injuries, premature birth, anoxia (lack of oxygen), Rh factor incompatibility, congenital malformations, and genetic factors.
3. Relationships among types of brain dysfunction: Suboptimal neural performance, causing impairment within an area of cerebral function produces either overt (gross) or borderline (minimal) manifestations that are sometimes referred to as hard or soft neurological signs, respectively.
4. Relationship between brain dysfunction and specific learning disorders: A child could exhibit (a) symptoms of brain dysfunction but no detectable learning disability, (b) both brain dysfunction and learning disability, or (c) a learning disability but no observable signs of brain malfunction. (Myers and Hammill 1976)
5. Other medical disorders (Kauffman and Hallahan 1976): More recently hypothesized causes include glandular disorders, hypoglycemia, narcolepsy complex, vitamin deficiencies, and allergies.

ENVIRONMENTALLY BASED ETIOLOGIES

1. Effect of emotional disturbance: Indications are that children with emotional problems tend to be poor in perception, speech, and academic subjects. (Myers and Hammill 1976)
2. Insufficient early experience: The sensorimotor processes need to be improved to increase perceptual abilities (perceptual motor programs often are implemented to improve perceptual skills). (Myers and Hammill, 1976)
3. Environmental deprivation (Kauffman and Hallahan 1976): There is a tendency for environmentally deprived children to exhibit learning problems that might be caused by inadequate learning experiences, poor teaching, or poor medical care that leads to brain damage.

CHARACTERISTICS OF SLD CHILDREN

Children with specific learning disabilities differ greatly from one another; however, some common types of characteristics have been observed. These characteristics are listed below to give teachers an indication of difficulties that SLD children might be experiencing; traits should not be used to label the child inappropriately. For instance, a child who is extremely easily distracted should not be considered learning disabled on that basis alone. Complete assessment and diagnostic procedures by qualified personnel are necessary before specific learning disabilities might be identified. One or more of the following characteristics might be exhibited. (Sherrill 1976 and Mann and Suiter 1974)

Poor Perceptual Abilities

Perception refers to cortical interpretation and organization of environmental sensory stimuli. Stimuli are interpreted in the brain as auditory, visual, olfactory (smell), gustatory (taste), cutaneous (tactile), kinesthetic (awareness of position and rate of movement of various parts of the body), and vestibular (location or position of the entire body in space) perceptions. (Myers and Hammill 1976)

Perceptual deficits do not include impairments in sensation. For example, visual acuity is considered an essential part of the visual sensory mechanism (eye), which provides sensory stimuli for interpretation into perceptual information. If there is a loss of visual acuity, this is not considered to be a learning disability. However, if the brain misinterprets the visual sensory input received, this is regarded as a visual perceptual deficit. Poor perceptual abilities might be observed in different areas.

Auditory perception. Deficits might occur in the auditory perceptual abilities described below.

- Auditory discrimination: Ability to differentiate between similar sounds, vowels, or consonants.
- Auditory closure: Ability to synthesize sounds or go from parts to the whole (for example, to hear part of a word and know what the entire word is).
- Auditory figure-ground: Ability to disregard irrelevant background sounds.
- Auditory localization and attention: Ability to locate source and direction of sound.

Among the more prevalent types of auditory perceptual deficits is auditory agnosia, the inability to recognize sounds or combinations of sounds with regard to their meaning. Another is auditory dissociation; sounds are heard and recognized but cannot be put into a meaningful whole.

Visual perception. Deficits might occur in visual perceptual abilities described below:

- Visual closure: Pattern completion, mechanism responsible for automatic completion of familiar visual symbols (for example, to see parts of an incomplete picture of a dog and know what the whole is).
- Visual discrimination: Ability to distinguish differences between similarly shaped objects, letters, or words ("b" and "d" appear to be different to a child).
- Visual form discrimination: Ability to distinguish differences between forms presented visually (for example, can distinguish between triangle and diamond forms pictured on cards).
- Visual figure-ground relationship: Tendency of one part of a visual configuration to stand out clearly while the remainder forms a background

(for example, can identify one entire figure of a girl from a picture of three similar figures of a girl superimposed on each other).

- Size perception: Ability to perceive a constancy in the size of an object.
- Depth and distance perception: Perception of length, depth, and distance of many stationary and moving objects seen.
- Object recognition: Ability to integrate visual stimuli into a meaningful whole or object.

One of the common types of visual perceptual deficits is visual agnosia, the loss of or impairment of the ability to recognize visually objects or events. Another is stereopsis, the inability to perceive objects in three dimensions. A third is visual dissociation, the inability to perceive visually things as a whole; the letter "w" might be perceived as separate lines rather than as one letter, for instance.

Tactile perception. The primary tactile perceptual ability observed is tactile discrimination, the ability to identify familiar objects or textures and locate the area of body being touched by someone else (by tactual input alone). Common problems relative to tactile perception include these:

- Astereognosis (tactile agnosia): Inability to identify familiar objects by touch alone.
- Finger agnosia: Inability to identify fingers as demonstrated by finger localization tests (examiner touches finger that child is supposed to identify without vision) or by self-drawings.
- Tactile defensiveness: Inappropriate, excessive response to tactual input, there may be a very negative response to being touched, a craving to be touched, or the avoidance of contact with surfaces that provide strong tactual input, such as carpeting and brushes.

Olfactory and gustatory perception. Little relationship to learning disabilities has been observed.

Body Awareness Difficulties

Body awareness is defined as the concept and awareness that people have of their own body and its relationship to the environment during movement behavior. Factors involved in the development of body awareness include kinesthesia (recognition of the orientation of the different parts of the body with respect to each other, as well as of the rates of movement of the different parts of the body) and assimilation of sensory input from vestibular and visual apparatus.

Difficulties in body awareness skills might occur in these areas:

- Spatial orientation: Awareness of space around the child in terms of distance, direction, and position.
- Laterality: Knowledge of left or right sides of the body.
- Verticality: Concept of upward and downward directions.
- Body image: Concept and awareness of body and its parts.
- Midline of body: Concept of vertical midline of body (separates body into two equal sides).

Problems often seen in body awareness include autotopagnosis, a disorder of body orientation and inability to identify body parts, and finger agnosia (also mentioned under tactile perception), the inability to identify fingers during finger localization tests.

Disorders of Motor Activity

Motor deficits often are observed in children diagnosed as learning disabled; it is possible that the motor problem and the learning disability have a common etiology (Myers and Hammill 1976).

Disorders of motor activity might be observed in

- Balance and postural maintenance: Difficulties in sitting, standing, postural maintenance, and specific balance.
- Locomotion and basic movement: Deficits might occur in skills such as walking, running, climbing, body mechanics, jumping, hopping, galloping, skipping, and gross body movement patterns.

The more prevalent types of motor disorders include these:

- Hyperactivity (hyperkinethesis): restless, erratic, random, and excessive mobility.
- Hypoactivity (hypokinethesis): Quiet, inactive, and insufficient motor activity.
- Clumsiness: Motor control difficulties with display of asynchronous and inefficient motor behavior in the form of physical awkwardness and lack of coordination.
- Apraxia (dyspraxia): Inability to initiate or voluntarily carry out motor planning to perform a complex movement pattern or task (such as a series of motor tasks to skip or hop).
- Perseveration: Automatic and often involuntary continuation of behavior that might be observed in speaking, writing, oral reading, drawing, and pointing.
- Adiadochokinesia: Inability to execute rapid and alternating movements.

Psychomotor response to specific perceptual abilities is another related area. Difficulties in psychomotor performance have been noted that are related to specific perceptual dysfunction. These include:

- Poor psychomotor response to auditory perception: specific auditory perceptual disabilities cause poor psychomotor response to auditory cues. For example, a child with deficient auditory discrimination might not be able to respond appropriately when the words "talk" and "walk" (similar sounds with different actions) are spoken.
- Poor psychomotor response to visual perception: Specific visual perceptual disabilities cause poor psychomotor response to visual cues. For instance, a child with faulty visual figure-ground relationship might not be able to distinguish a white ball high overhead against the background of the sky and, accordingly, might not catch the ball well.
- Poor psychomotor response to tactile perception: Inadequate psychomotor response to tactile cues is caused by faulty tactile discrimination. For example, the child might not be able to distinguish (by picking up while blindfolded) two nickels from a grouping of two nickels and two quarters on the table.

Another area where difficulties may be present is manipulation. Inadequate fine manual motor skills used in manipulation might be observed especially if extensive eye-body coordination and precise handling of such items as pencils or crayons are required.

Inappropriate Levels of Attention

Deficits in attention levels have been observed as either insufficient attention or excessive attention. Appropriate attention levels are prerequisites to desirable motivation and successful performance. There are two inappropriate attention levels. One is insufficient attention, the inability to screen out superfluous extraneous stimuli, often termed distractibility, hyperawareness, hyperirritability, or short attention span. The other is excessive attention, abnormal fixations of attention on unimportant details while disregarding the essentials of the event or situation.

Social or Emotional Difficulties

Emotional instability often accompanies a type of learning disability. Emotional difficulties may be due to prolonged dependency on others as a result of motor disorders, frustrations caused by lack of successful contact with others, and disturbed patterning of impulses. In addition, the child might have inadequacies in social perception, which would be observed as the inability to recognize meaning and significance of the behavior of others with resultant poor social adjustment.

Disorders of Memory (Imagery)

Difficulties in short-term and long-term memory might occur in the assimilation, storage, and/or retrieval of information that might be associated with difficulties in tactual, visual, auditory, or other learning systems. For instance, a child might not be able to associate accurately the auditory memory of a word he has heard with the same word he hears at a later time. Similarly inabilities to revisualize, reproduce, or use visual information are considered types of impairments in visual memory. Potential problems in various memory systems are quite numerous and might be demonstrated as poor recall, inaccurate reproduction, deficient association, improper sequencing with other sensory input, and/or translation to motor output.

Symbolization Difficulties

Problems might arise in the representation of experience symbolically (symbolization) of both nonverbal and verbal symbolic processes. Killen (1975) described nonverbal symbolism as receptive (seeing a flag or hearing a sound), inner thought (inner incorporation of auditory, visual, and tactile-kinesthetic components into symbol of experience), and expressive (drawing a picture or pantomiming). Nonverbal inner thought leads to development of inner thought for verbal symbols. Verbalization of the word *car* is based upon the previous nonverbal symbols developed regarding a car(s). From the system of integrative inner verbal thought, verbal reception and expression develop. Verbal symbolism is involved in listening, speaking, reading, and writing.

There are numerous problems that might occur in varying degrees in one or more areas of symbolization. A few of these are given below.

1. Receptive-auditory symbolization: The child may not understand the spoken word or confuses verbal commands. Examples include:

- Echolalia: Echoing speech heard in a parrot-like manner without comprehension.
- Receptive aphasia: Spoken language is heard but not understood; this disorder might cause child to be nonverbal.

2. Receptive-visual symbolization: The child may not understand what he reads. Examples include:
   - Strephosymbolia: Visual memory for a word pattern and letter orientation is confused or reversed (word blindness).
   - Visual dyslexia: Inaccurate association between visual input of written words and/or letters and auditory image of what is read. Similarly shaped letters such as o, e, c, b, p, d, h, and n could be transposed in reading (*pot* could be read as *top*).
3. Expressive-oral symbolization: The child cannot verbalize meaningfully about objects or describe their function, has inadequate syntax, and/or is unable to express ideas verbally. Examples include:
   - Dysnomia: Inability to recall words appropriate for objects. *Milk* might be expressed as *water*.
   - Syntax and formulation difficulties: Inability to organize words into appropriate linguistic patterns or grammatically correct verbalization. The child might say "mother car go" instead of "mother is going in the car."
4. Expressive-motor symbolization: The child cannot express himself well in speech, in writing, or in manual gestures or facial expressions. An example is dysgraphia, an inability to express thoughts in writing; letters might be omitted or words written inaccurately.

Conceptualization Problems

Difficulties often occur in the ability to categorize and classify experience, which is the highest level of cognitive development (conceptualization). Mann and Suiter (1974) described the different levels of concept development as concrete (an apple and an orange are both round), functional (an apple and an orange can both be eaten), and abstract (an apple and an orange are both fruit).

ADAPTATION OF PHYSICAL ACTIVITY PROGRAM

Consideration of the many different types of specific learning disabilities that might be manifested in children and youth indicates that an individualized program approach is necessary. The program must be comprehensive since these participants need the contributions of a well-developed physical activity program the same as all other individuals their age. Of course, the total program should include, and stress if necessary, any remedial activities indicated for alleviation of specific learning deficits that have been diagnosed.

During recent years, overemphasis has been placed upon perceptual motor training programs for the learning disabled child to the exclusion of other physical activities, such as physical fitness development, aquatics, rhythms, and leisure-time skills. A review of the literature concerning physical education programs for children with learning disabilities reveals that the primary thrust of research investigations and program materials has been in the area of perceptual motor training. Perceptual motor training is highly controversial, and no definite answer is available at this time regarding its effectiveness (see chapter 13 for a detailed discussion of this topic).

Perceptual motor training programs often present a shotgun approach; educators implement a total program of a perceptual motor theorist that may or may not hit upon the specific deficit the child is experiencing. Actually a child may have a specific learning disability that is not a distinct perceptual deficit, such as strephosymbolia (poor visual memory), and may not need a perceptual motor remediation program. Use of an existing perceptual motor training program that is not exactly related to the deficit demonstrated usually is a waste of time and money for the persons involved.

Even when a type of perceptual motor training program is needed—if, for example, the child has autotopagnosis (disorder of body orientation and inability to identify body parts)—a relevant program may not exist. Available perceptual motor testing and training programs usually cover a limited number of factors and are insufficiently comprehensive. This forces teachers to study various perceptual motor theories, test items and batteries, and training programs and to use an eclectic approach in developing an individualized program for each participant.

Some of the deficits discussed previously might be exhibited by a participant, and a myriad of additional and/or more complex disorders might be present. Therefore, it is essential that evaluative procedures be followed, in conjunction with educational and therapeutic personnel, to ascertain functional levels of the child.

It is difficult to identify many of the types of learning problems in particular, those that are involved with cortical integrative function. Also it is difficult for the teacher to know exactly what the problem is when a child demonstrates an obvious motor problem such as inability to bat a ball. The child could be having difficulty in the sensory input processes, or in cortical integration, or in the motor output system, or a combination of several deficits. It is necessary to identify, as much as possible, the dysfunction that is occurring in the total learning process. In that way, an appropriate physical activity program might be designed to assist in remediating the specific disorder in addition to providing a complete program.

The teacher should select the appropriate age range section of the *Geddes Psychomotor Inventory (GPI),* part I and the appropriate checklist(s) from part II for assessment of psychomotor performance levels. In the case of a 12-year-old child who has a diagnosed or suspected learning disability, the teacher would use the Intermediate Level age range of the GPI part I and the checklist "*Individuals with Specific Learning Disabilities.*" If the student was exhibiting behavioral difficulties, the teacher would also use the checklist "*Individuals with Behavioral Disabilities.*" In addition, the child should be assessed on the portion of the GPI part I for Primary Level, which is concerned with perceptual abilities and body awareness skills. Results of these evaluative procedures in addition to other teacher-selected assessment instruments would then be utilized to complete the *GPI Profile* and the *Psychomotor Individualized Educational Program (IEP)* form. The IEP form indicates the activities that should be provided from the *Geddes Psychomotor Development Program (GPDP).*

Some specific program suggestions follow:

- It is important to work closely with all related educational and therapeutic personnel to understand the child completely, to communicate information, and to employ special methods and techniques that have been effective in educational or therapeutic situations.
- Provide physical activities based upon individual functional levels and needs so that the child might have appropriate movement experiences to learn about the environment, himself, and others in addition to gaining the benefits of vigorous physical exercise.

- If a perceptual motor program is necessary, employ an eclectic approach in developing it. Be knowledgeable of and select from existing perceptual motor training programs in accordance with the specific deficit. In addition, use regular physical education activities such as movement exploration or rhythms to alleviate specific perceptual or body awareness disabilities. For example, provide the child with laterality difficulties with rhythmic activities in which she must use right and left sides of the body ("Hokey-Pokey").
- Identification of the specific learning disability will indicate the avenue of learning that might be employed. For instance, if the child has visual, perceptual or memory problems, use of auditory cues and kinesthetic input will constitute a good learning strategy. Knowledge of effective learning strategies for use with various children will give ideas for potentially successful activities, assist in organizing homogeneous class subgroups, and identify teachers or aides who would be desirable to work with the child because of their own styles of teaching and leading.
- Many times, the child needs a structured program to the extent that she knows the routines usually followed and has a sense of security regarding activities to be performed. If necessary, have the child respond promptly to teacher command and move to and from a clearly identified spot in the gymnasium.
- The whole child should be considered. Because of previous experiences imposed by her learning disorder, the child might be confused, lonely, anxious, frustrated, have a poor self-concept, lack confidence, and have poor social relationships with peers and other people. To the extent that any of these deficits can be improved, important general benefits can be expected.
- Select appropriate experiences in which the child might be successful. If a child has a problem with fine eye-hand coordination, provision might be made for gross motor activities such as swimming, bowling, running track, or jumping rope.
- If the participant is apprehensive about participating in competitive activities such as games or relays, do not force this participation. Gradually develop the motor skills and psychosocial competencies that are prerequisites for competition. Supplementary game skill instruction should be provided for successful participation. Assist the participant to progress from individual to dual to small-group to large-group activities.
- Reduce the stimuli in the physical activity situation that tend to distract, irritate, or undesirably arouse the child. Approaches to consider include removal of all equipment or supplies currently not in use, presentation of a neutral atmosphere, elimination of unnecessary noises, and individual play isolated from other students.
- If the student is demonstrating any of the characteristics described in the preceding section of this chapter—poor body awareness, perhaps, or deficient psychomotor response to specific perceptual abilities—appropriate activities should be offered to improve these abilities.
- Program organization and group placement depend upon the individual participant's needs. Consideration should be made of placement in regular, separate, or combinations of special and mainstreamed situations. Activities should be taught using aides, volunteers, resource teachers, and supplementary instruction. These arrangements should be flexible and allow for schedule and/or group placement changes when indicated.

REFERENCES

Anderson, Robert P., and Halcomb, Charles G. eds. *Learning Disability/Minimal Brain Dysfunction Syndrome—Research Perspectives and Applications.* Springfield, Ill.: Charles C. Thomas, 1976.

Gearheart, Bill R. *Learning Disabilities Educational Strategies.* St. Louis: C. V. Mosby Co., 1977.

Geddes, Dolores. *Physical Activities for Individuals with Handicapping Conditions.* 2d ed. St. Louis: C. V. Mosby Co., 1978.

Hallahan, D., and Cruickshank, W. *Psychoeducational Foundations of Learning Disabilities.* Englewood Cliffs, N.J.: Prentice-Hall, 1973.

Hallahan, Daniel P., and Kauffman, James M. *Exceptional Children: Introduction to Special Education.* Englewood Cliffs, N.J.: Prentice-Hall, 1978.

Kauffman, James M., and Hallahan, Daniel P. *Teaching Children with Learning Disabilities, Personal Perspectives.* Columbus, Ohio: Charles E. Merrill Publishing Co., 1976.

Killen, James R. "A Learning Systems Approach to Intervention." In Helmer R. Myklebust, ed., *Progress in Learning Disabilities,* 3: 1–17. New York: Grune & Stratton, 1975.

Kirk, Samuel A. *Educating Exceptional Children.* Boston: Houghton Mifflin, 1972.

Mann, Philip H., and Suiter, Patricia. *Handbook in Diagnostic Teaching: A Learning Disabilities Approach.* Boston: Allyn & Bacon, 1974.

Myers, Patricia I., and Hammill, Donald D. *Methods for Learning Disorders.* New York: John Wiley, 1976.

National Advisory Committee on Handicapped Children. *First Annual Report. Special Education for Handicapped Children.* Washington, D.C.: U.S.O.E., Department of Health, Education, and Welfare, 1968.

Sherrill, Claudine. *Adapted Physical Education and Recreation: A Multidisciplinary Approach.* Dubuque, Iowa: Wm. C. Brown, 1976.

Waugh, Kenneth W., and Bush, Wilma Jo. *Diagnosing Learning Disorders.* Columbus, Ohio: Charles E. Merrill Publishing Co., 1971.

8

BEHAVIORAL DISABILITIES

Many children and youths exhibit different types of behavioral and emotional disabilities. These disturbances might be associated with another handicapping condition (such as mental retardation or a specific learning disability) or they might be manifested as the only disability. Teachers will encounter such participants in both regular and special physical activity programs since these people would be placed educationally in accordance with the severity of the condition.

Most of those with behavioral disabilities at a mild level of severity are found in the regular or mainstreamed program, while those with a moderate behavioral disability are placed in either or both regular and special classes. Quite severe disturbances in children would be observed in special situations.[1] Presumably, however, the impact of legislation for the education and treatment of handicapped persons will cause additional occurrences of more severely disturbed persons in the regular program.

Behavioral disabilities are evidenced by a variety of complex and interacting surface behaviors that are so extreme in deviation from normal behavior that the person and others are negatively affected. These behavioral disturbances are expressed because of antagonism within the person and with the world around him. Such dissension also interferes with the child's learning ability and performance on psychometric tests. Many behaviorally disturbed children score in the slow learner and mildly retarded ranges of intelligence test scores.

There is little agreement among educators regarding the definition of the most commonly used label for these children, emotionally disturbed.[2] However, common factors underlying most definitions include extreme long-term behavior and behavior that violates or does not meet the expectations of social or cultural standards. Bower (1969) defined emotionally handicapped children as those who exhibit some of the following characteristics in an extreme and chronic fashion:

---

1. Extremely severe disturbances such as schizophrenic, psychopathic, and psychotic behavior are not included in this chapter.

2. Other categorical terms include maladaptive social-emotional behavior, behaviorally disordered, educationally handicapped, and psychologically disordered.

- learning problems which cannot be explained by intellectual, sensory, or health factors;
- poor interpersonal relationships with peers and teachers;
- inappropriate types of behavior or feelings;
- general, pervasive mood of unhappiness or depression; and
- tendency to develop physical symptoms, pains, or psychological fears associated with personal or school problems.

PREVALENCE

The estimate of prevalence of children and youths with behavioral disabilities varies according to the person making the calculation, the definition used, the reason for estimating, and the evaluative criteria employed (Reinert 1976). The majority of persons have mild to moderate behavioral disabilities.

Estimates range from 2 to 22 percent of school-age children, with greater identification of boys than girls. Since girls are more apt to demonstrate passive or withdrawn behaviors than boys are, it is assumed that girls are not identified as readily. Aggressive, acting-out behavior is displayed more prevalently by lower-class than middle- or upper-class children (Graubard 1969).

CAUSES

Investigations into causes for behavioral disorders can be considered in terms of rationales concerning biological or organic deficits, psychological or psychodynamic disorders, environmental conflicts, and maladjustment of socioadaptive behavior (Reinert 1976; Garrison and Force 1965). Conceptual approaches could overlap and might be similar in some aspects, although different terminology is used.

Biological or Organic Deficits

Organic deficits alone or in combination with environmental factors produce behavioral disorders. A child with a central nervous system dysfunction or a biochemical disorder may exhibit a variety of behavioral disturbances. In addition, environmental factors such as poor nutrition or lack of sleep will aggravate the effects of physical defects such as hormonal imbalance, brain damage, schizophrenic genotype, or enzyme defect. Biological or organic deficits are not easily identified although it seems that quite severe conditions, such as autism and schizophrenia, are more likely to have a biological etiology than are more mild conditions.

Psychological or Psychodynamic Disorders

Psychological or personality problems often are observed in children and youths. Theoretical rationale to explain causation for this behavior often is made in terms of the Freudian psychoanalytic model (imbalance of the id, ego, and superego) and humanistic psychological approaches described by theorists such as Adler, Maslow, Allport, Combs, and Rogers (Reinert 1976).

Some advocates of psychoanalysis believe that early negative interactions between parent and child, and in particular, mother and child, are the primary causes for severe emotional problems. Parents who are lax in disciplining their children but who react to misbehavior in a cruel, hostile, or rejecting manner are likely to have aggressive or delinquent children. However, deviant children may influence their parents as much as parents influence them (Hallahan and Kauffman 1978).

Environmental Conflicts

Societal pressures upon the child and unsuccessful interaction of the child to the cultural environment often produce deviant behaviors. Also, the child might not understand her role in society or she might be reacting negatively toward prejudices expressed toward her as a member of a minority group or as a handicapped person. A person often reacts to these forces in terms of breaking societal rules or laws and rebelling against authority.

Maladjustment of Socioadaptive Behavior

Socioadaptive behavior is considered to be reactions and adjustments that an individual makes in response to the environment and life experiences. Factors underlying socioadaptive behavior include developmental maturation, social adjustment, and learning ability. If a person deviates chronically from the normal range of progression in socioadaptive behavior, then this is considered to be a maladjustment or maladaptive behavior. Poor parent-child and peer relationships and attitudes are major causes for this type of maladjustment. Sometimes the situation becomes more aggravated after the child starts school if poor interaction of the child with peers and/or teacher(s) occurs.

These causal perspectives often interact as contributing factors toward the development of a behavioral disturbance so that it is difficult to identify any single reason for the problem. Identification of or speculation about causes for behavioral disorders also indicates the type of treatment program that would be used. For example, if a child is experiencing psychological problems that have been interpreted by a psychoanalytic model, it would be more important to emphasize treating the fundamental psychodynamic causes rather than the current surface behaviors. On the other hand, if a child is demonstrating maladjustment of socioadaptive behavior as described by a behavioral model, the treatment approach would stress modifying the learned inappropriate behaviors rather than correcting underlying causes.

TYPES OF SURFACE BEHAVIORS

Surface (observable) behaviors are reflections of inner feelings such as anger, sense of failure, fear, frustration, anxiety, poor self-concept, insecurity, poor self-acceptance, identity problems, and sense of rejection by others. These behaviors are often accompanied by additional problems like academic failure or stuttering.

Surface behaviors primarily are aggressive, withdrawing, or defensive in nature. In addition, some severely and profoundly disturbed persons become out of touch with reality.

Aggression

Aggressive or acting-out behavior is often observed in the form of hostility, belligerency, yelling, crying, temper outbursts, teasing, disruptiveness, hyperactivity, vandalism, resistance to adult authority, delinquency, physically striking others, and refusing to cooperate.

Withdrawal

Withdrawing behaviors are not very noticeable and are often overlooked by teachers. In fact, participants who are withdrawn often are considered to be well behaved since they do not actively confront the teacher. Common withdrawal behaviors are passivity, daydreaming, immaturity, thumb sucking, extreme fear, failure to talk, reluctance to socialize, playing alone, complaining of feeling ill, not responding when spoken to, self-stimulating behavior, and being easily depressed.

Defensive Behavior

Defense mechanisms are behaviors that serve to protect a person from psychologically dangerous situations. These mechanisms are used by all persons in the general population but are utilized excessively by behaviorally disabled persons who seek to defend themselves against the world around them. Examples of defense mechanisms are:

- Projection: Blaming others for one's own faults or deficiencies.
- Regression: Reverting to infantile behavior.
- Escape: Daydreaming or fantasizing to escape from reality.
- Rationalization: Using substitute reasons rather than the real reasons for actions.
- Repression: Inhibition or lack of memory regarding particularly painful or stressful events.
- Compensation: Developing a specific skill or talent to adjust to a deficit or shortcoming.
- Identification: Assuming the characteristics of someone who is greatly admired.

Other typical defensive behavioral characteristics have been observed; these include absenteeism, running away, tardiness, lying, cheating, stealing, irresponsibility, losing things, and avoiding work.

PSYCHOSOCIAL IMPLICATIONS OF ADDITIONAL HANDICAPPING CONDITIONS

Multitudinous interactions between physical activity and psychosocial development occur that have specific implications for an individual with a handicapping condition in addition to a single behavioral disability. The person with an additional handicapping condition has the same needs as other persons for the contributions of physical activity; in fact, these needs are compounded.

The body of knowledge specific to the relationship between physical activity in the physical education setting and mental health development of disabled persons is quite limited; most information focuses upon mentally retarded persons. However, more inquiries into psychosocial factors have been accomplished in the therapeutic recreation area since this field historically has placed greater emphasis upon human development in the affective domain.

Geddes (1976) analyzed almost five hundred studies regarding mental health development of mildly to moderately mentally retarded individuals:

> Specific contributions of active participation in physical activity programs to facets of a mentally retarded child's development have been reported. Self-concept has in-

> creased in the stress-free, noncompetitive and accepting environment of these programs that were helpful to the individual in building confidence and becoming better able to deal with stresses of everyday life. (p. 104)

> Social relationships, peer acceptance and other indicators of true group interaction and integration do not automatically result for retarded children through active participation in physical education, recreation, and related activities. Although some studies have shown positive relationships among a variety of physical/motor and social characteristics, several others have shown retarded youngsters in both regular and special physical education programs to be less accepted and more rejected at the end of such experiences than at the beginning. (pp. 104–105)

> Motivation and individual success are cornerstones for a successful overall program; success breeds success and often leads to reversal of the failure frustration cycle in which so many retarded persons have been locked. (p. 105)

Analyses of about forty studies (Geddes 1976) regarding mental health development of severely to profoundly mentally retarded persons revealed that:

> although little research has been accomplished in this area, it is assumed that many of the findings indicated for the mildly to moderately mentally retarded level are applicable to this lower level.... Social-emotional-adaptive performance levels are assumed to be much lower. There are extreme individual differences seen among these participants: mental health characteristics that are observed include exaggerated defense mechanisms, especially aggression and withdrawal; little self-motivation to move or play; dependence upon others; mental health problems such as autism, schizophrenia and psychosis; and deficient socio-adaptive behavior. (p. 106)

Psychological reaction to a handicapping condition differs from one person to another and is related to each individual's life experiences and environment. Maladaptive behavior might occur in some persons, while others would not feel handicapped by the disability. Sometimes the psychosocial problem resulting from frustration and poor social relationships leads to a more debilitating handicap than the original handicapping condition.

ADAPTATION OF PHYSICAL ACTIVITY PROGRAM

For determining the current psychomotor functional levels of behaviorally disabled students, the teacher should select the appropriate age range section of the *Geddes Psychomotor Inventory (GPI),* part I, and the appropriate checklist(s) from part II. Since it is anticipated that these students will function close to chronologic standards in psychomotor development, the age range of part I to be selected should be in accordance with actual chronologic age. The checklist "*Individuals with Behavioral Disabilities*" should be selected from part II. Data gained from these evaluative procedures would be analyzed to complete the *GPI Profile* and the *Psychomotor Individualized Educational Program (IEP)* form. The IEP form indicates the activities that should be provided from the *Geddes Psychomotor Development Program (GPDP)*. However, the strongest emphasis in the physical activity program should be given to the social-emotional development of the student.

Physical activity programs contribute to social-emotional development of participants in terms of (Geddes 1976):

- Human happiness or inner satisfaction such as sense of well being, enhanced self concept, increased self confidence, self actualization and improved body awareness;

- Social development such as socially acceptable attitudes, values, personality, and traits in character; social adjustment, and desirable social relationships with other persons in their environment;
- Emotional development such as improved emotional stability and well being, and desirable expressions of emotional feelings; and close relationship between organic health and social adjustment as part of the principle of mind-body unity. (p. 103)

The type of program that each participant should receive will depend partially upon the determinant(s) of the surface behaviors and the severity of the deviations. For example, if a child suffered a biological or organic deficit that resulted in a behavioral disturbance, then the treatment program would be developed in relation to this etiology. In this instance, many persons would not consider employing a behavior modification program since that approach does not consider cause(s) for surface behaviors. On the other hand, many behaviorists do not feel that it is important to consider the underlying cause(s) for the surface behavior. This is an important point since behavior modification programs are provided extensively to youngsters in the behavioral disabilities group.

Physical activity programs developed in direct relationship to or toward the amelioration of biological or organic deficits and psychological or psychodynamic disorders are not considered in the scope of this book. Therefore the following general suggestions are given primarily for improvement of the socioadaptive behavior:

- Provide activities that develop good sportsmanship, democratic relationships, and citizenship.
- Offer physical activities that ensure successful experiences with accompanying awards or certificates so that the person has satisfying and fulfilling experiences.
- Provide activities such as game situations, relays, tag games, dances, and sports to improve such problems as the need to establish short-term goals (since long-term goal cannot be planned), inadequate participation as an individual in a group, lowered leadership ability, social immaturity, and overeagerness for approval.

Approaches to consider for all participants, regardless of type of surface behavior, are these:

- Play therapy: Play activities are employed for a therapeutic purpose in terms of (1) providing opportunities for the child to express himself, (2) establishing a warm, friendly relationship between teacher and child, (3) allowing the child the time and freedom to solve his own problems, (4) acceptance of the child, and (5) respect for the child's ability to cope with the situation (Reinert 1976).
- Dance therapy: Dance therapy utilizes rhythmic movement experiences for therapeutic purposes on an individual basis. Goals include getting the child to relate to the environment and other persons, in addition to expressing himself.
- Behavior modification (operant conditioning): Behavior modification is a voluntary process employed in the educational setting that reinforces observable, operant behaviors (conscious responses to environment) so that these behaviors are repeated or extinguished. Behaviorists are concerned with overt behavior that might be modified rather than with internal causation such as poor self-concept or intrapsychic conflicts.

Behaviorists would employ positive reinforcement (considered by many people to be the best technique), negative reinforcement, or punishment.

A reinforcer of behavior is considered *positive* if the behavior it followed is maintained at a high level or is strengthened. For example, a teacher who immediately says "Great teamwork, Mary!" or "That's really good, Henry!" following observation of an appropriate behavior is giving a positive reinforcement. The reinforcement is positive *if* the desired behavior is continued at a high level or is increased and *if* the reinforcement really is something positive to or considered favorable by the child. This is important since the teacher might presume that a particular reinforcement would be positive to the child but in reality it is not. For instance, the teacher might present a piece of candy to the child after the desired behavior. If the child does not want the candy since she has just eaten or does not like candy, then the reinforcement would not be positive to this child. It is crucial that the teacher know if she is giving positive reinforcement for behaviors displayed by the students. If a child acts out (for example, by disrupting the class) and if the teacher scolds or yells at him, this could be positive reinforcement to the student if he is getting the attention that he wants.

A reinforcer of behavior is *negative* if its removal causes the appropriate behavior to become stronger. For example, if the removal of a shock that is given each time the bed is wet causes the child to increase bladder control, then the shock was a negative reinforcer.

Punishment is considered to be different from positive or negative reinforcement in that it is aimed toward decreasing specific behaviors. Punishment may be the presentation of aversive stimuli (such as shock, spanking, or loud noises) that the person wants to avoid or end. The teacher must know that the stimulus is indeed aversive rather than simply assuming that it is. For example, the teacher must decide whether spanking is something the child does not want or whether it gives the child the attention that he desires. Another aspect to consider is that a spanking will not make much impression on the child who is spanked to an extreme or hostile degree at home. Punishment also might be the removal of a positive reinforcer. For example, if the student likes physical education (positive reinforcer) but acts out, the child might be taken out of the class temporarily *(time-out)*.

The teacher who wishes to employ a behavior modification program should consider the following:

- The development of a behavior modification program should be accomplished in cooperation with personnel with this type of expertise, such as school psychologists, therapists, or qualified teachers. It is important that the behavior modification program be properly established so that it is both appropriate and effective and not hazardous to the child.
- The consequences (reinforcers) of behaviors must be immediate, consistent, and specific. The child needs to know exactly the behavior that is being reinforced. The teacher might say, "That's good, Tom; you took your turn."
- Start with primary reinforcers and progress from reinforcing every response to intermittent reinforcement. Subsequently use intangible reinforcers such as social rewards (praise and attention). Also the person's own self-satisfaction will serve as a reinforcement.

Consider the following reinforcers to *increase* behavior:

- Verbal praise: "You really hit the ball well, John."
- Approval: A pat on the back, a hug, or a smile.

- Attention: Give immediate attention to actions of that person.
- Special privileges: Assisting the teacher, lunch with the teacher, leading the exercises, being team captain, carrying out equipment, free time, extra playground time, keeping score, officiating, and going on field trips.
- Special rewards: Sweatbands, toys, bean bags, and balls.
- Primary reinforcers: A snack that the child particularly enjoys.
- Token reinforcers: Tokens (plastic chips, beans, stars, points) exchangeable for prizes, food, special rewards, or special privileges. The points can be given at the beginning of class and taken away for inappropriate behavior. Or the child can start without points and then gain them as desirable behavior is observed. Go from short-term to long-term goals. For example, a child earns points for appropriate behavior that apply toward a certificate given out after several months, which can be redeemed for a hamburger and drink. This approach has been used in the Los Angeles area under the sponsorship of a local fast-food franchise.
- Modeling: Teachers and peers serve as models for appropriate behavior.
- Contracts: The student agrees to achieve a long-term or short-term behavioral goal that is written down on a contract form. If and when the desired behavior is reached, the teacher signs the contract with praise and gives it to the child.
- Self-control: The student is told what is the desired behavior and works toward that goal. A chart might be used for the child to complete.

Consider the following reinforcers to decrease behavior:

- No reinforcement: The teacher ignores undesirable behavior (unless it is dangerous) and praises appropriate behavior.
- Rewarding behavior incompatible with undesired behavior: The teacher involves the child in physical activities so that he will not have time to disrupt the class or hit other children.
- Reprimands: Use softly spoken reprimands in a calm and firm manner so that other children cannot hear. Do this at the beginning of poor behavior.
- Time-out: Give time-out from physical activity. Have the student go to a small, isolated, screened-off section of the gymnasium or to a classroom. The student would lose the time if physical activity is a positive reinforcer. However, if physical activity is not greatly desired, the student would owe the teacher the amount of time-out and have to make it up later.

Suggestions are given below to give ideas to teachers who must select approaches or activities on an individual basis for persons who are aggressive, withdrawn, or defensive. These suggestions are not intended for use with all children. It is up to the teacher to determine the feasibility or desirability of using any of the program ideas.

These approaches deal with aggressive behavior:

- Have the person move as slowly as possible in movement exploration and rhythms or play freeze tag, which demands control of movement.
- Provide relaxation activities. (1) Have children lie down on their backs, close their eyes and, think intensively "about being ice cream slowly melting on the sidewalk because the sun is very, very hot." (2) Have students tighten up parts of their body and then loosen or relax these parts while lying on their backs in a quiet atmosphere. Start from the top of

the head and progress down to the toes. (3) Use Jacobson's (1938) techniques for progressive relaxation.

- Be aware of medication that a child might be taking for hyperactivity since this drug might cause drowsiness.
- Manually guide participants through physical activities to develop the kinesthetic sense of what is to be done.
- If the child is distractible, maintain contact and insist upon complete attention to you during instruction, or physically restrain the participant by holding his arms and speaking directly to him.
- Remove unnecessary equipment or distractions in the activity area.
- Increase attention span by providing short time periods of activity, which are gradually increased in duration.
- Start with gross-motor activities before fine-motor skills to avoid unnecessary frustration because of coordination problems.
- Have teacher or aide serve as a model showing nonaggressive responses to aggressive behavior of students.
- Have children role play nonaggressive behavior during story plays or movement exploration.
- Make aggressive children squad leaders and assign them definite responsibilities in performing this job.
- Use the names of the children frequently, particularly when first entering room and following appropriate behavior by the child.
- Use games or relays with definite boundaries such as hopscotch or shuttle relay.
- Encourage a behavior that is in conflict with inappropriate behavior—such as participation in sports or athletics so students will have less time for acting-out behavior.
- Have students contract for an amount of work to be done in the activity period in order to have free time to enjoy special privileges or activities of special interest.
- Use satiation techniques, for example, if a participant throws a ball out of the activity area, have him do this over and over following ball retrieval until she no longer desires to do so.
- If a participant frequently runs from the room, station yourself between him and the door to stop him from leaving.
- Keep rules to a minimum and established for easy understanding. Exact consequences to rule breaking should be clearly understood and enforced.
- Give praise or approval to the student in a low voice so others will not hear and use nonverbal cues such as a pat on the back or a smile as much as possible whenever appropriate behavior is displayed.
- Provide games or rhythms that require concentration, listening, and responding, such as musical chairs or squirrels in the trees.
- Break up perseveration or rigid patterns of behavior by channeling them into more flexible movement patterns such as in movement exploration or rhythms.
- Allow participants free play time following very structured or authoritarian techniques.
- Have participants perform activities such as walking a low balance beam so that concentration is given to task at hand or the participant will fall off.
- Structure the environment while working toward a goal that is known by participant.
- Provide the same daily routine for class organization; for example, have participants come into the room or gymnasium, go to their places, per-

form exercises, go though the activity of the day, do relaxation activities, and then be dismissed for the next class.

- Present one activity at a time using one primary avenue of sensory input—for example, verbal command.
- Establish a systematic routine for participants to follow rules and respond to instructions.
- Have a participant work in a small, screened-off area of the activity area or in an area with specific boundaries, such as on a mat or in a hoop.
- Be relaxed and calm but enthusiastic while working with participants.
- Give short and simple commands to participants. Give them time to think and make a decision and urge them into action if they do not move quickly enough; for example, say "Now, John!"
- Place students in a progression from individual to dual to small-group to large-group situations according to levels of socioadaptive behavior.
- Give instructions to the participants from the same place every day.
- Use the same signals daily to start various activities—perhaps blowing a whistle once or twice.

These approaches deal with withdrawn behavior:

- Physically guide participants through the activity—for example, through the performance of a forward roll.
- Establish individual activities to develop physical fitness and improve the physical appearance of each participant.
- Be aware that participants should not be forced into activities such as swimming, tumbling, or apparatus work if they are fearful or anxious about this participation.
- Invite the child to participate in the activity and then progressively increase her attention to the activity and try to keep her in the group.
- Present multiple sensory stimulation in order to obtain one response; verbal, visual, and tactile cues can be used for one specific performance, for instance.
- Establish time periods for active participation and free play alone.
- Bring the participant into group activity where she can contribute in an inconspicuous manner.

These approaches deal with defensive behavior:

- Emphasize activities in which the participant might achieve success.
- Emphasize nonverbal reinforcement such as body gestures, smiles, and a pat on the back whenever desired behavior is seen.
- Establish a program that will entice the participant to be present.
- Establish stations of different activity in the gymnasium so that persons will be able to choose the activities that are least threatening.

REFERENCES

Bower, E. M. *Early Identification of Emotionally Handicapped Children in School* 2nd Ed. Springfield, Ill.: Charles C Thomas, 1969.

Cruickshank, William M., and Johnson, G. Orville, eds. *Education of Exceptional Children and Youth.* Englewood Cliffs, N.J.: Prentice-Hall, 1959.

Gallagher, James J., ed. *The Application of Child Development Research to Exceptional Children.* Reston, Va.: Council for Exceptional Children, 1975.

Garrison, Karl C., and Force, Dewey G. *The Psychology of Exceptional Children.* New York: Ronald Press, 1965.

Geddes, Dolores. "Physical Activity for Impaired, Disabled and Handicapped Individuals." In Timothy T. Craig, ed., *The Humanistic and Mental Health Aspects of Sports, Exercise and Recreation,* pp. 103–107. Chicago: American Medical Association, 1976.

Graubard, P. S., ed. *Children against Schools.* Chicago: Follett, 1969.

Hallahan, Daniel P., and Kauffman, James. *Exceptional Children: Introduction to Special Education.* Englewood Cliffs, N.J.: Prentice-Hall, 1978.

Hewett, Frank M. *The Emotionally Disturbed Child in the Classroom: A Developmental Strategy for Educating Children with Maladaptive Behavior.* Boston, Mass.: Allyn & Bacon, 1970.

Jacobson, E. *Progressive Relaxation.* Chicago: University of Chicago Press, 1938.

Long, Nicholas J.; Morse, William C.; and Newman, Ruth G., eds. *Conflict in the Classroom: The Education of Emotionally Disturbed Children.* Belmont, Calif.: Wadsworth Publishing, 1969.

O'Leary, K. Daniel, and O'Leary, Susan G. *Classroom Management: The Successful Use of Behavior Modification.* New York: Pergamon Press, 1977.

Reinert, Henry R. *Children in Conflict: Educational Strategies for the Emotionally Disturbed and Behaviorally Disordered.* St. Louis: Missouri: C. V. Mosby Co., 1976.

9

AUTISTIC-LIKE PERSONS

Autism was described in 1943 by Kanner (1943) when he reported a syndrome called early infantile autism. Kanner's syndrome consisted of common characteristics observed in a group of children who were exhibiting abnormal behavioral patterns. These characteristics included extreme withdrawal from contact with people, strong attachment to objects, good potential in cognition, mutism or language disorders, desire for perseveration of sameness, attractive appearance, unusual abilities in memory, and superior performances in specific motor tasks.

Although some authors feel that this specific syndrome is in operation today (Rimland 1964, 1971; Kanner 1973), many others (Creak 1964; Rutter 1972) argue for a much broader view of autism. A common view that many hold is that the term *autistic-like* should be used to describe persons afflicted with profound aphasia, childhood psychosis, severe language disorders, behavioral disturbances, and inability to relate appropriately to others. This description includes but is not limited to Kanner's syndrome. Additional problems that might be observed include perceptual and cognitive deficits that cause problems in comprehension, communication, learning, and socialization. A general definition that covers all of these characteristics is provided by the National Society for Autistic Children (NSAC 1975): "persons, regardless of age, with severe disorders of communication and behavior whose disability became manifest during the early developmental stages of childhood."

PREVALENCE

Autism is a relatively rare condition; approximately two to five cases per 10,000 population are diagnosed (Oppenheim 1974). Estimates regarding autistic-like children vary depending on the definition used; however, an extensive study done in Middlesex, England reported that there were between four and five autistic children per 10,000 aged 8, 9, and 10 (Wing et al. 1967). The sex ratio is approximately four boys to one girl (Rimland 1964). In addition, many authors feel that parents of autistic children are likely to be middle class or above and professionally qualified (Wing et al. 1967; Kanner, 1973).

CAUSES

Autism was commonly viewed in earlier times as psychogenic in origin in which case parents, particularly the mother, were thought to be emotionally cold toward the infant, thus depriving the child of affection and happy experiences. A later version of this earlier theory was that the unresponsive nature of a child caused parents to treat him in a cold, mechanical manner. Currently this premise is not widely accepted since parents of autistic children seem to behave the same as other parents. However, some authors (Bettelheim 1967; Eisenberg 1967) specify types of parental failure that are reflected in the child's autistic behavior.

Some of the current research investigations into the etiology of autism include possibilities of biochemical error or central nervous system disturbance (Rimland 1971; Rutter and Bartak 1971; Rutter 1968; Chess 1971). Some researchers feel that these types of disturbances give the child a distorted picture of reality, causing improper responses to the world around him. Rimland (1964) views the hyperkinetic behavior of these children as indicative of improper functioning of the reticular activating system, which causes overarousal in the child. Ornitz (1974) feels that strange motility patterns could not be readily explained by either postulated states of overarousal or insufficient sensory stimulation. He considers the dysfunction of the modulation of motor output to be related in some way to faulty modulation of sensory input.

TYPES OF AUTISTIC-LIKE BEHAVIOR

A child with the label of autism could be exhibiting the classic Kanner's syndrome or one or more types of autistic-like behavior. The behaviors described below by Wing (1976) would rarely appear totally in one child although it could be expected that some of these characteristics would be seen:

- Language problems—problems in comprehension of speech, lack of speech, echolalia (repetition of words just heard), confusion over use of personal pronouns (may not use "I"), and pronunciation difficulties.
- Poor nonverbal communication—poor comprehension or lack of use of gesture, facial expression, and bodily posture.
- Abnormal responses to sensory experiences—inappropriate, indifferent, over-reactive, or frustrated response to auditory, visual, tactile, or cold temperature sensory input.
- Abnormal visual inspection—more use of peripheral than central visual field and "looking-through" people or at them only in brief glances.
- Problems in motor imitation—difficulty in copying movements and confusion of laterality and directionality.
- Problems of motor control—jumping, flapping limbs, rocking and grimacing when excited, springy tip-toe walk without arm/leg opposition, odd posture when standing, and erratic skill in movement patterns.
- Other problems—poor sleeping patterns and erratic eating and drinking habits.
- Unusual memory—recalls unimportant phrases or events exactly as originally experienced.

- Indifference to people—aloofness to other people, especially peers.
- Resistance to change in routines and attachment to objects—fascination with objects and repetitive routines.
- Poverty of imagination—inability to play creatively.
- Attention to trivial things or events—attending to minor aspects of environment rather than the total scene.
- Repetitive activities—repetitive, stereotyped movements, actions and sometimes self-abusive behavior.
- Socially immature behavior—screaming, kicking or inappropriate behavior.

ADAPTATION OF PHYSICAL ACTIVITY PROGRAM

Autistic-like persons enrolled in motor development programs usually are of a very heterogeneous nature and manifest a variety of behaviors. Since the participants differ greatly from each other, motor performance levels should be evaluated by selection of the appropriate age range section of the Geddes Psychomotor Inventory (GPI) part I and by the checklist *"Individuals with Autistic-like Conditions"* in part II. Since an autistic child probably will have a combination of below-age, at-age, and above-age performances in the psychomotor functioning area, the teacher should assess psychomotor performances using the age range section of the GPI part I in accordance with actual chronologic age. Then depending upon the child, other age range sections that are below age and above age should be employed. Information gained should be used to complete the *GPI Profile* and the *Psychomotor Individualized Educational Program (IEP)* form. The IEP form indicates the activities that should be offered from the *Geddes Psychomotor Development Program (GPDP)*. These activities will need to be greatly modified because of the autistic-like condition of the student. Therefore it is important that available literature concerning education and physical education for autistic-like persons be reviewed to determine which modifications should be made.

The literature suggests the following regarding the implementation of the program (Ayres 1973; Dewey 1972; NSAC 1975; Oppenheim 1974; Geddes 1977; AAHPER 1976; Best and Jones 1974; Davis, 1975; Everard 1976; Ornitz 1974).

Participants might be manifesting deficiencies in motor skills that are based upon language development (writing and drawing) or communication of pattern to be performed (riding a tricycle or hopping in a specific pattern) or appropriate relationship to objects (ball handling and kicking).

Participants might function at age in gross movement patterns, balance skills, and postural maintenance (walking, running, and climbing) since these motor skills are not dependent upon language development or specific relationships to surrounding environment.

Ayres's (1973) sensory integrative therapy approach is frequently employed to modify neurological dysfunctions interfering with learning. This approach assumes that the brain can be trained to perceive, remember, and motor plan better. The *Southern California Sensory Integration Tests* (Ayres 1972) are used in conjunction with the sensory integrative therapy program.

Emphasize motor activities in accordance with the type of specific perceptual deficit that the person might have, such as problems in laterality, directionality, verticality, spatial orientation, body awareness, and identification of body parts.

Channel bizarre behavioral patterns such as rocking the body back and forth or flapping hands into more meaningful motor activity. Break up perseverative patterns in movement.

Provide body stimulation activities in which the person becomes more aware of his body as it moves in the environment. These programs stimulate senses of touch, taste, and other areas of sensory input, in addition to enhancing the kinesthetic (physical) sense that the person has of his body.

Employ methods such as part-whole teaching, simple to complex progression, and physically guiding the person through a motor task.

Behavior modification techniques have been successfully used in educational situations; the physical activity teacher should employ the same types of behavioral modification techniques used by the classroom teacher or therapist. It is a good idea to observe or participate in the classroom activities to become familiar with the techniques used for each child.

A structured program is considered a successful approach. Constraints are put on the behavior of students, who know exactly what is expected of them. The environment is limited, planned, and organized by the teacher.

Maintain control. If the participants are literally rebounding off the walls and going off in all directions, utilize control approaches such as command teaching, staying in one place until time for performance, and obeying instructions. Extremely hyperactive persons might be better off in a small room with few distractions. If the participant demonstrates the other extreme in activity and is quite passive, try to motivate him to move and become interested in the activities offered.

Intrude on the withdrawal or detachment of a person and force him to participate in the ongoing activity.

Get the attention of the participant. Although it is possible that the problem of inattention might be due to a neurological or arousal problem, strive to obtain the attention of the participant to you and to the activity desired. If necessary, call out "look," or "John," make a loud noise, clap your hands loudly, or slap your hands on a table. Work on getting and increasing eye contact.

Assist the person to relate to people rather than objects. Change objects if necessary and substitute persons in their place during game situations or in rhythmics. If a person is obsessed with a particular object, change the manner in which the object is used. For example, if the person perseverates in handling a ball, add one more ball at a time so that several balls are utilized together in a more meaningful fashion or in a game situation. If the participant is obsessed with a string, add other strings so that a simple craft such as knotting string is performed. If it is necessary to remove an object from a child's manipulation, the object should be removed or substituted with other objects gradually over a period of time.

Motivate the child to use toys or objects in appropriate ways. If the child is obsessed with the wheels of a toy truck, work on playing with the truck in a normal fashion.

Assist the person in reacting appropriately to environmental changes.

It is essential that physical activities be related with the classroom or therapy program so that information regarding the participant is exchanged and common educational goals are identified.

Consult with the classroom teacher, therapist, and other related personnel who might have identified certain language disorders and who probably are working on alleviating these problems. Provide activities in which language development can take place, and use the language skill techniques that are being employed by the therapist. Realize that the student may not understand your instructions.

Employ a low student-teacher ratio. Additional assistance might be obtained from aides, volunteers, or students from other classes.

Begin with individual activities and work toward more cooperative play or motor performance. Assist the person to the highest level possible in socialization. Work from individual activity, dual activity, small-group activity, to large-group activity. As the person participates in group activities, he will be forced to maintain a certain amount of eye contact and to relate to other persons. Provide many opportunities for peer group relationships to be developed if this is appropriate. Be aware, though, that activities such as games and relays may be inappropriate if social skills have not developed to the state of a competitive spirit or understanding of competition.

Swimming is considered to be an excellent activity. Individual progress has been observed in participants who initially were fearful and apprehensive about touching the water.

Many autistic children do not know how to play so play skills may have to be taught.

Many autistic children have a good sense of rhythm and enjoy rhythmic activities although they might not sing well with a group.

Utilize dance therapy procedures such as mirroring an autistic child's movements so that the teacher is "blended" with the child; then progressively change minor movement patterns so that eventually the teacher is separate from the child. The goal is to have the child gradually realize that the teacher is there and is separate from himself.

REFERENCES

American Alliance for Health, Physical Education and Recreation. *Physical Education, Recreation, and Related Programs for Autistic and Emotionally Disturbed Children.* Washington, D.C.: The Alliance, 1976.

Ayres, A. J. *Southern California Sensory Integration Tests.* Los Angeles, Calif.: Western Psychological Services, 1972.

———. *Sensory Integration and Learning Disorders.* Los Angeles, Calif.: Western Psychological Services, 1973.

Best, J. F., and Jones, J. G. "Movement Therapy in the Treatment of Autistic Children." *Australian Occupational Therapy Journal* 21 (1974): 72–86.

Bettelheim, Bruno. *The Empty Fortress.* New York: Free Press, 1967.

Chess, S. "Autism in Children with Congenital Rubella." *Journal of Autism and Childhood Schizophrenia* 1 (1971): 33–47.

Creak, M. "Schizophrenic Syndrome in Childhood: Further Progress Report of a Working Party." *Developmental Medicine and Child Neurology* 6 (1964): 530–535.

Davis, D. "The Balance Beam: A Bridge to Cooperation." *Teaching Exceptional Children* 7 (1975): 94–95.

Dewey, M. "The Autistic Child in a Physical Education Class." *Journal of Health, Physical Education and Recreation* 43 (April 1972): 79–80.

Eisenberg, L. "Pyschotic Disorders in Childhood." In L. D. Eron, ed., *Classification of Behavior Disorders.* Chicago: Aldine Press, 1967.

Everard, M., ed. *An Approach to Teaching Autistic Children.* Oxford: Pergamon Press, 1976.

Geddes, D. "Motor Development of Autistic Monozygotic Twins: A Case Study." *Perceptual and Motor Skills* 45 (1977): 179–186.

Kanner, L. "Autistic Disturbances of Affective Contact." *Nervous Child* 2 (1943): 217–250.

———. *Childhood Psychosis: Initial Studies and New Insights.* Washington, D.C.: Winston, 1973.

National Society for Autistic Children. *Working Definition of Autistic Children.* Albany, N.Y.: NSAC, 1975.

Oppenheim, R. C. *Effective Teaching Methods for Autistic Children.* Springfield, Ill.: Charles C. Thomas, 1974.

Ornitz, E. M. "The Modulation of Sensory Input and Motor Output in Autistic Children." *Journal of Autism and Childhood Schizophrenia* 4 (1974): 197–215.

Rimland, B. *Infantile Autism: The Syndrome and Its Implications for a Neural Theory of Behavior.* New York: Appleton-Century-Crofts, 1964.

______. "The Differentiation of Childhood Psychoses: An Analysis of Checklists for 2,218 Psychotic Children." *Journal of Autism and Childhood Schizophrenia* 1 (1971): 161–174.

Rutter, M. "Concepts of Autism: A Review of Research." *Journal of Child Psychology and Psychiatry* 9 (1968): 1–25.

______. "Childhood Schizophrenia Reconsidered." *Journal of Autism and Childhood Schizophrenia* 2 (1972): 315–337.

Rutter, M. L. and Bartak, L. "Causes of Infantile Autism: Some Considerations from Recent Literature." *Journal of Autism and Childhood Schizophrenia* 1 (1971): 20–32.

Wing, J. K.; O'Connor, N.; and Lotter, V. "Autistic Conditions in Early Childhood: A Survey in Middlesex," *British Medical Journal* 3 (1967): 389.

Wing, L. "Assessment: The Role of the Teacher." In M. Everard, ed., *An Approach to Teaching Autistic Children*, pp. 10–11, 25. Oxford, Pergamon Press, 1976.

IV

GEDDES PSYCHOMOTOR DEVELOPMENT PROGRAM (GPDP)

A Psychomotor Individualized Educational Program

10

GEDDES PSYCHOMOTOR DEVELOPMENT PROGRAM (GPDP)

Primary Level Activities

From the following activities, select those that are indicated by the completed *Psychomotor Individualized Educational Program (IEP)* form.[1] Emphasize the activities associated with competencies recorded as "Improve." Give minimal emphasis to activities related to competencies recorded as "Maintain." Modify the activities according to the students' functional age levels and information given in the chapters on handicapping conditions. Activities that are repeated for several performance competencies are described at the end of this chapter in the section "*Description of Selected Activities.*"[2]

1. Describe additional activities on the blank program activities form provided in appendix C for selected performance competencies from the Infant or Early Childhood Levels of the Geddes Psychomotor Inventory (GPI), part I.

2. The page numbers in parentheses following each performance competency statement refer to the GPI long and short forms.

Figure 10–1. Walks forward on balance beam.

WALKS (on balance beam) (GPI pp. 64, 70)

Alternates steps forward on balance beam

Equipment: As indicated or items italicized

1. Walk forward, backward, and sideways:
   - balancing *bean bag* on head.
   - holding *heavy object* out to one side with outstretched hand.
   - catching thrown *yarn balls* and *foam balls*.
   - while visually focusing on one spot at the end of beam.
   - while bouncing a *ball* off floor on one side of beam.
   - while standing on toes.
   - stepping over *obstacles* on beam.
   - while *blindfolded*.
2. Walk forward to middle of beam, turn on both feet, and return to beginning end of beam.
3. Stand on one foot on beam as long as possible.
4. Stand on beam with arms close to sides of body.
5. Stand on beam, bend down and touch toes, then stand up again.
6. Walk on other surfaces on which it is difficult to maintain balance (such as *foam shapes* and *inner tubes*).
7. Other:__________

PRIMARY LEVEL ACTIVITIES (2)

Figure 10–2. Runs in physical activities (in games, runs with ball).

RUNS (GPI pp. 64, 70).

Runs in physical activities

Equipment: As indicated or items italicized

1. Run in game situations, relays, or tag games such as Back to Back; Wild Horses; Brownies and Elves; Call Ball; Run-Stop; Walk, Walk, Run; Huntsman; Simple Tag; Cat and Rat; and Basic Relay. See activities 1, 2, 3, 5, 6, 10, 12, 18, 21, and 50 on pages 172–174 and 180.
2. Run in movement exploration activities in response to questions posed by the teacher. See activities on page 167.
3. Play Follow the Leader emphasizing running. See activity 51 on page 180.
4. Run to music of *rhythms records* designed for running.
5. Run in creative drama and story plays, such as "the wind is blowing through the trees in a forest" or "the horse is running through the meadow."
6. Run with apparatus such as *hoops* or *wands.*
7. Other:______________________________________
____
____

PRIMARY LEVEL ACTIVITIES (3)

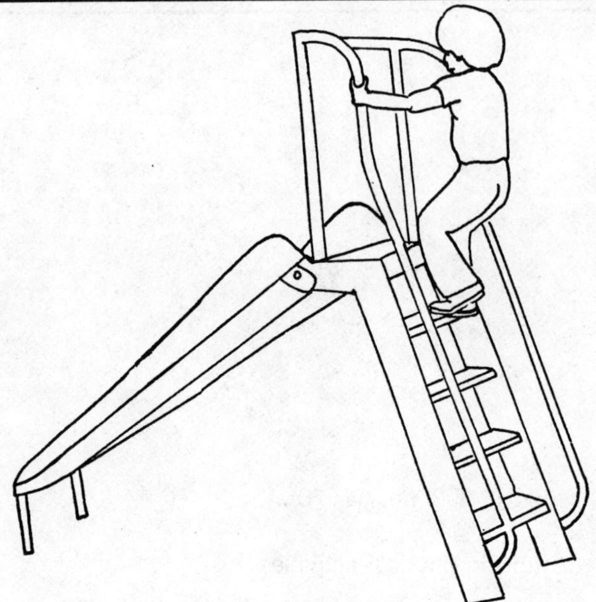

Figure 10–3. Climbs up steps to top of playground slide.

CLIMBS (GPI pp. 64, 70)

Climbs on apparatus

Equipment: As indicated or items italicized

1. Play on *Lind Climber.*
2. Play on *playground gym.*
3. Play on *climbing frames.*
4. Climb *ladders.*
5. Climb *1½" thick climbing ropes* for short distances (use a spotter and *landing mat*).
6. Climb up steps to top of *playground slide.*
7. Climb on *boxes* and jump down (need soft landing area).
8. Other:____________________

Figure 10–4. Lifts moderately heavy baskets.

BODY MECHANICS (GPI pp. 64, 70).

Lifts and carries moderately heavy objects

Equipment: As indicated or items italicized.

PRIMARY LEVEL ACTIVITIES (4)

1. Practice lifting *moderately heavy baskets* by bending at knees and using leg muscles to return to upright position. Carry boxes a specified distance keeping boxes close to body at trunk level.
2. Pick up moderately *heavy objects* (baskets, chairs, or medicine balls) from the starting line and put them down on goal line in Basic Relay. See activity 50 on page 323.
3. Pretend to pick *heavy objects* in movement exploration activities ("how do you pick up a heavy boulder?")
4. Act in story plays about picking up *heavy objects* ("giant picks up the house").
5. Other:____________________

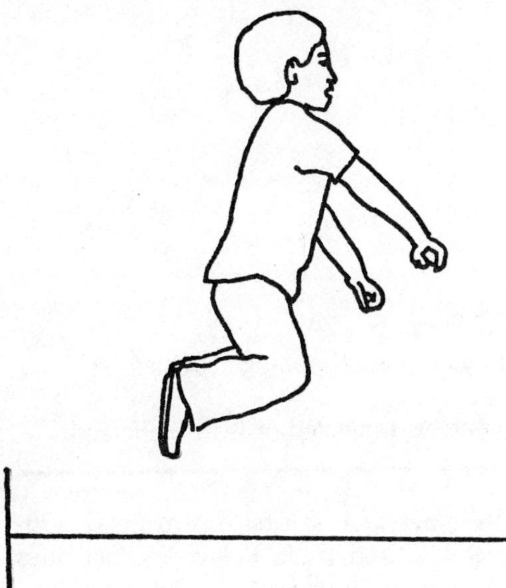

Figure 10–5. Standing broad jump.

JUMPS (GPI pp. 65, 70)

Jumps with and without equipment

Equipment: As indicated by items or tasks italicized.

1. Practice *standing broad jump.*
2. Compete with a partner in *standing broad jump.*
3. Attempt to land on a spot (an X made with *colored tape*) on floor by performing a standing broad jump.
4. Compete with other children in trying to mark highest level chalk mark on *chalkboard* by performing vertical jump.
5. Practice *short rope* jumping.
6. Jump *short* and *long rope* in time to slow and fast *music.*
7. Practice *vertical jump.*
8. Compete with a partner in *vertical jump.*
9. Attempt to touch suspended *balloon* or grab a *toy* held overhead.
10. Jump *long rope.*
11. Jump through *hula hoops* lying on the floor.
12. Jump over *low obstacles.*

Figure 10–6. Vertical jump.

PRIMARY LEVEL ACTIVITIES (5)

13. Jump in Follow the Leader. See activity 51 on page 180.
14. Play Frog in the Sea, substituting jumping for stepping, *Obstacle* Relay (modified), and Jump the Brook. See activities 11, 42, and 46 on pages 173 and 178–179.
15. Jump in movement-exploration of activities in response to questions posed by teacher. See activities on page 167.
16. Jump on *jump boards* or *mini trampolines*.
17. Jump off *jumping box* in variety of patterns.
18. Other:____________________

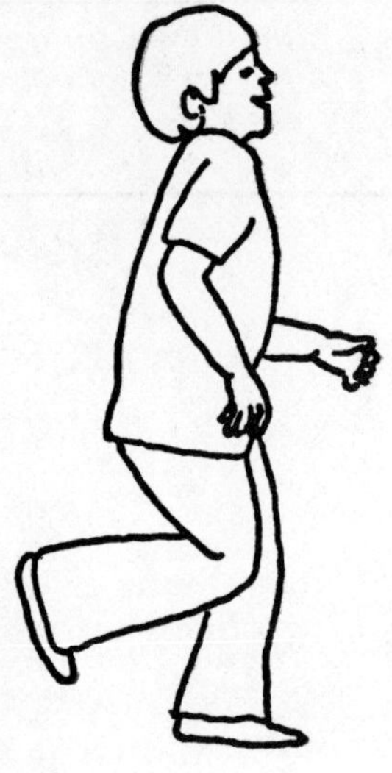

Figure 10–7. Practice hopping pattern.

HOPS (GPI pp. 65, 70)
Hops in games and hopping activities

Equipment: As indicated or items italicized.

1. Practice hopping pattern.
2. Hop in movement exploration activities in response to problems posed by teacher. See activities on page 296. Also pose the following problems:
   - How far can you hop in three hops?
   - Can you hop __steps forward and __steps backward?
   - Can you turn around while hopping in place?
   - Can you hop in one place?
   - Can you hop like a kangaroo [grasshopper, frog, rabbit]?
   - Can you hop on one foot and then on the other foot?
3. Hop in relays such as *Chalkboard* Relay, *Obstacle* Relay, and Basic Relay. See activities 28, 42, and 50 on pages 176, 178, and 180.
4. Hop to music of *rhythms records*.
5. Hop in game situations such as Run-Stop (modified), Animal Race, and Lame Man. See activities 6, 15, and 24 on pages 172 and 174–175.
6. Play Follow the Leader, emphasizing hopping. See activity 51 on page 180.
7. Play Hopscotch. See activity 47 on page 179.
8. Other:____________________

PRIMARY LEVEL ACTIVITIES (6)

Figure 10–8. Practice galloping.

GALLOPS (GPI pp. 65, 70)

Gallops in games and galloping activities

Equipment: As indicated or items italicized.

1. Practice galloping with and without the teacher.
2. Gallop in movement exploration activities in response to problems posed by the teacher. See activities on page 167. Also pose the following problems:
   - Can you gallop like a horse?
   - Can you gallop around the room without touching other children?
3. Gallop to music, using *phonograph records* designed for galloping.
4. Gallop in relays such as Animal Race (modified into relay), *Chalkboard* Relay, *Obstacle* Relay, and Basic Relay. See activities 15, 28, 42, and 50 on pages 174, 176, 178, and 180.
5. Play Duck, Duck, Goose (see activity 4 on page 172) substituting galloping for running.
6. Play tag games such as Wild Horses, Simple Tag, Run for Your Supper, and Freeze Tag. See activities 2, 18, 26, and 49 on pages 172, 174–175, and 180), substituting galloping for running.
7. Play Follow the Leader emphasizing galloping. See activity 51 on page 180.
8. Other:____________________

PRIMARY LEVEL ACTIVITIES (7)

Figure 10–9. Skips.

SKIPS (GPI pp. 65, 70)

Skips in games and skipping activities

Equipment: As indicated or items italicized.

1. Practice skipping with and without the teacher.
2. Skip in movement exploration activities in response to problems posed by teacher. See activities on page 167.
3. Skip to music, using *phonograph records* designed for skipping.
4. Skip in relays such as *Chalkboard* Relay, *Obstacle* Relay, and Basic Relay. See activities 28, 42, and 50 on pages 176, 178, and 180.
5. Play games such as Wild Horses, Drop the *Handkerchief,* Animal Race, and Crows and Cranes. See activities 2, 9, 15, and 31 on pages 172–174 and 176.
6. Skip in tag games such as Simple Tag, Squat Tag, Partner Tag, and Freeze Tag. See activities 18, 19, 32, and 49 on pages 174, 177, and 180.
7. Play Follow the Leader, emphasizing skipping. See activity 51 on page 180.
8. Other:____________________

Body Awareness

Concept and awareness that a person has of his or her own body and its relationship to the environment during movement behavior.

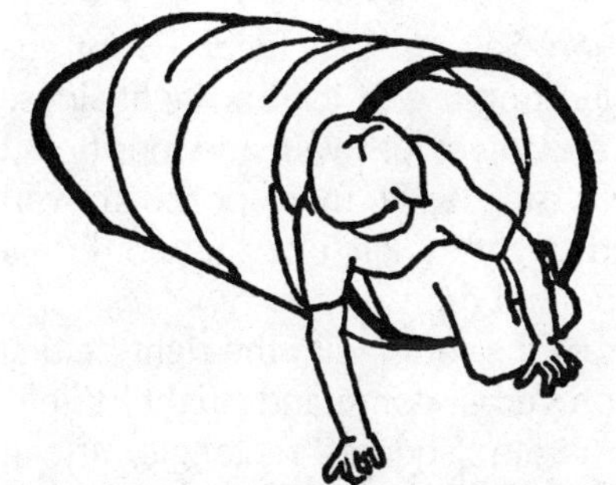

Figure 10–10. Negotiate tunnels without touching sides.

SPATIAL ORIENTATION (GPI pp. 65, 70)

Awareness of space around the child in terms of distance, direction, and position.

Equipment: As indicated or items italicized.

1. Go through obstacle course of *chairs, boxes, hula hoops,* and other objects arranged so that the child goes over, under, and between items.
2. Practice tumbling skills such as forward roll, backward roll, and cartwheel. See activities 1, 2, and 3 on pages 166–167.
3. Perform stunts and self-testing skills such as log roll, elephant walk, thread the needle, wring the dishrag, seal crawl, bear walk, tip-up, crab walk, egg roll, frog hop, inch worm, jump and slap heels, knee lift, step over the wand, balance stand, forearm headstand, handstand with support, and tripod. See activities 1–7, 9–19 on pages 167–171.
4. Play *parachute* activities such as walking in a circle, changing places with others across the circle, and making a dome and going under it.
5. Move quickly in movement exploration activities in response to problems posed by teacher. See activities on page 167.
6. Negotiate *tunnels* without touching sides.
7. Step into *hula hoop* lying on the floor, bend down, and pull it up and over the head without it touching the body.
8. Move to appropriate location when instructed "stand by the *chair* next to the *wall*" or "stand next to me."
9. Other:____________________

Figure 10–11. Position right or left side to wall on verbal command or after reading right or left on poster.

LATERALITY (GPI pp. 65, 71)

Knowledge of left and right sides of the body

Equipment: As indicated or items italicized

PRIMARY LEVEL ACTIVITIES (9)

1. Play Hokey-Pokey using *phonograph record.* Use other records that emphasize knowledge of left and right.
2. Perform movement exploration activities in response to problems posed by the teacher:
   - Can you run [walk, jump, hop, gallop, skip] to the left and then to the right?
   - Can you sway like a tree to the left [right]?
   - Can you lie down on your left [right] side?
   - Can you touch your left [right] foot [eye, hand, ear, leg, elbow]?
   - Can you turn in a circle to the right [left]?
3. Practice kicking [throwing, catching] balls on verbal command "left" ["right"].
4. Hop on right [left] foot on right [left] *footprints* made of *contact paper* that are on the floor.
5. Practice reading the word *right [left]* on *posters*, on *cards*, in *books*, and raising the right [left] hand when the word is read out loud.
6. Reach out and touch a *suspended*, swinging *ball* with the right [left] hand in response to the verbal command "right" ["left"].
7. Hop on right [left] foot in a relay in response to verbal command "right" ["left"].
8. Play Simon Says (see activity 65 on page 182, requesting use of left and right sides.
9. Run to an *object* or *wall* and position the right [left] side to it in response to verbal command "right" ["left"] or the word "right" ["left"] printed on a poster.
10. Slide across the room with the right [left] side leading on verbal command "right" ["left"].
11. Draw a circle [square, rectangle, triangle] from right to left [left to right] in response to verbal command "right" ["left"].
12. Walk, raise right [left] leg, and clap hands under that leg.
13. Clap right [left] hand of partner with your right [left] hand in response to verbal command "right" ["left"].
14. Play *Eraser* Relay. (See activity 35 on page 177.)
15. Turn a *long rope* to the right and then to the left.
16. Other: ____________________

Figure 10–12. Move up or down after reading word on poster.

VERTICALITY (GPI pp. 66, 71)

Concept of upward and downward directions

Equipment: As indicated or items italicized.

PRIMARY LEVEL ACTIVITIES (10)

1. Raise *hula hoops* up [down] in response to verbal command "up" ["down"] or after reading word "up" ["down"] on *poster*.
2. Jump up and down, saying the appropriate words "up" or "down" as it is performed. Vary routine by closing eyes.
3. Move up or down in response to seeing arrows pointing up or down that are drawn on *posters*.
4. Run through obstacle course, going up or down as *tables* marked "up" or "down" are negotiated. Climb up and down *ladders or steps*, saying "up" or "down" when appropriate.
5. Perform movement exploration activities in response to problems posed by the teacher:
   - Show me what a jack-in-the-box does.
   - How does toast pop up?
   - How does bacon fry?
   - Can you move one part of your body up and down?
   - Can you jump up and turn in the air?
   - Can you reach up to the sky and then down to the ground?
   - Can you jump up and down like a frog?
6. Perform stunts such as Jump and Slap the Heels, Squat Tag, Turk Stand, and Partner Get Up and Down. See activities 13, 19, 20, and 21 on pages 169 and 171.
7. Other: ______________________

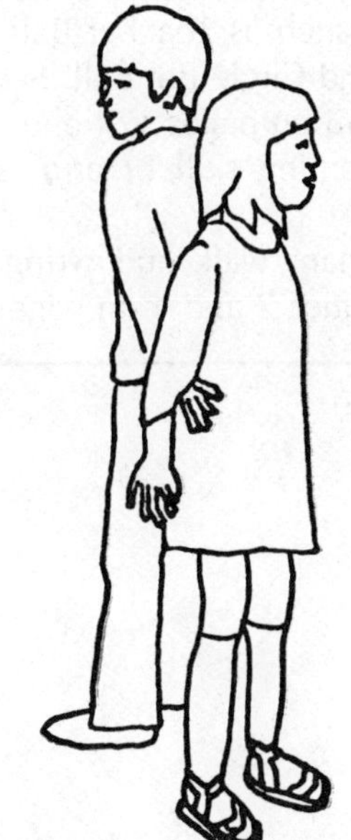

Figure 10–13. Play games such as Back to Back.

BODY IMAGE (GPI pp. 66, 71)

Concept and awareness of body

Equipment: As indicated or items italicized

1. Play games such as Back to Back, Have You Seen My Dog, and Japanese Tag. See activities 1, 23, and 39 on pages 172, 175, and 178.
2. Draw outlines of other children as they lie down on *large sheets of paper* on the floor.
3. Draw and cut out figures of boys and girls from *construction paper*.
4. Assemble human figures on *flannel boards*.
5. Tense, then relax the body starting from the head to the toes.
6. Perform movement exploration activities in response to questions posed by teacher:
   - Can you make your body look like a ball [building, piece of paper, carpet]?
   - Can you make your body big [little, tall, skinny, fat]?
7. Cut out pictures of people illustrated in old *magazines*.
8. Other: ______________________

PRIMARY LEVEL ACTIVITIES (11)

Figure 10–14. Perform exercises such as Wind Mill.

MIDLINE OF BODY (GPI pp. 66, 71)

Concept of vertical midline of body that separates body into two equal sides

Equipment: As indicated or items italicized.

1. Perform gross movement patterns such as twisting, turning, swinging, pushing, pulling, and swaying.
2. Touch body parts on left side with the right hand and vice versa.
3. Turn a *long rope* while someone else jumps it.
4. Perform exercises such as Wind Mill.
5. Dance in rhythmic activities such as the Hora in which the legs are swung across the midline of the body.
6. Trace shapes on *chalkboard* or on a *template board* that require crossing the midline (large circle, triangle, rectangle, and so forth).
7. Move arm in a parallel path to a *suspended, swinging ball.*
8. Twist arms and body while on a *Twist Board.*
9. Practice *chalkboard* activities designed to have student cross the midline.
10. Play games that require throwing or striking across body, such as Teacher Ball, Toss and Catch Ball, and Circle Bat Ball. See activities 16, 17, and 58 on pages 174 and 181.
11. Practice swimming skill of arm pull of the front crawl.
12. Perform elephant walk and wring the dish-rag. See activities 2 and 4 on page 167.
13. Other: ______________________

Figure 10–15. Touch different body parts. Play Simon Says requesting that students touch different body parts.

IDENTIFY BODY PARTS (GPI pp. 66, 71)

Concept and awareness of parts of one's own body

Equipment: As indicated or items italicized.

1. Bounce *balloons* on different body parts in response to verbal commands: "head," "knee," "nose," "ears," etc.
2. Place different body parts in *hula hoops* placed on the floor, in response to verbal commands.
3. Play Simon Says (see activity 65 on page 182), requesting that the students touch different body parts.
4. Point to different body parts of children and have them move that part.
5. Copy the movement of body parts that is being performed by a partner.
6. Attach *jingle bells* or *weights* to body parts such as wrists or ankles to call attention to that part if child is experiencing difficulty identifying it.
7. Tell story plays regarding the function of different body parts such as stories about hearing with the ears and seeing with the eyes.
8. Perform movement exploration activities in response to questions posed by teacher:
   - Can you bend one part of your body?
   - Which parts of your body can you swing?
   - Can you push with a part of your body?
   - Can you balance with a part of your body?
9. Other: ______________________________

PRIMARY LEVEL ACTIVITIES (13)

Perceptual Abilities

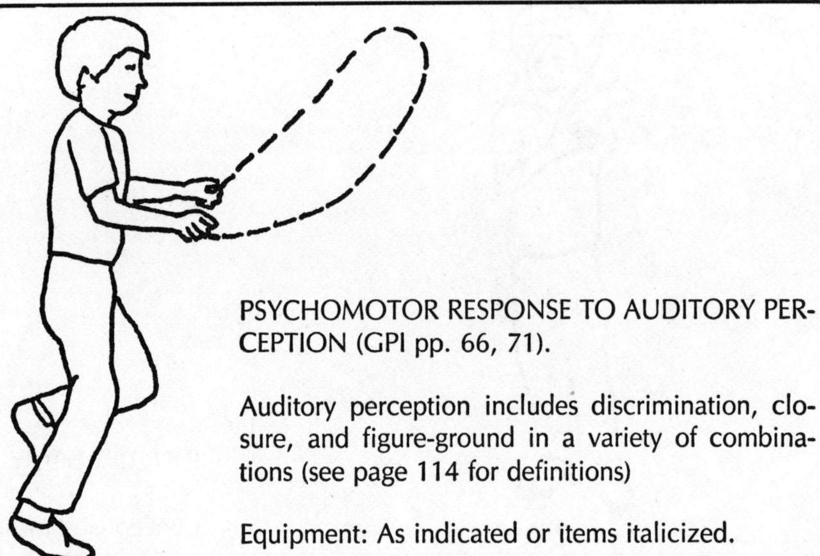

Figure 10–16. Jump rope to music.

PSYCHOMOTOR RESPONSE TO AUDITORY PERCEPTION (GPI pp. 66, 71).

Auditory perception includes discrimination, closure, and figure-ground in a variety of combinations (see page 114 for definitions)

Equipment: As indicated or items italicized.

1. Play games or relays in which auditory perception is important such as Back to Back, Wild Horses, Brownies and Elves, Call Ball, Midnight, Blind Man's Bluff, Crows and Cranes, and Red Light-Green Light. See activities 1, 2, 3, 5, 25, 29, 31, and 33 on pages 172 and 175–177.
2. Arrange body in the shape of a geometric form upon verbal command (work with others to make shapes).
3. Perform dances such as Bingo or London Bridge.
4. Perform stunts on verbal command such as log roll, elephant walk, seal crawl, bear walk, and crab walk. See activities 1, 2, 5, 6, and 9 on pages 167–169.
5. Play Musical *Chairs.*
6. Act out story plays.
7. React to poems read aloud.
8. Move in creative dance patterns to *music* played, *percussive instruments* sounded, or songs sung.
9. Move appropriately when words or verbal commands are heard, such as "walk," "talk," or "jump like a rabbit."
10. Jump *rope* to *music.*
11. Perform movement exploration activities in response to problems verbally posed by teacher:
    - Can you make yourself small and then tall?
    - Can you move one part of your body forward and another part backward at the same time?
    - Can you move like a clock hand around the clock?
    - Can you move in and out of a circle formed by other students?
    - Can you make the bottom half of your body get shorter then taller?
12. Run and retrieve the correct shape of *foam* (circle, square, rectangle, triangle, etc.) upon verbal command.
13. Tell which noise is loud or soft (bounce a *ball,* blow a *whistle,* and clap hands with different intensities).
14. Go outside and name out loud the sounds that are heard (bird, water, dog, and wind).
15. Perform various movement patterns in a series after verbal command.
16. Play Simon Says and I Say Stoop. See activities 38 and 65 on pages 177 and 182.
17. Write words or letters on *paper* (*chalkboard*) that are dictated by teacher.
18. Name objects on the basis of the sound that they make such as *rocks* in a *can, drum, horn,* and *whistle.*
19. Other: ____________________

PRIMARY LEVEL ACTIVITIES (14)

Figure 10–17. Touch a swinging ball.

PSYCHOMOTOR RESPONSE TO VISUAL PERCEPTION (GPI pp. 66, 71)

Visual perception includes closure, discrimination, form discrimination, figure-ground relationship, size perception, depth and distance perception, and object recognition in a variety of combinations (see pages 114–115 for definitions)

Equipment: As indicated or items italicized.

1. Play games such as Teacher Ball, Toss and Catch Ball, Indians, Child and Teacher Drill, Circle Kickball, and Throw against Wall Drill. See activities 16, 17, 37, 56, 60, and 61 on pages 174, 177, and 181.
2. Move in creative dance patterns to interpret reactions to things seen in environment:
   - *Colors* such as red, yellow, brown, black, blue, and white.
   - *Paintings* or *sculptures*.
   - *Shapes* such as curves, wavy lines, circles and straight lines.
3. Play Stepping Stones (step on different *tiles* or *blocks*, such as step on red tiles with right foot and blue tiles with left foot).
4. Practice skills that emphasize visual perception, such as catching or batting a *ball*.
5. Negotiate *obstacle courses* of different forms and colors.
6. Negotiate a *ladder* on the floor (step through the rungs).
7. Read *posters* and move accordingly (for example, read "go" and move forward).
8. Copy geometric forms seen on *cards*.
9. Point to the geometric form on the *table* that is the same as the form drawn on a *card*.
10. Select a geometric *form* and place it on a similar form (substitute *colors* placed on same color).
11. Reproduce a given pattern of *beads* or *blocks* that is on the table (substitute by reproducing the pattern from memory).
12. Find the correct path through a maze and follow it with a *pencil*.
13. Touch a swinging *ball* that is suspended in front of a person.
14. Strike a *yarn ball* with a *paddle* that has been tossed to person.
15. Place forms in a *form board*.
16. Throw a *bean bag* onto the correct *letter* or *form* after seeing it displayed on a *card*.
17. Perform a gross motor skill the number of times indicated by a number displayed on a *card*. Run in a relay race to retrieve the correct *letter* or *form* after seeing it displayed on a *card*.
18. Perform movement patterns designated by a color code displayed on a *card* (for example, green means to skip and blue to gallop).
19. Throw *bean bags* onto different *shapes* and name the shapes touched by bean bags.
20. Run and retrieve *balls* with *numbers* on them after reading the number on a *poster*.
21. Throw a *bean bag* on a *grid* containing different letters and then writing on the *chalkboard* the letter that is touched by the bean bag.

PRIMARY LEVEL ACTIVITIES (15)

22. Run [hop, skip, gallop] until an estimated distance of fifteen feet is covered.
23. Run [hop, skip, gallop] from one location to another in accordance with a *chart* that is read.
24. Trace the foreground *figure* that is superimposed on a similar background.
25. Color *pictures* that are color coded (for example, a "1" means to use green).
26. Place similar *dominoes* on top of each other.
27. Play American Hopscotch. See activity 47 on page 179.
28. Other: ________________

Figure 10–18. Close eyes and manipulate small objects such as nickels or dimes.

PSYCHOMOTOR RESPONSE TO TACTILE PERCEPTION (GPI pp. 67, 71)

Tactile perception includes discrimination (see page 115 for definition)

Equipment: As indicated or items italicized.

1. Close eyes and manipulate small objects such as *nickels, dimes, pencils,* and *thimbles,* and identify verbally each of these. Repeat with different shapes.
2. Rub *coarse textures,* pieces of *carpeting, loofah sponges, ice,* etc. on the skin and verbally identify each of these.
3. Interlace fingers of both hands and press hands together. After teacher presses more strongly on left or right hand, identify verbally or move the hand emphasized.
4. Trace forms and figures in the *sand.* Close eyes and identify by tactile input alone the form manipulated.
5. Wear *weights* on wrists or ankles. Raise the body part with the weight on it.
6. Move in creative dance patterns to interpret different surfaces touched, such as rough *sandpaper, carpeting, water, ice, sand, smooth fabric, foam,* or *hard plastic.*
7. Close eyes and raise the finger that is touched by another person (hands should be resting on *table* in front).
8. Close eyes and perform Row Boat (alternate pushing and pulling hands with a partner while both are seated on the floor).
9. Pick out all of the hard [soft] objects on a *table* (*wood, metal, glass,* etc. for hard and *cotton, silk, fur,* etc., for soft).
10. Trace letters or words constructed of *sandpaper* and name those identified.
11. Hold balls of different weights (*whiffle ball* and *medicine ball*) and describe whether it is heavy [and which is heavier than the other].
12. Trace letters or words on the palm of another student's hand to see if he can identify that which is written.
13. Other: ________________

PRIMARY LEVEL ACTIVITIES (16)

Eye-Body Coordination (includes visual-motor match)

HAND PREFERENCE (GPI pp. 67, 71)

Also see manipulation activities in next section.

Equipment: As indicated or items italicized.

1. Perform fine manual motor tasks such as manipulation of *small objects* or writing and drawing with *pencil* or *crayon*.
2. Perform throwing and striking pattern activities.
3. Perform laterality activities designed to emphasize right and left hands.
4. Play musical instruments such as a *horn* or *tambourine* that are held primarily in one hand.
5. Perform *arts* and *crafts* activities.
6. Manipulate apparatus such as *wands, ropes,* and *hoops*.
7. Play *darts*.
8. Play special games such as Scoops (catch tossed *balls* or *yarn balls* in *plastic Clorox bottles* that have been cut open).
9. Bowl with *plastic ball* and *pins*.
10. Catch a *cane* released from an upright position on the floor before it falls down on the floor.
11. Other: ______________________

EYE PREFERENCE (GPI pp. 67, 71)

Equipment: As indicated or items italicized.

1. Play with *kaleidoscope*.
2. Look through *telescope*.
3. Other: ______________________

FOOT PREFERENCE (GPI pp. 67, 71)

Also see kicking activities

Equipment: As indicated or items italicized.

1. Perform kicking activities.
2. Perform laterality activities designed to emphasize knowledge of left and right feet.
3. Perform locomotor patterns that emphasize a dominant foot, such as hopping or galloping.
4. Play American Hopscotch. See activity 47 on page 179.
5. Other: ______________________

PRIMARY LEVEL ACTIVITIES (17)

Manipulation (includes visual-motor match)

Figure 10–19. Practice copying forms displayed on cards.

WRITING AND DRAWING (GPI pp. 67, 71)

Equipment: As indicated or items italicized.

1. Practice copying forms displayed on *cards*: Draw on *paper*, trace in *sand*, draw on *chalkboard*, and arrange body in that shape.
2. Practice copying words and letters on *paper*, on the *chalkboard*, and arranging bodies in that shape.
3. *Finger paint.*
4. Perform in movement exploration activities in response to problems posed by teacher:
   - Can you walk in a circle [square, diamond, triangle, etc.]?
   - Can you walk in the pattern of the letter "C" ["X," "Z," etc.]?
5. Practice writing and drawing such as being performed in the classroom.
6. Other: ______

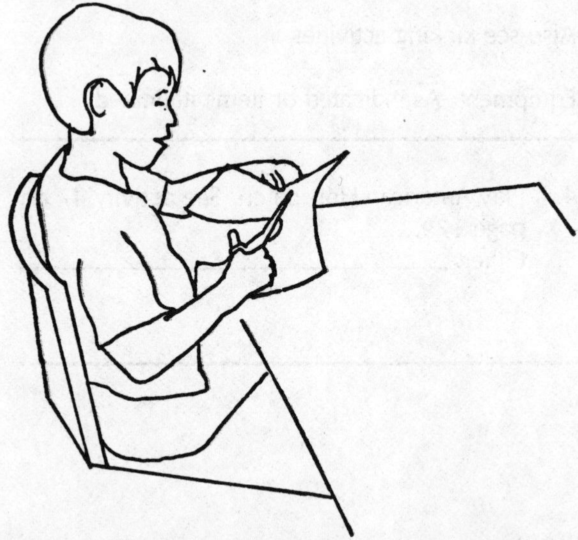

Figure 10–20. Practice cutting circles and triangles out of construction paper.

MANIPULATES OBJECTS (GPI pp. 67, 71)

Equipment: As indicated or items italicized.

PRIMARY LEVEL ACTIVITIES (18)

1. Practice cutting circles and triangles out of *construction paper* by use of *scissors*.
2. Play games such as *Bean Bag* Tag and Drop the *Handkerchief*. See activities 8 and 9 on page 173.
3. Tear, knead, roll, and manipulate *clay*.
4. Make *puppets* for hands and fingers.
5. String *beads*.
6. Stack *blocks* or *Tinkertoys*.
7. Tie *shoelaces*, buckle *buckles*, button *buttons*, fasten *hooks* and *eyes*, snap *snaps*, close *zippers*, and shoot *marbles*.
8. *Paste paper* or *material* together.
9. Tear *paper* into various shapes.
10. Fold *paper* into various shapes.
11. Play *Jacks*.
12. Perform exercises such as
    - Open and close fists.
    - Place hands flat on a surface and alternate raising and lowering fingers.
    - Oppose fingers and thumb of each hand in sequences.
13. Play games with *strings* such as Cat's Cradle.
14. Crumble a sheet of *paper* with one hand.
15. Play *cards*.
16. Throw *bean bags* at *targets*.
17. Perform rhythmic activities with *wands*.
18. Open and close *clothespins*.
19. Screw and unscrew *nuts* and *bolts*.
20. Turn pages in a *book* singly.
21. Open and close lids or tops on containers such as *milk cartons* or *screw-top jars*.
22. Make *yarn* balls.
23. Make figures of *pipe cleaners*.
24. Other: ____________________

Performs on Apparatus

RIDES BICYCLE (GPI pp. 67, 71)

Equipment: As indicated or items italicized.

1. Practice riding *bicycle* appropriate for size around street corners or obstacles.
2. Other: ____________________

MOVES ALONG HORIZONTAL LADDER (GPI pp. 67, 71).

Equipment: As indicated or items italicized.

1. Practice single rung traveling on *horizontal ladder*.
2. Practice alternate rung traveling on *horizontal ladder*.
3. Practice various hanging positions (use a spotter) on a *horizontal ladder*.
4. Other: ____________________

PRIMARY LEVEL ACTIVITIES (19)

Ball Handling

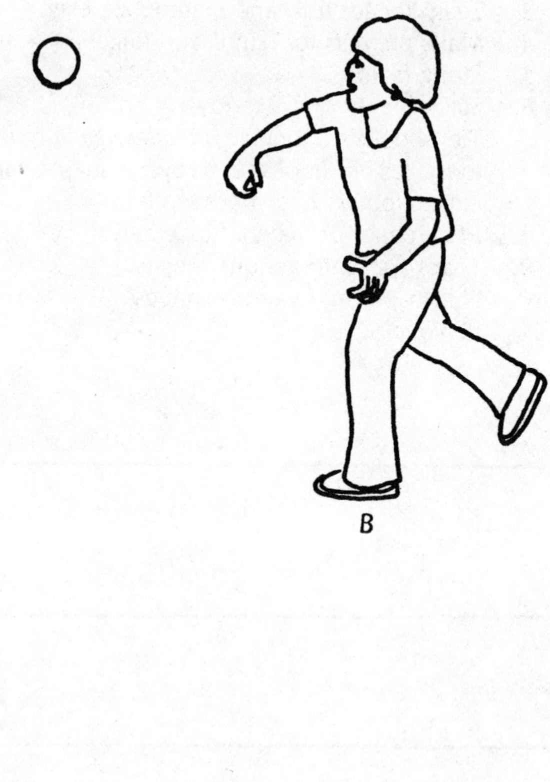

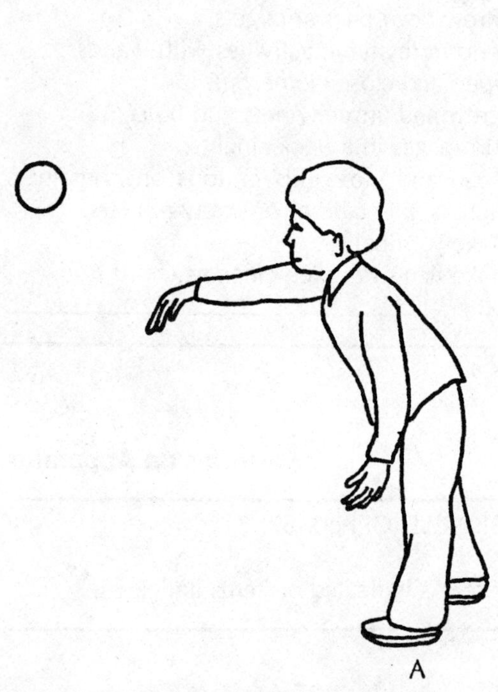

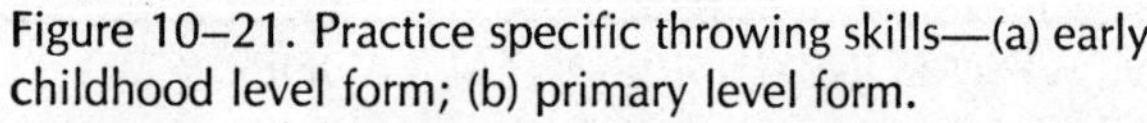

Figure 10–21. Practice specific throwing skills—(a) early childhood level form; (b) primary level form.

Throws (GPI pp. 68, 71)

Equipment: As indicated or items italicized.

1. Play games such as Call *Ball*, Teacher *Ball*, Toss and Catch *Ball*, Boundary *Ball*, Spot *Basketball*, Clean Up Your Own Backyard, Over the *Net*, Chase, Child and Teacher Drill, Circle Toss Drill, and Leader of the Class. See activities 5, 16, 17, 30, 43, 52, 53, 54, 56, 62, and 63 on pages 172, 174, 176, and 180–181.
2. Practice specific throwing skills in relays and drill formations such as Zig-zag Formation, Shuttle Formation, *Softball* Throw Relay, *Basketball* Relay, and Throw Against the *Wall* Drill. See activities 3, 5, 7,8, and 61 on pages 202–203 and 181.
3. Throw different types of *balls* and *bean bags* at different targets, such as *clown faces, boards with holes* in them, targets that fall over (*plastic bottles*), or targets that make noises (*aluminum foil pie plates*).
4. Other: ______________________

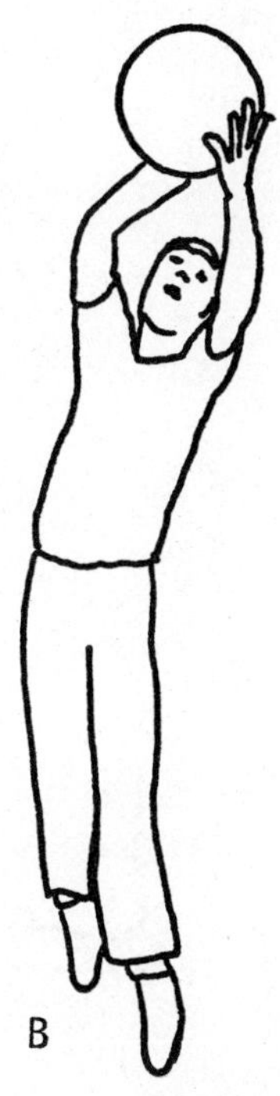

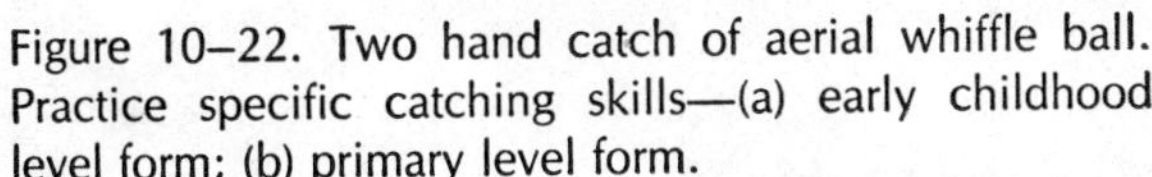
Figure 10–22. Two hand catch of aerial whiffle ball. Practice specific catching skills—(a) early childhood level form; (b) primary level form.

CATCHES (GPI pp. 68, 72)

Equipment: As indicated or items italicized.

1. Play games such as Call *Ball*, Teacher *Ball*, Toss and Catch *Ball*, Spot *Basketball*, Clean Up Your Own Backyard, Chase, Child and Teacher Drill, Circle Toss Drill, and Leader of the Class. See activities 5, 16, 17, 43, 52, 53, 56, 62, and 63 on pages 172, 174, and 178–182.
2. Practice specific catching skills in relays and drill formations such as Zig-zag Formation, Shuttle Formation, *Softball* Throw Relay, *Basketball* Relay, and Throw against the *Wall* Drill. See activities 3, 5, 7, 8, and 61 on pages 202–203 and 181.
3. Toss and catch *rhythmic balls* or *small balls* to music.
4. Catch in movement exploration activities in response to questions posed by teachers:
   - Can you toss the *ball* above your head and catch it before it bounces?
   - Can you toss the *ball* above your head, let it bounce once, and then catch it?
   - Can you toss the *ball* above your head, turn around once, and catch the ball?
   - Can you bounce the *ball* once, turn around once, and catch the ball?
   - Can you throw the *ball* against the *wall* and catch it before the ball bounces?
   - Can you throw the *ball* against the *wall* and then catch it after one [two] bounces?
5. Other: ____________________

PRIMARY LEVEL ACTIVITIES (21)

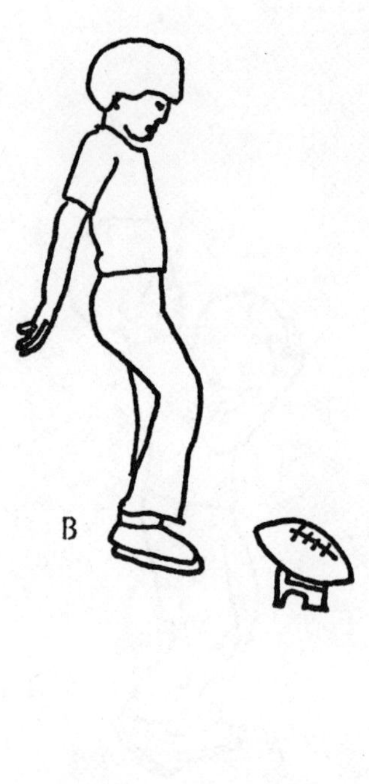

Figure 10–23. Perform kicking activities—(a) early childhood level form; (b) primary level form.

KICKS (GPI pp. 68, 72)

Equipment: As indicated or items italicized.

1. Play games such as Kick and Run, *Soccer* Keep-away, *Kickball* Croquet, and Circle *Kickball*. See activities 44, 45, 59, and 60 on pages 179 and 181.
2. Practice specific kicking skills in relays and drill formations, such as the Fan Formation, Shuttle Formation, and Soccer Dribble Relay. See activities 2, 5, and 6 on pages 202–203.
3. Perform kicking activities:
   - Kick a stationary *ball*.
   - Kick a moving *ball*.
   - Kick a *ball* dropped from hands.
4. Kick in movement exploration activities in response to questions posed by teacher:
   - How far can you kick a *ball*?
   - How many times can you kick a *ball* against the *wall*?
   - How high can you kick a *ball*?
   - Can you kick a *ball* while you run?
   - Can you kick a *ball* to a partner?
   - Show me how you kick different balls (display *9½" and 16¼" playground balls, small whiffle ball, soccer ball,* and *football*).
5. Other: ______________________

PRIMARY LEVEL ACTIVITIES (22)

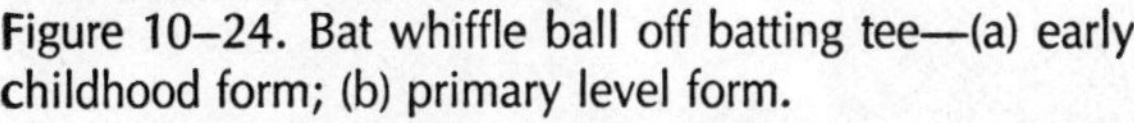
Figure 10–24. Bat whiffle ball off batting tee—(a) early childhood form; (b) primary level form.

STRIKES (GPI pp. 69, 72).

Equipment: As indicated or items italicized.

1. Play games such as Longest Volley, Circle Bat *Ball*, and Four Square. See activities 57, 58, and 64 on pages 181 and 182.
2. Practice specific striking skills in relays and drill formations, such as the Fan Formation and Circle Bat *Ball*. See activities 3 and 58 on pages 181 and 202.
3. Play Tether Ball (strike a suspended ball around a pole) with different balls such as a *tether ball, whiffle ball,* or *foam ball.*
4. *Bat whiffle balls* off *batting tee* to a partner [to target].
5. Fungo hit (toss *ball* up in air and *bat* it before it lands) a ball to other students (more appropriate for 8–9 yrs.).
6. Other: ______________________

DESCRIPTION OF SELECTED ACTIVITIES

Tumbling Skills

1. Forward roll (6–7, 7–8, 8–9 yrs.[2])
Squat down and place hands (shoulder width apart) on mat, fingers pointing forward. Keep elbows inside legs and tuck chin to chest. Push off with hands and feet. Roll forward like a ball. Support body weight with arms keeping head off mat. Note: Teacher should "spot" child through forward roll by holding back of neck and raising thighs.

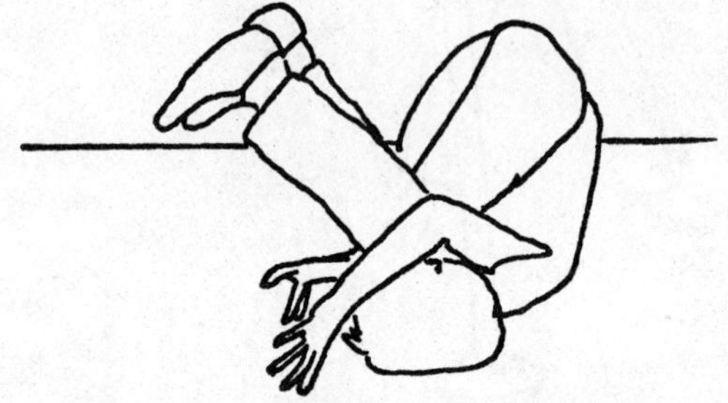

Figure 10–25. Forward roll.

Figure 10–26. Backward roll.

2. Backward Roll (7–8, 8–9 yrs.)
Squat down and roll backward on rounded back with chin and knees tucked to chest. Place hands at shoulders, palms up, thumbs beside neck. When fingers touch mat, push off from mat to lift head clear as body completes backward roll to feet. Note: Teacher should "spot" child through backward roll by lifting shoulder when legs are overhead and by guiding back of thigh through the roll.

Figure 10–27. Cartwheel.

3. Cartwheel (7–8, 8–9, 9–10, 10–11, 11–12 yrs.)
Stand with side facing length of mat. Bend down and place hands on mat while pushing off with one and then the other foot. Legs are swung in an arc overhead down the length of the mat while arms are extended and supporting the weight of the body. Push off from mat with hands, bring legs down, and regain upright position (go from crouching to standing position). Note: Teacher should "spot" child by holding trunk at waist level while child is upside down.

Movement Exploration

1. Problems posed by teacher to develop locomotor patterns (6–7, 7–8, 8–9 yrs.):
   - How fast can you run [walk, jump, hop, gallop, skip]?
   - Can you run [walk, jump, hop, gallop, skip] in a large circle without bumping into others?
   - Can you run [walk, jump, hop, gallop, skip] with very long [short] steps?
   - Can you run [walk, jump, hop, gallop, skip] to that line and then back to me?
   - Can you run [walk, jump, hop, gallop, skip] high [low, fast, slow]?
   - Can you run [walk, jump hop, gallop, skip] with two other children [with a partner]?
   - How do you run [walk, jump, hop, gallop, skip] if you are happy [sad, mad, tired, etc.]?
   - Can you run [walk, jump, hop, gallop, skip] around other students in a smaller area?
   - Can you run [walk, jump, hop, gallop, skip] very low and end up very high?
   - How would you run [walk, jump, hop, gallop, skip] on a slippery sidewalk?
   - Can you run [walk, jump, hop, gallop, skip] forward [backward, sideward]?
   - Can you clap your hands each time you run [walk, jump, hop, gallop, skip]?

Stunts and Self-Testing Skills

1. Log roll (6–7 yrs.)
Lie on mat with arms and legs fully stretched out so that body is like a log. Roll like a log down the length of the mat and then return to beginning place.
2. Elephant walk (6–7 yrs.)
Bend forward at waist with arms extended and hands clasped like a trunk of an elephant. Walk forward with straight legs, with "trunk" swinging from side to side.
3. Thread the needle (6–7 yrs.)
Extend arms in front of body with finger tips together. Step through arms one leg at a time. Reverse pattern to return to starting position.
4. Wring the dishrag (6–7 yrs.)
Two children face each other holding hands. Raise one set of hands and

Figure 10–28. Log roll.

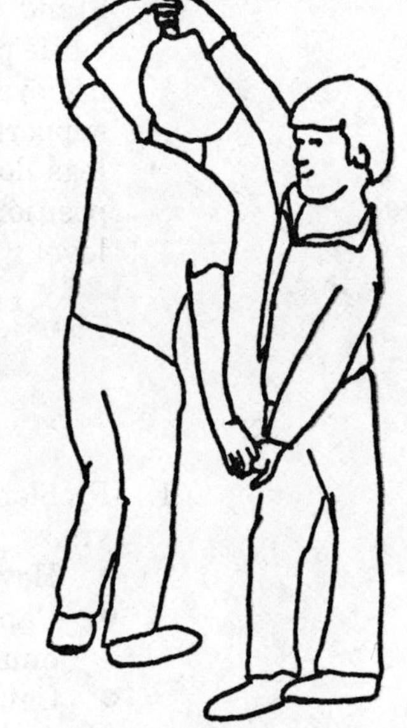

Figure 10–29. Wring the dishrag.

both children rotate in that direction until a full turn is taken to the original facing position (bodies go under arms).

5. Seal crawl (6–7, 7–8, 8–9 yrs.)
   Extend body forward on mat with both arms fully extended. Move arms forward in alternation so that body is propelled forward like a seal. Keep legs extended behind body and let them drag on mat.

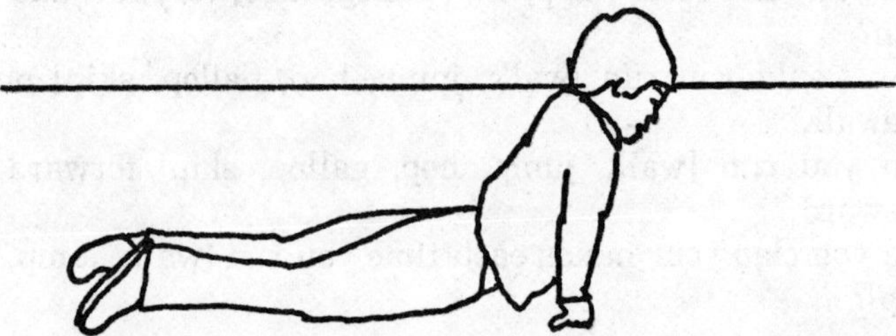

Figure 10–30. Seal crawl.

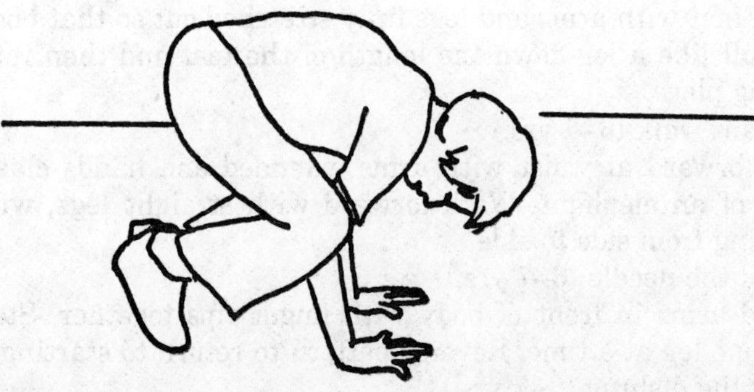

Figure 10–31. Bear walk.

6. Bear walk (6–7, 7–8, 8–9 yrs.)
   Place hands on floor and walk like a bear with extended arms and legs. Alternate left arm and leg with right arm and leg.

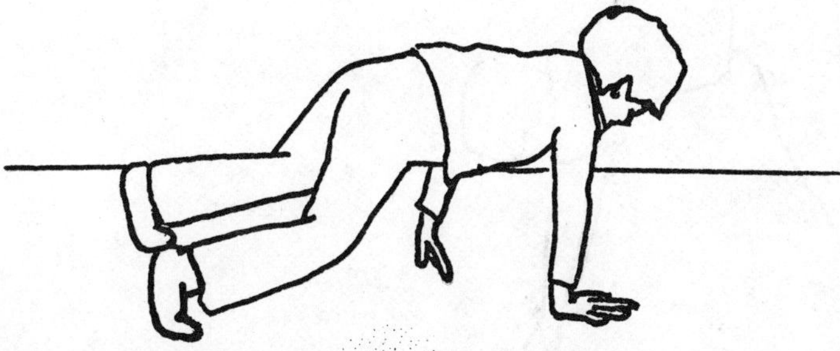

Figure 10–32. Tip-up.

7. Tip-up (7–8 yrs.)
   Squat down on mat, placing hands flat with fingers facing forward. Lean forward, placing knees upon platform formed by flexed elbows. Slowly transfer weight until forehead touches the mat. Go back to starting position.
8. Backward kick (7–8 yrs.)
   Jump in place three times. On the fourth jump, jump backward and start repetition again.

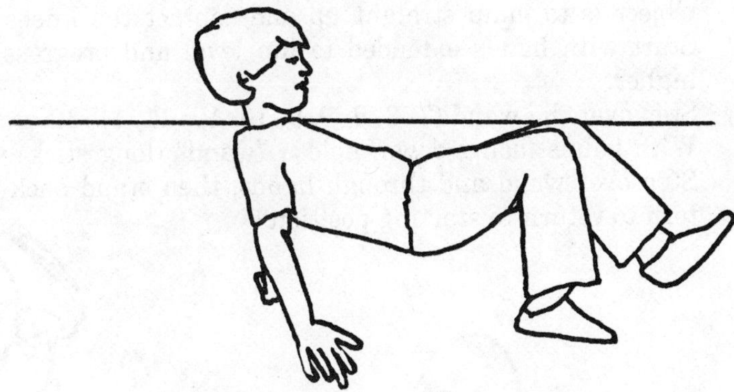

Figure 10–33. Crab walk.

9. Crab walk (7–8, 8–9 yrs.)
   Lie supine on floor and raise body off floor with arms and legs. Walk like a crab using right arm and right leg together alternated by left arm and left leg. Move forward and backward.
10. Egg roll (7–8, 8–9, 9–10, 10–11, 11–12 yrs.)
    Lie on mat with arms crossed over chest and legs crossed. Bend knee and roll like an egg down the mat.
11. Frog hop (7–8, 8–9, 9–10, 10–11, 11–12 yrs.)
    Squat, placing hands on the floor and between legs. "Hop" by placing hands in front of feet and bringing feet up to meet hands.
12. Inchworm (7–8, 8–9, 9–10, 10–11, 11–12 yrs.)
    Start in a push-up position with legs extended and arms supporting. Slowly walk, leaving the hands stationary, so that the feet meet the hands. Now walk foward with the hands, keeping legs stationary until the body is fully extended again. Repeat, inching the way across the floor.

Figure 10–34. Inch worm.

13. Jump and slap heels (7–8, 8–9, 9–10, 10–11, 11–12 yrs.)
Jump up, bringing heels up to side. Slap right heel with right hand and left heel with left hand.
14. Knee lift (7–8, 8–9, 9–10, 10–11, 11–12 yrs.)
Extend arms to the front of the body so palms of hands are facing down. Object is to jump straight up and contact the knees with the hands. Start with hands extended to hip level and progressively move them higher.
15. Step over the wand (7–8, 8–9, 9–10, 10–11, 11–12 yrs.)
With palms facing down, hold a "wand" (long stick) with both hands. Step over wand and through hands; then stand back up. Reverse pattern to return to starting position.

Figure 10–35. Balance stand.

Figure 10–36. Forearm stand.

16. Balance stand (8–9 yrs.)
Stand on one leg, with other leg in the air and knees slightly bent. From waist up, the body is parallel with the floor and the arms are extended in front of body.
17. Forearm headstand (8–9 yrs.)
Place forearms, palms down, on mat while in kneeling position. Place forehead between hands. Kick one leg, then the other, up vertically overhead until both legs are balanced overhead in headstand position.
18. Handstand with support (8–9 yrs.)
Stand upright, lean over, and place both hands flat on mat shoulder-width apart. Kick one leg, then the other, vertically overhead in a handstand position. Teacher assists child in maintaining balance for the handstand.

Figure 10–37. Handstand with support.

Figure 10–38. Turk stand.

19. Tripod (8–9 yrs.)
Kneel on mat placing both hands flat on mat (shoulder-width apart) and flex elbows so that a platform is made with both arms. Place right knee on right arm above the elbow and left knee on left arm above elbow. Hold head off mat while balancing in tripod position.
20. Turk stand (8–9, 9–10 yrs.)
Sit with arms folded across body and legs crossed. Lean forward and rise to a standing position. Return to original sitting position.
21. Partner get up and down (8–9, 9–10 yrs.)
Partners sit back to back on floor. By interlocking elbows and pushing against one another, they rise to a standing position and then return to sitting position.

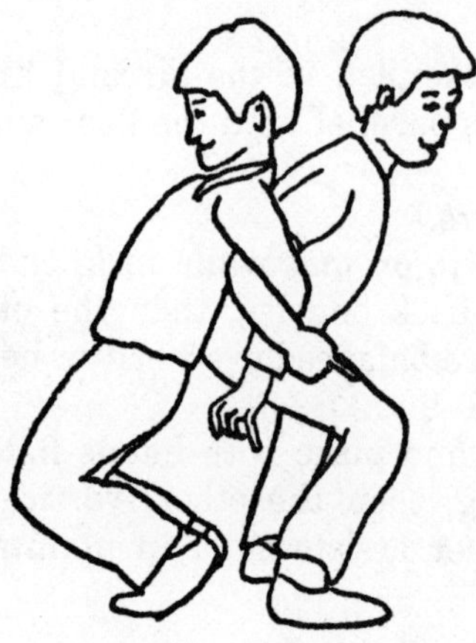

Figure 10–39. Partner get up and down.

Game Situations, Relays, Tag Games and Drills

1. Back to Back (6–7, 7–8, 8–9 yrs.)
   Children scatter throughout area with a partner. One extra person is It and calls out commands such as "back to back," "front to front," "side to side," "knees to knees," "head to head," etc. When the call is given, children must run to another partner and match up the body parts called out. It tries to get a partner when exchanges are made. The child who ends up without a partner becomes It, and game starts again.
2. Wild Horses (6–7 yrs.)
   Children pretend that they are Wild Horses resting at edge of river. One extra person is behind the group acting as a Wild Lion. The Lion "roars" and/or chases the Horses, who try to get across the river to safety. The river edges are marked lines. The river may be widened (the distance between lines may gradually increase) at any time. Repeat, designating another child to be the Wild Lion.
3. Brownies and Elves (6–7, 7–8 yrs.)
   Children are grouped into Brownies, standing at one marked goal line, and Elves standing at the opposite marked goal line. Each group has its back to the other group. Upon signal from the teacher, the Brownies turn around and silently sneak up behind the elves. When the teacher calls out, "The Brownies are coming," the children designated as the Elves turn around toward the Brownies and chase them. The Brownies try to get back to their goal line, where they are safe, without being tagged by an Elf. If a Brownie is tagged before reaching safety, then that child becomes an Elf. Repeat, letting Elves sneak up on Brownies.
4. Duck, Duck, Goose (6–7, 7–8 yrs.)
   Children sit in a circle. One extra child is It and walks around the outside of the circle, touching each person's head or shoulder. As each person is tapped, It calls out either "Duck" or "Goose." A tapped child called a Duck remains sitting. If the tapped child is a Goose, that child stands and chases It around the circle before It has gone completely around to sit in the vacant place left by Goose. If It gets tagged by Goose, then It remains It. If It gets around the circle and is seated without being tagged, the Goose becomes It.
5. Call Ball (6–7, 7–8, 8–9 yrs.)

Children stand in a circle, facing inward, with one child standing in the center of the circle. The child in the center is It and bounces a ball to one of the children standing on the circle. Simultaneously It calls out the name of the person to whom she is throwing the ball. The ball-receiving child must catch the ball before the second bounce. If the child is successful, then he goes to the center and becomes It. If the ball-receiving child misses the ball, then he remains in his place, and the original It continues tossing to other children.

6. Run-Stop (6–7 yrs.)
Children are scattered throughout a designated area. When the teacher calls out "Run!" the children run in any direction as long as they do not bump into anyone or step out of designated boundaries. The teacher then calls out "Stop!" and the children immediately stop wherever they are. The children run again when the teacher calls out "Run!" again. Variations may be used, such as substituting "Hop!" for "Run!" etc. Other variations include having children doing a movement after they have stopped, such as clapping their hands.

7. Charlie over the Water (6–7, 7–8 yrs.)
Children join hands forming a circle. One child is Charlie and stands in the center of the circle. The children on the circle move in one direction while chanting:

    Charlie over the water,
    Charlie over the sea,
    Charlie caught a blackbird
    But he can't catch me!

The children quickly squat as they say "me." Charlies tries to tag a person before the person sits down. If Charlie succeeds in tagging, then the person tagged becomes the new Charlie. The old Charlie exchanges places, and the game begins again.

8. Bean Bag Tag (6–7 yrs.)
Children are scattered, with one child being It. It starts running with a bean bag in her hand. She may choose to toss the bean bag to another child at any time. The other children chase It and try to tag her. The person who tags It before she tosses the bean bag becomes the new It and is chased by the other children.

9. Drop the Handkerchief (6–7, 7–8 yrs.)
Children stand in a circle, facing inward, with one child standing on the outside of the circle. The child who is alone on the outside of the circle is It and carries a handkerchief in his hand. It runs around the circle and drops the handkerchief directly behind one of the other children. It continues running in same direction, while the child with the handkerchief behind him picks up the handkerchief and runs in the opposite direction of It. Both children race to the vacant place left by the child with the handkerchief. The last child there becomes It, and the game begins again.

10. Walk, Walk, Run (6–7, 7–8 yrs.)
Children stand in a circle formation, facing inward. One extra child is It and walks around the outside of the circle, touching each person's head or shoulder. As each person is tapped, It calls out either "Walk" or "Run." If It says "Walk" then the person tapped remains standing. If the tapped child is told "Run!" then the child turns around and chases It around the circle. If the chaser tags It before It has reached the vacant place left by the Chaser, then It must be in the "mush pot." The

"mush pot" is in the center of the circle, and It must remain there until another child has been tagged and replaces her. If It reaches the chaser's vacant place without being tagged, then It remains in that place and the chaser becomes It. The game begins again.

11. Frog in the Sea (6–7, 7–8 yrs.)
One child, the Frog, sits cross-legged in the center of a circle approximately six feet wide. The other children step in and out of the circle, chanting:

Frog in the sea
Can't catch me!

The Frog in the center tries to tag another child *without leaving his sitting position.* If the Frog is successful, then the person he tags exchanges places with him and the game begins again.

12. Huntsman (6–7, 7–8 yrs.)
Children line up behind one child who is designated as the Huntsman. Everyone follows the Huntsman's footsteps as she calls out, "Come with me to hunt." Huntsman leads the other children away from a predetermined goal line. The children turn and run to the goal line when Huntsman calls out "Bang!" Huntsman tries to tag as many children as possible before they reach the goal safely. She calls out each child's name as she tags them. One of the children who reaches the goal line without being tagged is chosen by the previous Huntsman to be the new Huntsman.

13. I Saw (6–7, 7–8, 8–9 yrs.)
One child stands in front of the other children, who are seated. The child standing, It, begins by saying, "On my way to school this morning I saw ____." It pantomimes what he saw. If a child guesses what It saw, then that child becomes It. If no one guesses correctly, then It may stay It. After a child is It two times, the teacher chooses another It.

14. Squirrels in Trees (6–7, 7–8 yrs.)
Groups of three children are scattered throughout area. Each child is numbered as "one," "two," or "three." "Ones" and "Twos" join hands to form a Tree, while number "Threes" stand in the middle of the trees and are the Squirrels. One extra child is a Squirrel and does not have a Tree. When the teacher says "Squirrels run!" all Squirrels change Trees and the extra Squirrel joins a Tree. There will again be an extra Squirrel remaining without a tree, since only one Squirrel is allowed per Tree. The game is continued.

15. Animal Race (6–7, 7–8 yrs.)
Children line up behind a line and race to a designated finish line. The locomotion used by the children is a type of an animal walk—for example, a bunny hop, a wild horse gallop, or a bird race.

16. Teacher Ball (6–7, 7–8 yrs.)
Children are in a line formation with one child as the Teacher in front of the lines. The Teacher faces the line and tosses a ball to the first child who in turn tosses it back to her. The Teacher then tosses the ball to the next person in line, and so on. If a squad member misses the ball, he must move to the end of the line. If the Teacher misses the ball, then she must also move to the end of the line, and the first member in the line becomes the Teacher and play continues.

17. Toss and Catch Ball (7–8, 8–9 yrs.)
Children stand in a circle with one extra child standing in the center of

the circle. The child in the center tosses the ball to any person standing in the circle, who tosses it back. Children who miss catching the ball are eliminated from the game. For variation, the center child can call out the name of the person to whom she is tossing the ball.

18. Simple Tag (6–7 yrs.)
Children are scattered throughout area, and one child is designated It. It tries to tag another child. The child tagged becomes the new It.
19. Squat Tag (6–7 yrs.)
Children are scattered throughout area, and one child is designated It. It tries to tag another child, but children assuming a squat position are safe and may not be tagged. When children are not in a squatting position, they may be tagged.
20. Balance Relay (6–7, 7–8, 8–9, 9–10 yrs.)
Each team member walks in a a relay procedure balancing an object on top of the head. If the object falls off, the player must stop and replace it.
21. Cat and Rat (7–8, 8–9 yrs.)
Children stand in a circle. One child is chosen to be the Cat and one child is the Rat. The Cat is on the outside of the circle and the Rat is on the inside of it. When the teacher calls out "Chase," the Cat tries to tag the Rat. The Rat may weave in and out of the circle, but the Cat must stay on the outside of the circle. When the Rat is tagged, the Cat becomes the Rat, and the Cat chooses another child to replace him.
22. Circle Stride Ball (7–8, 8–9 yrs.)
Approximately fourteen children stand in a circle with one child standing in the center with a soft ball. Children in circle stand so each foot is touching the foot of child next to them (a "stride" position). The child in the center, It, tries to roll the ball between the legs of a person standing in the circle without that person reaching down with his hands and stopping the ball. Players in the circle may reach only with hands and may not move their feet. If It is successful in rolling the ball out of the circle, then the player letting the ball through becomes It. If the ball passes between two people, then the ball is retrieved, and play is resumed with the same It.
23. Have You Seen My Dog? (7–8, 8–9 yrs.)
Children either stand or sit in a circle, with It standing on the outside of the circle. It walks around the circle, stops behind someone on the circle, and asks, "Have you seen my dog?" The child being asked (child 1) replies, "What does she look like?" It then describes another child on the circle (child 2). Child 1 tries to guess who child 2 is, and as soon as he does he chases child 2 around the circle and tries to tag her. It steps into child 1's place and remains there during entire chase. If child 1 succeeds in tagging child 2 before child 2 runs around circle and returns to her original place, then child 2 becomes It. If child 1 does not tag child 2, then child 1 becomes It. The game is repeated with the new It.
24. Lame Man (7–8, 8–9 yrs.)
One child, the Man, stands inside a circle on the floor that is about one-third of the playing area. The other children run across the circle which is in the center of the playing area, calling out, "Lame man! Lame man! Can't catch anybody!" The Man may take three steps out of the circle in efforts to tag another child. After taking three steps, the Man is allowed to hop on one foot. If the Man puts his other foot down, he must return to his circle before he can try tagging again. He may also return at any time to rest. Any child he tags becomes the Man, and the game

starts over with the new Man. As a variation, anyone whom the Man tags must join him until all other players are tagged and the last one tagged becomes the starting Man.

25. Midnight (7–8, 8–9 yrs.)
All children are Chickens. One extra child is designated as the Fox. A small space, the fox's den, is marked at one end of the playing area, while at the opposite end of the area is a goal line. When the Fox is in the den, the Chickens advance toward her, asking, "What time is it?" The Fox starts calling out any clock time. When the Fox says "Midnight!" the Chickens run and try to reach their goal line before being tagged. Only when the fox says "Midnight!" may she chase the Chickens. Each Chicken tagged must go to the den and assist the Fox in tagging when she again answers "Midnight." The game is continued until all Chickens have been tagged.

26. Run for Your Supper (7–8, 8–9 yrs.)
Children stand in a circle, facing inward. One extra person is It and walks around the outside of the circle. It stops between two children on the circle and says, "Run for your supper!" The two children then turn to the outside of the circle and run in opposite directions around the circle. The first child to reach the place vacated by the other takes that place. The other child becomes the new It.

27. Water Sprite (7–8, 8–9 yrs.)
Children spread themselves out behind two marked goal lines. One extra child, the Sprite, stands in the middle of the area between the goal lines. The Sprite begins play by calling out the name of a child. That child quickly calls out the name of another child behind the opposite goal line. Both these children try to run across the area to the opposite goal without being tagged by the Sprite. If the Sprite tags one of them, then the child he tags becomes the Sprite and the old Sprite goes to the goal line to which the child he tagged was running.

28. Chalkboard Relay (8–9 yrs.)
Children stand in relay lines, facing a board. When signal is given, the first person in each line runs up to the board and writes a number on it, runs back, and hands the chalk to the next player in line. Each member does the same until the last child, who must add up all the numbers written by the team. The winning team is the first one back that has the correct addition of their numbers.

29. Blind Man's Bluff (8–9 yrs.)
Children stand in a circle. One child, the Blind Man, stands in the center of the circle blindfolded. Children in the circle join hands and walk in one direction of the circle until the Blind Man claps her hands. Everyone stops when she claps and she points to someone, calling out the name of an animal. The child who is pointed to must make the sound of the animal that the Blind Man named. The Blind Man has three tries to guess who the person is making the noise. If she is successful, then the child on the circle becomes the Blind Man and the previous Blind Man takes the child's place on the circle. If the Blind Man does not guess correctly, then the game continues with the same Blind Man. A variation may be played by having a child step into the circle with the Blind Man trying to catch him. The Blind Man tries to guess who the person is if caught.

30. Boundary Ball (8–9 yrs.)
Children are divided into two teams. Each team must stay in its own end area. The two end areas are separated by an equally large central

or neutral area. These three sections make up the play space, which is approximately the size of a basketball court. The object of the game is to throw or roll the ball so that it crosses over the opponent's rear boundary line. To begin play, a player from each team stands behind her own rear boundary line and throws in her ball. Every ball is thrown from the place of interception in the end areas. When the ball goes out of bounds, it is brought into the end area at the point where it left. The central area is out of bounds. Each ball thrown successfully over the opponent's rear boundary line counts as one point. The game may be played up to five points or simply the first team to get the ball over the opponent's rear boundary line.

31. Crows and Cranes (8–9 yrs.)
Children divide equally into a team of Crows and a team of Cranes. To begin each tagging race, the children are in a stride-stand position with one foot touching their own starting line. The two starting lines are six feet apart and each is marked about twenty-five to thirty feet from the two goal lines. Play begins when the teacher calls out either "Crows!" or "Cranes!" If she calls out "Crows!" then the Crows run from their starting line toward their goal line for safety, while the Cranes chase them. If a Crow is tagged before reaching her goal line, then she becomes a Crane. If the teacher calls out "Cranes!" then the Crows chase the Cranes. The object is to have the most members on a team at the end of the predesignated playing time.

32. Partner Tag (7–8, 8–9 yrs.)
Each child has a partner that she has linked elbows with. Two extra children do not link elbows; one becomes the runner and one is the chaser. The chaser tries to tag the runner before the runner links elbows with another child. The partner of the child with whom the runner links elbows with must quickly unlink and become the runner. This new runner is now chased. If a runner is tagged, then the runner becomes the chaser and the chaser becomes the runner.

33. Red Light, Green Light (7–8, 8–9 yrs.)
Children spread out behind a designated starting line. One extra child is It and stands at the other end of the playing space with her back to the other children. When It says "Green light!" the players walk toward It, trying to reach the goal line where It is standing. When It calls out "Red Light!" the children advancing must stop before It turns and faces them. If It turns and sees anyone moving their feet after she has called out "Red Light!" then that player is sent back to the starting line. The object is to be the first player over the goal line. Play continues until everyone has reached the goal line. The last player over becomes the new It, and the game starts again.

34. Dodge Ball (8–9 yrs.)
Children divide into six different teams. Teams 1–4 form a circle around teams 5 and 6. Teams 1–4 on the circle try to hit the teams on the inside of the circle with a soft ball. The hits must be below the waist. A player who is hit joins the circle. The last one left inside the circle is the winner. Begin play again with two different teams standing inside the circle.

35. Eraser Relay (8–9 yrs.)
Children are seated in rows in the schoolroom or play area. An eraser is placed on the floor to the right of each row. When the teacher signals, each child at the end of the row next to the eraser picks up the eraser with his right hand and places it on the floor with his left hand. The

next child (on the first child's left) picks up the eraser with her right hand and places it on the left with her left hand. The first row to place the eraser on the left-hand outside aisle wins.

36. Hill Dill (8–9 yrs.)
Children number off 1 through 6. Numbers 1–3 stand behind one goal line, and numbers 4–6 stand behind the opposite marked goal line. One extra person is It and stands in the center, between the two goal lines. When It calls "Hill Dill! Come over the hill!" all of the children run to their opposite goal trying not to be tagged by It. A tagged child must go to the center and help It tag the remaining children when It calls out "Hill Dill!" again. Game continues until all of the children have been tagged.

37. Indians (8–9 yrs.)
Six children, the Indians, leave the room. They enter again in a line. They circle the other children once and then leave the room again. The first child in the room to guess correctly the order in which they entered and circled becomes the new Indian. The new Indian picks five other Indians, they exit the room, and the game is repeated.

38. I Say Stoop (8–9 yrs.)
Children are in aisles facing the front of the room. It stands in front of the children facing them and calls out, "I say stoop!" or "I say stand!" The children do the action It calls out, not the action It does. It may either stand or stoop, no matter what she calls out. The first child to disobey It's command becomes the new It.

39. Japanese Tag (8–9 yrs.)
Children are spread throughout the playing area. One child is designated It and tries to tag another player. Wherever the child is tagged, she must hold her hand there and be the new It. The game is the same as Simple Tag, except It holds her hand on the spot It was tagged while trying to tag a new It. Game is continuous.

40. Lemonade (8–9 yrs.)
Children are in two equal groups. Each group stands behind its marked goal line, which is opposite the other group's goal line. The first group thinks of a "trade" and then approaches the opposite goal line calling out, "Here we come!" The second group asks, "Where from?"

First group: "New Orleans."
Second group: "What is your trade?"
First group: "Lemonade!"
Second group: "Show us some!"

The first group then proceeds to pantomime the trade they thought of. (The teacher may help suggest trades such as sweeping the floor, fishing, sawing wood, etc.) When the second group guesses correctly, the children in group 1 turn and run toward their goal line, trying not to be tagged. Any child tagged by group 2 members before reaching safety behind the goal line must join group 2. The game continues with group 2 thinking of a trade and approaching group 1.

41. Posture Relay (7–8, 8–9 yrs.)
Children are in file formation. The first child of each file starts the relay with a bean bag on his head. Each line faces a marked goal line. The first player runs to the goal line and back to his file with the bean bag on his head and then passes the bean bag to the next player. The next player puts the bean bag on her head and does the same thing. The first

file (team) to have every player run up and back with the bean bag on their head is the winner.

42. Obstacle Relay (8–9 yrs.)
Children are in equally numbered teams in file formation. There are three obstacles each child must pass before running back and tagging the next player in the line. The first obstacle is to pick up a jump rope in the designated circle, jump once, and set it back down in the circle. The second obstacle the child runs to is a box with a rubber ball inside. The child must take out the ball, bounce it three times, and return it to the box. The third and last obstacle is a circle that is divided equally into four sections. The child must hop from the first section to the second section, to the third section, to the fourth section, and then out of the circle. The child then runs back to her team, and the next player in line does the same race. The first team to have all players complete the obstacle race is the winner. Obstacle Relay may be modified by substituting various locomotor patterns, such as walking, jumping, hopping, galloping, or skipping.

43. Spot Basketball (8–9, 9–10 yrs.)
Children are grouped into two opposing teams. A circle, three feet in diameter, is drawn on the floor at each end of the basketball court. The game begins with one team member receiving the ball from the referee at his team's end line. The children pass the ball from one to another of their own teammates, trying to place it in the opposing team's circle (spot). The team that places the ball in the opponent's circle scores one point each time this is done. After each score, the nonscoring team receives the ball at its end line. The game continues. The players may pass or bounce the ball to each other but may not take more than one step when in possession of the ball. Dribbling is not permitted, nor is unwarranted roughness or possession of the ball by one team member in excess of five seconds. If any of the above fouls occur, any score made does not count, and the opposing team is given the ball at the point where the foul was committed.

44. Kick and Run (6–7, 7–8 yrs.)
Children are in two teams, one up to kick and the other fielding. Play begins with one child from fielding team on the field and one child from the kicking team up to kick (at home plate). The child up to kick places the ball on the ground and kicks the ball into the field. The fielder retrieves the ball, runs to home plate, and calls out "Home!" The kicker runs around bases and back to home plate. The kicker scores one point for each base she touched before the fielder called out "Home!" Each child is up to kick once, with a different fielder for each kicker. After everyone has had a chance to kick, the kicking team becomes the fielding team and the fielding team is up to kick. Score may be kept individually and by team. Highest score wins.

45. Soccer Keep-away (8–9, 9–10 yrs.)
Children are in two teams. Without touching ball with hands, the team beginning with the ball tries to keep the ball away from the opposing team. Children may pass the ball by dribbling it with the inside of foot. Children may not have contact with another player.

46. Jump the Brook (8–9, 9–10 yrs.)
Divide the children into groups of up to ten and draw a "brook" for each group. Two chalk lines will do, starting about three feet apart and gradually widening to about four-and-a-half feet apart, depending upon the age and skill of the children. Forming a line, the players take turns

running and jumping over the brook at the narrowest point. As soon as one width of the brook is jumped by a child, she moves down to a spot a little wider than before. The child who jumps the farthest is the winner.

47. American Hopscotch (8–9 yrs.)
Draw a rectangle [approximately four feet by twelve feet. Then divide the rectangle's twelve-foot side into two two-foot sections, followed by a four-foot section, and then two more two-foot sections. In the second and fourth region, divide the area in half making two two-foot squares. Then, divide the center section into four parts by making an X that reaches each corner. Label the parts with numbers from one to ten as shown in the diagram on the next page.] Place about six to eight players on each team, and give each one a bean bag or other small object. Arrange the teams in single file with the first player facing area number 1 with a bean bag in hand. Standing on one foot, the player tosses the bean bag into square 1 and then leaps over that square, landing with one foot in 2 and one in 3 in a spread-eagle position. He then hops on one foot in 4, two feet, spread-eagle, in 5 and 6, and so on, hopping twice in 10 in order to turn around. Going back the way he came, the player stops in 2 and 3, picks up the bean bag, and hops out. The next time through the player tosses the bean bag into area 2 and proceeds

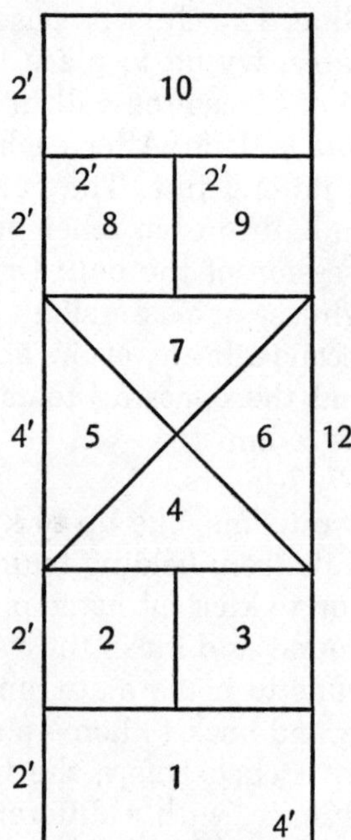

Diagram 10–1. American Hopscotch

the same as before, only leaving 2 alone instead of 1. Stepping on a line, tossing the bean bag into the wrong area, touching a hand to the ground, or landing on the wrong feet are errors, and the child must end his turn there and go to the end of the line.

48. Flag Tag (7–8, 8–9 yrs.)
Each child wears a handkerchief (the Flag) hanging down in back from a belt. On teacher's signal, children run to grab as many Flags as possible while trying to dodge other children trying to get their Flags. The child with the most Flags at the end of two minutes wins.

49. Freeze Tag (6–7, 7–8, 8–9 yrs.)

Children run away from It. If It tags them, they must freeze like a statue in the position in which they were tagged.

50. Basic Relay (6–7, 7–8, 8–9 yrs.)
Relay teams stand on starting line, run to opposite line, and run back to starting line, touching the outstretched hand of the next player in line. Waiting players run in sequence to and from the opposite line. The first team that finishes wins the relay.

51. Follow the Leader (6–7, 7–8, 8–9 yrs.)
One student or the teacher serves as the leader, and all others follow the leader around the room or through various obstacles.

52. Clean Up Your Own Backyard (8–9 yrs.)
Two teams face each other and are separated by a line. Evenly divide 9½" balls between the teams with approximately one ball for every two children. When the teacher says "Go," the balls are thrown at the opposing team and then thrown back as quickly as possible. When the teacher says "Stop," the children cease throwing, and the side with the fewest balls is the winner.

53. Chase (8–9 yrs.)
The children form a circle about ten feet apart from each other. The game is played with two 9½" rubber balls. The first ball is thrown from player to player around the circle. Once it gets halfway around, the second ball is started. Both balls travel in the same direction, and the children try to get the second ball to catch up to the first.

54. Over the Net (8–9 yrs.)
Two equal teams are divided by a net that is approximately five feet high. The children try to throw the ball over the net. Every time the ball is successfully thrown over the net, the team that threw it receives one point. The receiving team does not have to catch the ball.

55. Target Throwing (8–9 yrs.)
Either suspend several hula hoops from the ceiling or support them on the floor so that they are standing on edge. Position the children about ten or fifteen yards away, and have them try to throw a 9½" ball through the hoops. The game can be made easier or more difficult by varying the distance between the children and the hoops. Have two equal teams of children and see which one can score the highest number of balls thrown through the hoops in a specified amount of time.

56. Child and Teacher Drill (7–8, 8–9 yrs.)
The child and teacher throw and catch different-sized balls from different distances, trying to increase the distance as time passes.

57. The Longest Volley (8–9 yrs.)
Students form groups of six or seven and get into circle formations. Using a 9½" rubber ball, the students bat the ball into the air with either their fists or open palms when the teacher says "Go." Each group tries to make the most consecutive hits without allowing the ball to hit the ground.

58. Circle Bat Ball (8–9 yrs.)
The entire class forms one big circle with their legs about two feet apart and feet touching the person next to them. The students try to bat the ball across the circle and make it go between the legs of a person on the other side. If the ball goes out of the circle by passing between someone's legs, that person is eliminated. Play continues until another player is eliminated and then that person takes the place of the first one. The first player who was eliminated rejoins the circle and play continues.

59. Kickball Croquet (8–9 yrs.)
A modified croquet course is set up using boxes with the bottoms removed instead of wire wickets. Using a 16¼″ rubber ball, the children try to kick the ball through the boxes in the same fashion as croquet. The game can be made more difficult by reducing the size of both the boxes and balls.

60. Circle Kickball (8–9 yrs.)
The class forms one large circle and uses a 9½″ rubber ball. The ball is kicked across and around inside the circle. The children try to keep the ball from going outside the circle.

61. Throw against Wall Drill (8–9 yrs.)
The child throws a ball against a wall using two hands and tries to catch it from about five feet away. Whenever a distance is mastered, the child moves back farther.

62. Circle Toss Drill (8–9 yrs.)
In a circle of four or five children, the teacher tosses the ball upward, claps her hands as the ball bounces, and then catches the ball with both hands. The children repeat this procedure around the circle.

63. Leader of the Class (7–8, 8–9 yrs.)
Divide the class into groups of five or six. One person in each group is the leader and stands facing the other group members who are about ten feet away in a row (not single file). The leader tosses the ball to each child and whoever misses goes to the foot of the line. Whenever the leader misses, the child at the head of the line becomes the new leader, and the play continues. To make the game more difficult, increase the distance between the leader and the line.

64. Four Square (8–9 yrs.)
Separate a large square, about sixteen by sixteen feet, into four equal four-foot squares and label them A, B, C, and D. One player stands in each of the squares, and player D starts the game. The ball is bounced and then hit with either one or two hands so that it lands in one of the other three squares. The play continues until a player fails to return the ball properly. That player then goes to the end of the line, and the players in the squares rotate one letter toward space D. The new player enters square A. The ball cannot be struck down at the ground by a player. It must be arched and cannot be held at any time. If a fair ball forces a player to return it from outside her own square, that is legal. An illegal ball is one that hits any line, is struck with closed fists, or hits a player who is standing in her own square.

65. Simon Says
See activity 13 in Intermediate-Level Activities.

11

GEDDES PSYCHOMOTOR DEVELOPMENT PROGRAM

Intermediate Level Activities

From the following activities, select those that are indicated by the completed Psychomotor Individualized Educational Program (IEP) form. Emphasize the activities associated with competencies recorded as "Improve." Give minimal emphasis to activities related to competencies recorded as "Maintain." Modify the activities according to the student's functional age levels and information given in the chapters on handicapping conditions. Activities that are repeated for several performance competencies are described at the end of this chapter in the section "Description of Selected Activities."[1]

1. The page numbers in parentheses following each performance competency statement refer to the GPI long and short forms.

INTERMEDIATE LEVEL ACTIVITIES (1)

Locomotion and Basic Movement (If indicated, select additional activities from Primary Level)

RUNS (GPI pp. 74, 78)

Runs in physical activities

Equipment: As indicated or items italicized.

1. Run in game situations, relays, and tag games such as Rescue Relay, Carry and Fetch Relay, Black House, Second Base Ball, Prisoner's Base, Run, Sheep, Run, One Old Cat, Last Couple Out, Streets and Alleys, Alley Soccer, Around the Bases, and Football Baseball. See activities 1, 2, 3, 14, 15, 22, 23, 25, 27, 34, 35, and 40 on pages 194, 196, and 198–202.
2. Run in rhythmic activities such as the Schottische or Polka.
3. Runs in drill formations such as Zig-Zag Formation, Shuttle Formation, Line Relay, Circle Tag, and File Relay. See activities 3, 5, 19, and 20 on pages 202–203 and 197.
4. Run in track and field such as the fifty-yard dash and the six-hundred-yard run-walk.
5. Other:________________

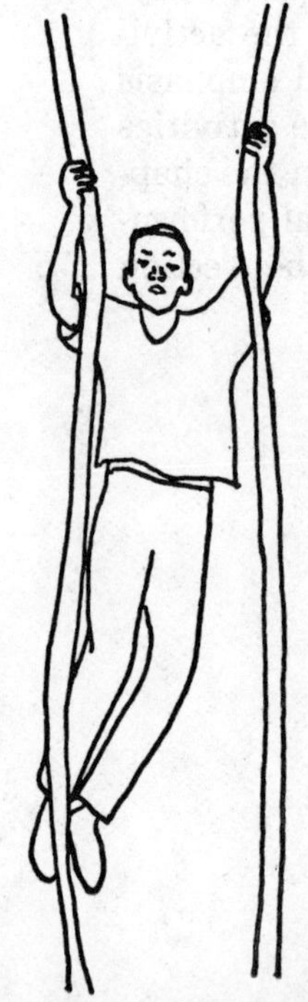

Figure 11–1. Climb climbing ropes.

CLIMBS (GPI, pp. 74, 78)

Climbs on apparatus

Equipment: As indicated or items italicized.

1. Play on *Lind Climber.*
2. Play on *climbing frames.*
3. Play on *playground gym.*
4. Climb *climbing ropes* to ceiling (use a spotter and *landing mat*).
5. Climb over *obstacles* in circuit training courses.
6. Other:________________

JUMPS (GPI pp. 74, 78)

Jumps with and without equipment

Equipment: As indicated or items italicized.

1. Practice *standing broad jump.*
2. Compete with others in *standing broad jump.*
3. Practice *vertical jump.*
4. Compete with others in *vertical jump.*
5. Practice jumping skills in drill formations such as line formation, fan formation, zig-zag formation, circle formation, and shuttle formation. See activities 1–5 on pages 202–203. Practice the jumping skills used in lead-up games such as the lay-up shot in *basketball* and blocking or spiking in *volleyball.*
6. Practice *short jump rope* jumping with and without music.
7. Play games such as Dodgeball, emphasizing jumping to dodge the *ball,* Keep Away (modified so ball is passed only overhead), and Jump the Shot. See activities 10, 21, and 26 on pages 195 and 197–198.
8. Jump in dances such as Bleking, Oxdansen, Tinikling, Hora, and Seven Jumps.
9. Other:____________________

HAS TOTAL BODY CONTROL (GPI pp. 75, 78)

Has total body control in physical activities

Equipment: As indicated or items italicized.

1. Practice stunts and self-testing skills such as egg roll, frog hop, inch worm, jump and slap heels, knee lift, step over the wand, mule kick, backward jump, bells, coffee grinder, human rocker, jump over the stick, grasp the toe, churn the butter, rocker, Chinese get-up, and Merry-Go-Round. See activities 1–17 on pages 191–193.
2. Practice tumbling skills such as cartwheel, dive over one, forearm handstand, handstand, headstand, and handspring progressions. See activities 1–6 on pages 193–194.
3. Other:____________________

Performs on Apparatus

INTERMEDIATE LEVEL ACTIVITIES (3)

Figure 11–3. Bird's nest.

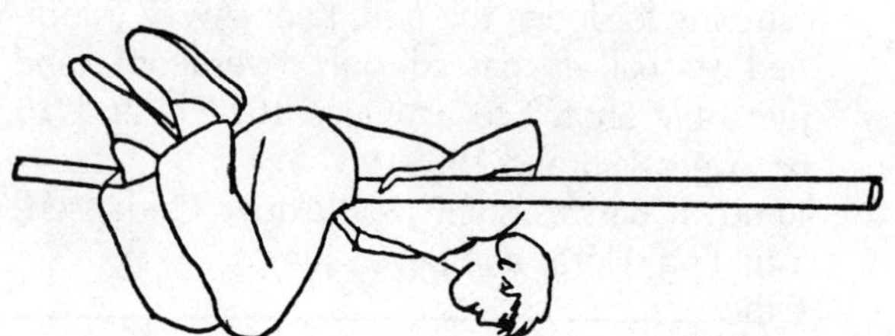
Figure 11–2. Pull-over

USES HORIZONTAL BAR (GPI pp. 75, 78)

Equipment: As indicated or items italicized.

1. Practice pull-over.
2. Practice bird's nest.
3. Other:____________________

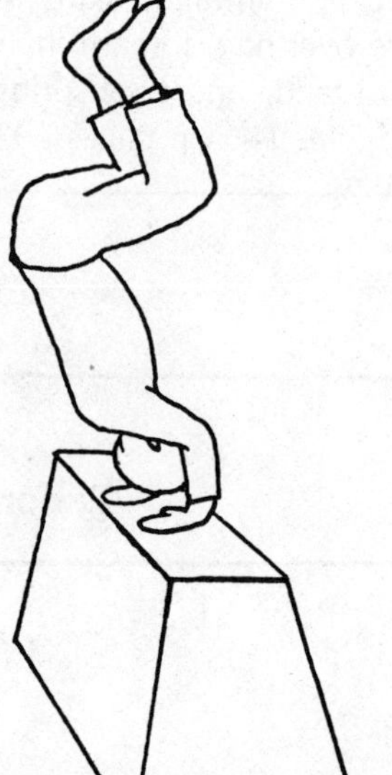
Figure 11–4. Front vault.

USES VAULTING BOX (GPI pp. 75, 78)

Equipment: As indicated or items italicized.

1. Practice front vault
2. Practice flank vault.
3. Practice squat vault.
4. Other:____________________

INTERMEDIATE LEVEL ACTIVITIES (4)

Aquatics

DOES DROWN-PROOFING SKILLS (GPI pp. 75, 78)

Equipment: As indicated or items italicized.

1. Practice survival floating, treading water, jellyfish float, and bobbing. Practice recovery techniques.
2. Other:____________________

DOES FLOATS AND GLIDES (GPI pp. 75, 78)

Equipment: As indicated or items italicized.

1. Practice front (prone) float, back float, front (prone) glide, and back glide. Practice recovery techniques.
2. Other:____________________

DOES ARM AND LEG STROKES (GPI pp. 75, 78)

Equipment: As indicated or items italicized.

1. Practice sculling, finning, arm and leg strokes, front crawl, back crawl, elementary backstroke, breast stroke, and sidestroke.
2. Other:____________________

DOES STYLES OF SWIMMING (GPI pp. 76, 79)

Equipment: As indicated or items italicized.

1. Combine arm strokes, leg strokes, and breathing for front crawl, back crawl, and elementary backstroke.
2. Other:____________________

INTERMEDIATE LEVEL ACTIVITIES (5)

Ball Handling
(If indicated, select additional activities from Primary Level)

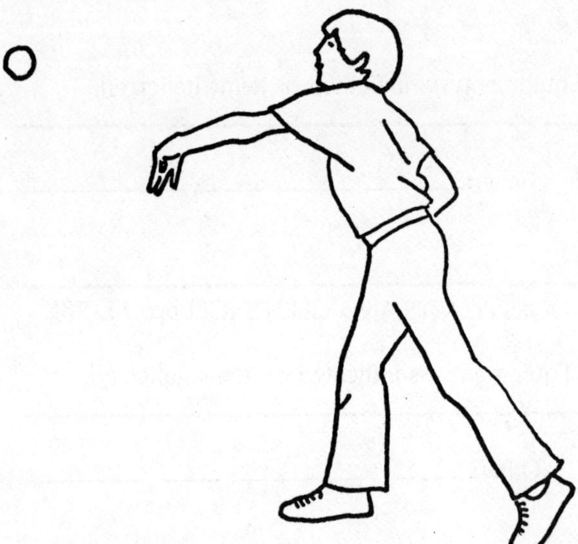

Figure 11–5. Softball throw.

THROWS (GPI pp. 76, 79)

Equipment: As indicated or items italicized.

1. Play games such as Kick Ball, Team Dodge Ball, Second Base Ball, Prisoner's Ball, End Ball, Keep Away, One Old Cat, Newcomb, Nine-Court Basketball, Half-court Basketball, Softball Fly Balls, and Long Ball. See activities 9, 10, 14, 16, 17, 21, 23, 24, 29, 30, 36, and 38 on pages 195–199, and 201.
2. Practice specific throwing skills such as overhand throw, underhand pitch *(softball)*, chest pass, two hand underhand pass, bounce pass, overhead pass *(basketball)*, and forward pass *(football)* in relays and drill formations such as line formation, fan formation, zig-zag formation, shuttle formation, throwing and catching drills, softball throw, basketball pass, teacher ball relay, and pitch at target. See activities 1, 2, 3, 5, 6, 7, 8, 11, and 37 on pages 194, 195, and 201–203.
3. Other:________________________

Figure 11–6. Two hand catch of softball.

CATCHES (GPI pp. 76, 79)

Equipment: As indicated or items italicized.

1. Play games such as Over and Under Relay, Fly Ball, Kick Ball, Second Base Ball, Prisoner's Ball, End Ball, Keep Away, One Old Cat, Nine-Court Basketball, Half-Court Basketball, Softball Fly Balls, Long Ball, and Kick Over. See activities 4, 8, 9, 14, 16, 17, 21, 23, 29, 30, 36, 38, and 39 on pages 194–199 and 201.
2. Practice specific catching skills such as catching chest pass, two-hand underhand pass, bounce pass *(basketball)*, catching overhead throw, fly ball *(softball)*, and catching forward pass *(football)* in relays and drill formations such as fan formation, zig-zag formation, shuttle formation, throwing and catching drills, softball throw, basketball pass, and teacher ball relay. See activities, 2, 3, 5, 6, 7, 8, and 11 on pages 194–195 and 202–203.

Figure 11–7. Kicks stationary ball (place kick soccer).

KICKS (GPI pp. 77, 79)

Equipment: As indicated or items italicized.

INTERMEDIATE LEVEL ACTIVITIES (7)

1. Play games such as Kick Ball, Second Base Ball, Soccer Dodgeball, Soccer in a Circle, Line Soccer, Alley Soccer, Kick Over, and Football Baseball. See activities 9, 14, 31, 32, 33, 34, 39, and 40 on pages 195–196 and 199–202.
2. Practice specific kicking skills such as place kick, punt *(football),* and dribble *(soccer)* in relays and drill formation such as fan formation, zig-zag formation, shuttle formation, soccer in a circle, and soccer dribble relay. See activities 2, 3, 5, 6, and 32 on pages 200 and 202–203.
3. Other:____________________

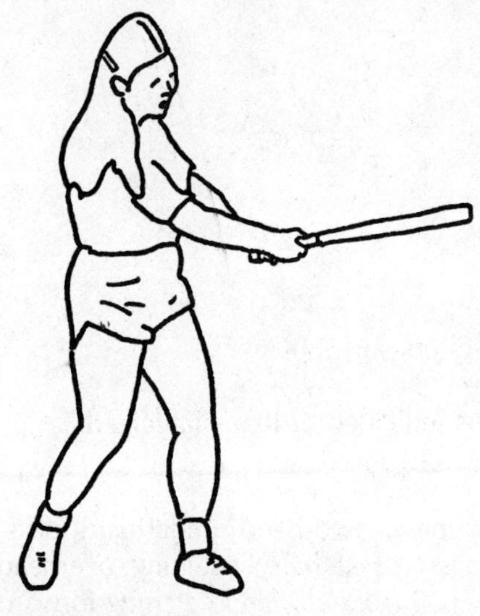

Figure 11–8. Bats pitched softball.

STRIKES (GPI pp. 77, 79)

Equipment: As indicated or items italicized.

1. Play games such as Fly Ball, One Old Cat, Long Ball, and Keep It Up. See activities 8, 23, 38, and 41 on pages 195, 198, and 201–202.
2. Practice specific striking skills such as batting underhand pitch *(softball),* forehand *(tennis),* and underhand serve *(volleyball)* in relays and drill formations such as circle bat ball and fan formation. See activities 2 and 58 on pages 181 and 202.
3. Other:____________________

DESCRIPTION OF SELECTED ACTIVITIES

Stunts and Self-Testing Skills

1. Egg roll (7–8, 8–9, 9–10, 10–11, 11–12 yrs.[2])
   Described under Primary Level Program Activities.
2. Frog hop (7–8, 8–9, 9–10, 10–11, 11–12 yrs.)
   Described under Primary Level Program Activities.
3. Inch worm (7–8, 8–9, 9–10, 10–11, 11–12 yrs.)
   Described under Primary Level Program Activities.
4. Jump and slap heels (7–8, 8–9, 9–10, 10–11, 11–12 yrs.)
   Described under Primary Level Program Activities.
5. Knee lift (7–8, 8–9, 9–10, 10–11, 11–12 yrs.)
   Described under Primary Level Program Activities.
6. Step over the wand (7–8, 8–9, 9–10, 10–11, 11–12 yrs.)
   Described under Primary Level Program Activities.
7. Mule kick (8–9, 9–10, 10–11, 11–12 yrs.)
   Bend over and place both palms on floor. With knees bent, kick both legs into the air like a mule.
8. Backward jump (9–10 yrs.)
   Stand at edge of mat with back facing the center of the mat. Using arms for momentum, jump backward as far as possible. Should land lightly on the mat.
9. Bells (9–10, 10–11, 11–12 yrs.)
   Hop on one foot while extending other leg to side and bringing foot being hopped on up to meet extended foot. Try to click two heels together.

Figure 11–9. Bells (heel-click).

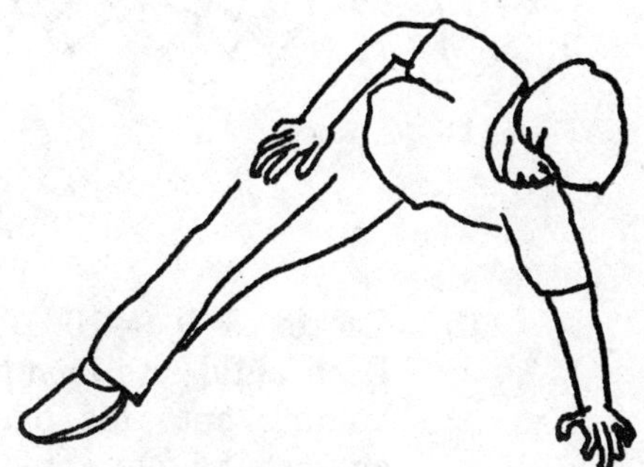

Figure 11–10. Coffee grinder.

2. Most appropriate age for activity.

10. Coffee grinder (9–10, 10–11, 11–12 yrs.)
Place the hand of an extended arm on a tumbling mat for support. Extend legs and walk with feet in a circle, using hand on mat as a pivot.
11. Human rocker (9–10, 10–11, 11–12 yrs.)
Lie with abdomen on a tumbling mat. While arching the back, grab left foot with left hand and right foot with right hand. Then rock forward onto chest and back onto thighs. Also try rocking without holding feet.
12. Jump over the stick (10–11 yrs.)
Hold stick (long rod) with both hands, knuckles facing upward. Bend and jump over the stick. Swing stick foward and jump over the stick in reverse direction.
13. Grasp the toe (10–11, 11–12 yrs.)
Stand on one foot and grab the other foot with both hands and attempt to touch the grasped foot to forehead by bending forward.

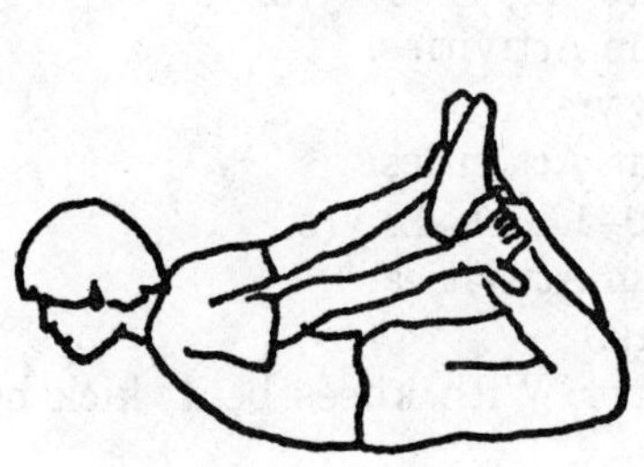

Figure 11–11. Human rocker.

Figure 11–12. Grasp the toe.

14. Churn the butter (8–9, 9–10, 10–11, 11–12 yrs.)
Each child has a partner. Partners face back to back and interlock elbows. When one partner bends over, the other child leans back on her partner so that her feet are off the floor. Alternately, one partner bends and the other leans back on the partner.

Figure 11–13. Rocker.

15. Rocker (8–9, 9–10, 10–11, 11–12 yrs.)
Each child sits facing a partner. Arms are extended so each child is holding onto his partner's upper arm. Each child presses his feet against the feet of his partner and rocks back and forth.
16. Chinese get-up (9–10, 10–11, 11–12 yrs.)
Children stand back to back with elbows locked to their partner. Part-

ners slowly go down to the floor and back up again by pressing against the back of her partner.

17. Merry-go-round (10–11, 11–12 yrs.)
Children form circles of eight or ten. Each child holds on to the wrist of the child next to her. Children number off so they are "even" or "odd." The children numbered even sit on the floor with legs together as spokes pointing to a hub of a wheel. The odd-numbered children remain standing, while the sitting children lift their hips so their bodies are straight. The odd-numbered children walk around the circle while the even-numbered children look like spokes of a wheel.

Tumbling Skills

1. Cartwheel (7–8, 8–9, 9–10, 10–11, 11–12 yrs.)
Described in Primary-Level Tumbling Skills.
2. Dive over one (9–10 yrs.)
With a short run, child does a forward roll to a standing position. Child may dive over a rolled mat to get height on dive.
3. Forearm handstand (9–10 yrs.)
Place head between hands on mat, with palms and forearms on mat for support. Walk toward forearms and kick up one leg. After securing balance, slowly raise other leg. Both legs finish together in a vertical position. Use spotters for safety.
4. Handstand (9–10 yrs.)
Extend arms, placing both hands on ground while keeping head off mat. Kick up with one leg and then the other until both legs are in a vertical position together over head. Arch the back slightly to maintain balance. Use spotters for safety.

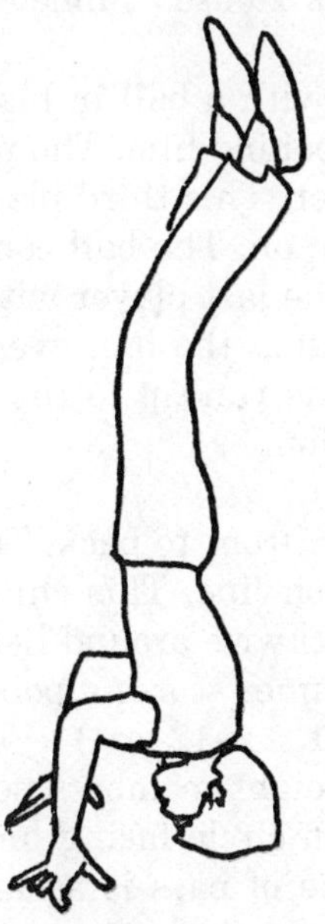

Figure 11–14. Headstand.

5. Headstand (9–10 yrs.)
Place head and palms of hands on mat. Head is slightly in front of the hands, so that the hands and head form a triangular base. Then extend legs vertically into the air (knees flexed and then extended). Use spotters for safety.

6. Handspring progressions (10–11 yrs.)
Do handstand, arch back, and let legs drop forward to mat. Push hard with hands to thrust to a standing position. Use spotters for safety.

Game Situations, Relays, and Tag Games

1. Rescue Relay (8–9, 9–10, 10–11, 11–12 yrs.)
A runner stands behind a goal line facing his team, which is lined up behind the starting line. The teacher says "Go," and the leader runs to the first player of his team, grasps him by the wrist, and runs back to the goal line. The rescued player runs back to get another player.
2. Carry and Fetch Relay (9–10 yrs.)
The first child in each team begins with a bean bag in her hand, runs up to a designated circle on the floor, and places the bean bag in the circle. Then she runs back and tags the next player on her team. After being tagged, the second player retrieves the bean bag and gives it to player 3. Player 3 (and all other odd-numbered children) does the same placement as the first child. Number 4 (and all other even-numbered children), after being tagged, retrieves the bean bag, and so on. First team with all players back in beginning position wins.
3. Black House (9–10 yrs.)
Children are in two equal groups, each standing behind one of two opposing goal lines. One extra player is It and stands in the center, between the goals. When It calls out "Black House!" the two groups of children change goals, trying not to be tagged by It. A child who is tagged becomes "It" and the game starts over. It can try to deceive the players by calling out "Blue House!" or "Brown House!" A player who jumps out at words other than "Black House!" immediately becomes It.
4. Over and Under Relay (9–10 yrs.)
First player in the relay line starts with a ball in his hand and passes the ball over his head to the player behind him. The next player passes it between her legs to the next player. This third player passes it over her head to the fourth player, and so on. The ball continues to go over and under through the entire line. The last player with the ball runs to the front of the line and begins passing the ball over her head again. Play continues until every player has run up to the front of the line, and the team is in the original position.
5. Line Relay (9–10, 10–11, 11–12 yrs.)
Teams number off consecutively from front to back. The teacher calls a number of one of the children in each line. This child runs out of the line to the right and runs counterclockwise around her team, returning to the original place in line. Each winner scores a point.
6. Throwing and Catching Drills (10–11, 11–12 yrs.)
Equal teams are formed with six to eight members per team. A player from each team is positioned inside a circle facing his own teammates lined up facing him. A different type of pass is assigned each player. The game begins with the players in the circles passing the ball to their own teammates using the assigned pass for that teammate who returns it to this player using the same type of pass. When the last teammate receives the ball, he replaces the first player in the circle, who takes his place in the line. The game is ended when all team members have had their turn in the circle. The team who gets all of its players back into their original positions first is the winner.

7. Twenty-one (10–11, 11–12 yrs.)
The children are divided into groups of four to six members. Each group has a basket and a basketball. Each player takes a turn in order, each turn consisting of three successive throws. A successful first throw (takes place at the free throw line) is worth five points; the second and third throws are worth three points and one point, respectively, if successful and are made from the spot where the ball is caught on the rebound. The first player to earn a score of twenty-one points is the winner. If the twenty-one points is exceeded by the player, her score goes back to zero, and she must begin to earn points again.
8. Fly Ball (10–11, 11–12 yrs.)
Groups of six to eight members are formed; one is the batter and the rest are fielders. The batter tosses the ball up and hits it out into the field as a "fly ball" or a grounder. If a fielder catches a fly ball or a grounder, she gets to be batter, and the batter returns to the field. The game continues as before.
9. Kick Ball (10–11, 11–12 yrs.)
This game is played by two opposing teams using a soccer ball, softball rules, and a softball diamond. The pitcher rolls the soccer ball to the batter, who kicks the ball out into the field. After three outs, the batters become fielders and the fielders become batters. The team with the highest score after an even number of innings is the winner.
10. Team Dodge Ball (9–10 yrs.)
Children are divided into two teams. One team forms a circle, with the other team standing in the middle of the circle. The team on the circle tries to hit the children on the inside of the circle with a soft ball. The hits must be below the waist. A player who is hit is out and stays out of the game until the teams change places at the end of the two-minute playing period. The team who puts out more of the opposing team during the playing period wins.
11. Teacher Ball Relay (9–10, 10–11, 11–12, 12–13 yrs.)
Divide students into teams of six. Each team is in a line, with one member starting as the Teacher or "leader." The Teacher stands facing her team with a ball, and the relay begins when Teacher tosses the ball to the person in the head position. (As Teacher faces the team, the child farthest left is at the head position, and the child farthest right is the foot.) The head child tosses ball back to Teacher, who tosses it to the next child and consecutively on down the line until the foot player. When the foot player receives ball, he runs with it to the Teacher position. Teacher runs to the head of the line and receives the first toss from the new Teacher. Play continues until every member has been the Teacher. When the original Teacher reaches her beginning position as Teacher again, the relay is over. The first team to do so wins. Lines are marked for Teacher position and team members' positions.
12. Modified Squat Tag (9–10 yrs.)
Children are scattered. One child is designated It and tries to tag another child, who then becomes It if tagged. Players cannot be tagged if in squat or deep-knee-bend position. However, children are only allowed three squats. After child has squatted and been safe three times, It can tag the child at any time, whether the child is squatting or not.
13. Simon Says (9–10 yrs.)
Children are in rows. One child, Simon, stands in front, facing the group of children. Simon calls out commands. If Simon begins the command with "Simon says," then all children must obey the command. If

Simon does not call out "Simon says" before the command, then children do not obey the command. If Simon sees children obeying the command when Simon does not precede the command with "Simon says," then Simon calls out the name of the person she saw and that child must sit down. After three players have been caught making mistakes, play begins again with a new Simon, and the three players stand up and join in the new game.

14. Second Base Ball (9–10 yrs.)
Children are in two teams, the kicking team and the fielding team. The first player up to kick places the soccer ball on home plate and kicks it into the field. (The field is marked as in baseball, except it has a modified second base. The second base is elongated, enabling more than one runner to stand on it.) After kicking, the player runs to second Base. Player may run directly home or wait on second base. If runner waits on second, she may run home only after a ball has just been kicked by teammate. The object is to run home without getting out. A player is out if the ball is kicked into the air and caught by a fielder before touching the ground or she is tagged if hit by the ball below the waist. Fielders cannot run with the ball; they may only pass to another fielder and can hold the ball for only three seconds. After three kickers are out, kickers become fielders and fielders become kickers. A point is scored for each player tagging home safely. The team with the most points at the end of an equal amount of innings wins.

15. Prisoner's Base (9–10 yrs.)
Behind each goal line of the play area there is a prison. Each of the two team's Base of safety is behind the goal line next to the prison for their opponent. The object is to tag all of the opposing team members and take them as prisoners. A prisoner may be freed if he is tagged by a player from his team. The player tagging the prisoner must have crossed the court without being tagged; if tagged she becomes a prisoner. A player may tag an opposing player only if the opposing player left her base line before the player tagging. Once a player has been captured or freed from prison, both players can walk freely to their respective prison or base. Players may return to their base line at any time if they have not been captured.

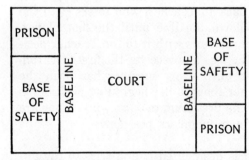

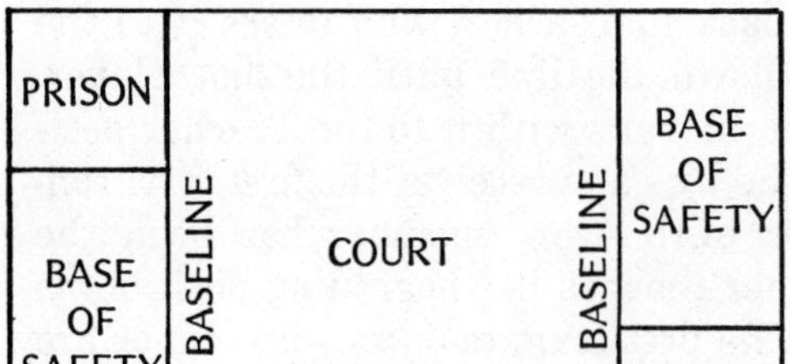

PRISON
BASE OF SAFETY
BASELINE
COURT
BASELINE
BASE OF SAFETY
PRISON

Diagram 11–1. Prisoner's Base

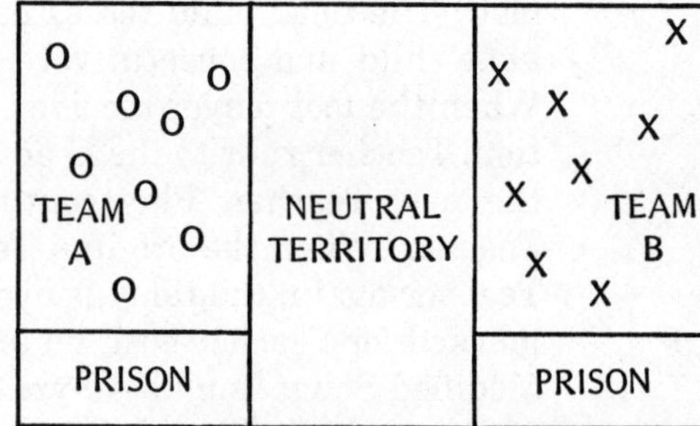

Diagram 11–2. Prisoner's Ball

16. Prisoner's Ball (9–10 yrs.)
Children are divided into two teams, and each team must stay in its designated area (on opposite sides of playing court). A neutral territory, which may not be stepped in, is marked between the two areas. The object is to put the opposing team members in prison. Each team has its prison marked beside its playing area at the far corner of the court. The players are numbered consecutively starting with one, until the last

player from each team has been given a number. The game begins when a player calls out a number and throws a basketball across the neutral area into the opposing team's court. If the ball is not caught by the opposing team before it bounces, then the player whose number was called out must go to prison. The game is continued by throwing the ball back and forth, calling out a player's number each time. A prisoner may be freed if "Prisoner number _____!" is called out by a teammate as the teammate throws the ball and if the opposing team fails to catch the ball. A player may not run with the ball, only pass it to a teammate.

ENDS	GUARDS	GUARDS	ENDS
X X X X X	O O O O O O O O O O	X X X X X X X X X X	O O O O O

Diagram 11–3. End Ball

17. End Ball (9–10 yrs.)
Children are in two teams. Each team has one-third of its members designated as ends, and the rest are guards. Teams remain in their side of the court, with the ends of each team at the opposite base line from their team. The ends have approximately a five-foot-wide area in which they must stay. The game is started with a center toss as in basketball. The object is for the guards to throw the ball over the opposing guards so that their own end catches the ball. The end must have both feet within the boundary. The end must quickly pass back to his own guard so that play is continuous. No player may run with the ball; they may only pass to a team player. A point is scored if the guard is successful in passing the ball to her teammate playing end. The ball may be either a basketball or volleyball. Teacher may want to introduce basketball terms and rules such as traveling, holding the ball, etc.
18. Line Tag (10–11, 11–12 yrs.)
Children are scattered. It tries to tag a player. If tagged, the child must join hands with It. Both children are It and can tag only with their free hands. Each successive player tagged must join hands with the child who tagged him or her. As the line grows, only the two people on the ends with their free hands may tag; and players must remain joined. Game continues until all children have been tagged.
19. File Relay (10–11, 11–12 yrs.)
Each player places her hands on the hips of the team member lined in front of her. Each relay team runs to a designated line and back. Variations include weaving around obstacles while joined, and dividing each relay into smaller units so the first part of the team has to run up and back and tag the second unit, who in turns run up and back and so on.
20. Circle Tag (10–11, 11–12 yrs.)
Children stand in a circle. When teacher calls out signal, all players run clockwise around the circle trying to tag the player in front of them. Each player tagged steps into the middle of the circle and waits until the end of the game. The last player to remain untagged wins.
21. Keep Away (10–11, 11–12 yrs.)
Children are in two teams scattered over the playing area. A ball is

thrown into the play area. The player who recovers the ball passes it to a team member. The opposing team tries to intercept the ball and, if successful, tries to keep the ball among their team members. Game is continuous, and no points are scored.

22. Run, Sheep, Run (10–11, 11–12 yrs.)
One team is the Sheep, the other team the Foxes. Each team picks a captain. The Sheep hide while the Foxes stand at the goal line and wait for the Sheep to hide. After the Sheep have hidden, the captain of the Sheep returns and accompanies the Foxes in their search. If a Fox finds a Sheep, the Fox tells his captain and the captain calls out "Run, Sheep, Run." All players from both teams must run to the goal line. The object is to be the first team to have all of its members over the goal line. If the Sheep captain feels the Fox team is farther away from the goal than his Sheep team, then the Sheep captain may call out "Run, Sheep, Run." If either captain calls out "Run, Sheep, Run," all players must respond and run to the goal line. The Sheep agree on signals so that their captain can warn them during the search. For example, the captain may call out "blue" to mean that the Foxes are far away so the Sheep should be prepared to run, "carrots" may mean to be careful because the Foxes are getting close, and so on.

23. One Old Cat (10–11, 11–12 yrs.)
A modified softball game for four or more children. Each player scores only for herself. The essential players are the pitcher, catcher, batter, and one fielder. Each additional player is a fielder. The object is for the batter to hit a fair ball, run to first base, and run to home plate without being put out. If the batter is put out, the players rotate positions: the catcher becomes the batter, the batter becomes the last fielder, the fielders move over one position, the first fielder becomes the pitcher, and the pitcher becomes the catcher. The batter is out if she makes three strikes, a fielder catches a fly or foul ball, or the catcher tags home plate with the ball before the runner touches the plate.

24. Newcomb (10–11, 11–12 yrs.)
Two teams of ten to twelve players each are scattered on opposite sides of the playing court. A rope or net about six feet high separates the two halves of the court. The object is to throw the ball over the net so that it hits the ground on the opponent's side of the court. A point is scored each time the ball hits the opponent's floor provided the ball does not touch the net as it goes over. The ball starts in play immediately after a point is scored, so that play is continuous. Players can throw the ball from anywhere on their side of the court. Teams change sides at the end of five minutes (half-time), and the second half begins with the team that did not start with the throw the first half. The team with the most points wins.

25. Last Couple Out (10–11, 11–12 yrs.)
Children are in pairs in a double file formation. One child designated as It stands about four feet in front of the line of couples and always remains with her back toward the other children. When It calls, "Last Couple Out!" the last couple in the line split up and run on the outside of the file toward It. "It" tries to tag one of the players before they run in front of her and join hands. The person whom It tags becomes Its partner and the other player becomes the new It. This newly formed couple stands at the head of the line and a new couple becomes the last couple to begin the game again. If It is not successful in tagging either player, then It remains It.

26. Jump the Shot (10–11, 11–12 yrs.)

One player, It, holds a rope and kneels in the middle of a circle of players. At the free end of the rope is a knotted towel for weight. The players standing in the circle jump over the weighted end of the rope as It turns the rope around. The momentum of the rope must be sufficient enough to keep the weighted end of the rope turning under the feet of the players. A player is out and must leave the circle if he fails to jump over the rope every time or touches the rope with his feet. The last player left in the circle is It, and the game is repeated.

27. Streets and Alleys (10–11, 11–12 yrs.)
Children divide equally to form several lines. Two extra children are It and the runner. It chases the runner through the "streets and alleys." "Streets" are the pathways formed when the children join hands and face front; "alleys" are the aisles formed when the children face to the side and join hands. When the leader calls out "Streets!" all players must immediately face front and join hands. When the leader calls out "Alleys!" the players must immediately face to the side and join hands. Two new players are chosen to take the place of It and the runner when the runner is tagged. The original two players take the new players' places in the lines and the game is repeated.

28. Around the World (8–9, 9–10, 10–11, 11–12 yrs.)
There are six to eight players on two or more teams. The object is to see which team can have the most members make baskets from designated spots on the gym floor. Each team member begins at the first spot and continues as long as he makes the basket. After a miss, the player may wait for his next turn and continue from the place where he missed or "risk it," which means that he gets another shot from where he missed. If he misses again, he starts over from the beginning on his next turn. If a player finishes, he starts over again. Each team participates at a different basket. The team completing the most "trips around the world" in an allotted time is the winner.

29. Nine-Court Basketball (11–12, 12–13 yrs.)
Any number of teams can play with nine players on each team. The court must be divided into nine equal parts. Each section is then numbered, with the center box being 9. A player from each team plays in each section and may not step out of that section. The forwards in the three sections closest to each basket try to score. Basketball rules apply, except that dribbling is not allowed. A jump ball in court 9 starts the game. After each basket is made, players rotate to the next higher numbered section, with number 9 going to number 1. Play is then resumed with another jump ball in court 9.

30. Half-Court Basketball (10–11, 11–12, 12–13 yrs.)
There are four to six players on two or more teams. Scoring is the same as in basketball, but only one-half of the court is used and both teams shoot at the same basket. Since only one basket is used, if the ball changes hands, the team gaining possession must take the ball behind a line extended from the free-throw line before the ball can be shot at the goal. The game can also be played having the scoring team keep possession of the ball until a shot is missed or the other team steals the ball.

31. Soccer Dodgeball (11–12, 12–13 yrs.)
Eight to ten players can play per team with an unlimited number of teams possible. One team stays in the middle of a circle formed by all of the other teams. The players making up the circle try to hit the players inside by kicking a soccer ball. A hit must be below the shoulders, and the inside players may not use their hands to deflect a shot. After being

hit, a player is not eliminated. Instead the number of hits is counted, and after a predetermined amount of time the teams change places. One point is given for each hit, and the team scoring the most hits is the winner.

32. Soccer in a Circle (11–12, 12–13 yrs.)
There are eight to ten players on two or more teams. Each team forms a semicircle with two opposing teams joining to form one circle. To score, a player must kick the ball below shoulder level between members of the other team. If the ball stays inside the circle, a player from that half of the circle may get the ball and start again. After each score, the players rotate one place to the right. Points are scored when the ball goes through the opponent's team below the shoulder level and when an opponent uses his hands to stop the ball.

33. Line Soccer (10–11, 11–12, 12–13 yrs.)
Eight to ten players can play on each team with an unlimited number of teams possible. The players on each team are assigned a number from 1 to 10. Two teams then line up facing each other and two of the numbers are called. The players with these numbers on each team become active and meet in the center. The ball is either dropped or rolled between them to start the game. Then only the active players try to score by kicking the ball through the opposing team below shoulder level. However, the players remaining on the line act as goalies and can use their hands. If the ball is caught by a linesman, he passes it to an active teammate and play continues. New members are called after each score. Line soccer can also be played with four teams, one lined up on each side of a square. When a number is called, the four persons with that number are against each other. Each player has the possibililty of scoring on either of three sides of the square.

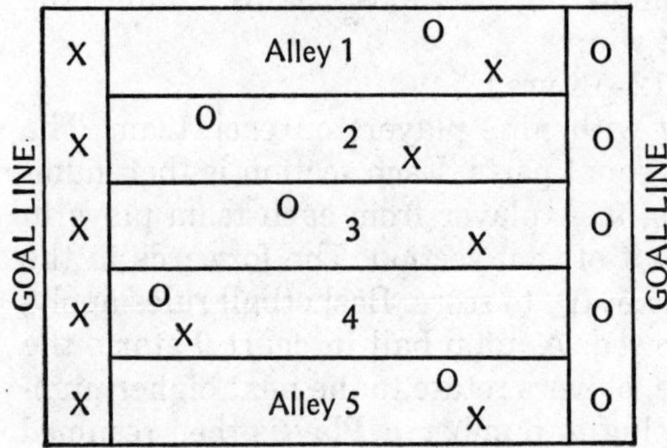

Diagram 11–4. Alley Soccer

34. Alley Soccer (11–12, 12–13 yrs.)
There are ten players on two or more teams. The playing surface is divided into five alleys. Each team sends out five alley players who must stay in their own alleys. The remaining players act as goalies and stand at opposite ends of the field. The alley players try to kick the ball below shoulder level over the other team's end line. The two center alley players start the game with a dropped ball at midfield. Each player may run the full length of the field, but only in her own alley. The penalty for going out of the alley is loss of the ball. The opposing team gets a free kick at the spot where the player committed the foul. Alley players and goalies exchange positions after each score.

35. Around the Bases (9–10, 10–11, 11–12, 12–13 yrs.)
Any number of teams can play with six players per team. A normal diamond is set up with four bases. The teams line up on the inside of the diamond facing opposite bases. The first person in each line runs one complete circuit of the bases. Then she touches the second player in her line, who does the same thing. The team that has everyone finish running the bases first is the winner.

36. Softball Fly Balls (10–11, 11–12, 12–13 yrs.)
There are six to eight players on two or more teams. Players on each team are assigned a number. One team is the fielding team, and one team forms a large circle. The fielders spread out in the center of the circle and try to catch the fly balls thrown to them by the throwing team. The members of the throwing team take turns throwing the ball, one at a time, as high into the air as possible. The player in the field who has the same number as the person who throws the ball attempts to catch it before it touches the ground. When everyone has thrown the ball, the teams change roles. One point is scored by the throwing team each time the ball drops in the circle without being caught.

37. Pitch at Target (9–10, 10–11, 11–12, 12–13 yrs.)
Place six players on each team. On a wall, mark a strike zone for each team. The teams then line up single file about forty-five feet from the wall. Each person takes one turn pitching underhand, trying to throw a strike. After retrieving his own ball, he then throws it to the next player in his line and goes to the rear of the line. The first team to pitch a certain number of strikes is the winner. If desired, the rules can be changed so that a player is allowed to continue pitching until he misses.

38. Long Ball (10–11, 11–12, 12–13 yrs.)
There are six to eight players on two or more teams. One team bats and one plays in the field. Bases are set up in a regular diamond, but first and third bases are used only to determine fair territory. A batter hits the pitched ball into fair territory and then runs to the far base (second base). She must reach the base either before the ball or before she is tagged with the ball. She can then stay on the base or try to return home. If she leaves the base when another player hits the ball, she cannot return unless it is a fly ball that is caught. Any number of runners can be on the far base as long as at least one batter is left. After all of the batters have had a chance to bat, the sides change. Long ball can also be played having the runner perform a stunt—for example, a forward roll—on her way to and from the base.

39. Kick Over (11–12, 12–13 yrs.)
There are six to eight players on a team, with any number of teams possible. Each team stands on opposite halves of the field. One point is scored for each uncaught soccer ball that is kicked over the opponent's goal line. One player puts the ball in play by kicking it from a point halfway between his team's goal line and the center line. If an opposing player catches the kick on the fly, he takes five steps forward and then kicks the ball as far toward his opponent's goal line as possible. If the ball is not caught, it is kicked from the point where someone first touched it. If the ball goes beyond the goal line but is caught, the player moves up to the goal line, takes five steps, and then kicks the ball as usual. The team that is scored upon puts the ball in play from the point between the goal line and center line. The kicking team must always stay behind the kicker, and the receiving team must be more than thirty feet from the kicker. This game can also be played using passing

instead of kicking.

40. Football Baseball (12–13 yrs.)
Eight to ten players are needed for each team. The game is played much like baseball, except a football is used. A batter stands at home plate, and a pitcher from her own team centers the ball to her. A line is drawn from first to third base, and two members of the fielding team are stationed just behind it. As the ball is centered, the two players rush the batter, who tries to kick the ball away cleanly. The ball must go beyond the line from first to third to be legal. After the batter kicks the ball, she runs the bases as in baseball. If the rushers block the kick or if the kicked ball is caught on the fly, the batter is out. Otherwise the game is played like baseball.

41. Keep It Up (9–10, 10–11, 11–12, 12–13 yrs.)
Children divide equally into teams and form large circles. A volleyball is tossed into the air for each circle, and the players try to keep it up by striking it into the air with both hands. The team that keeps the ball up the longest wins one point. No player may hit the ball more than once in succession. The team with the most points wins. By counting each contact that is made as one point, a winner can also be determined by the greatest number of points that a circle gets before the ball falls to the ground.

Skill Relays and Drill Formations (9–10, 10–11, 11–12, 12–13 yrs.)[1]

1. Line formation
All children on one team are in line behind the leader. Good for basket shooting and all types of relays.

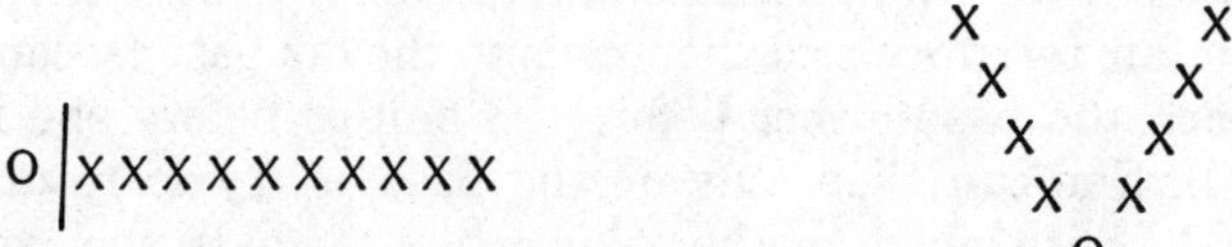

Diagram 11–5. Line Formation

Diagram 11–6. Fan Formation

2. Fan formation
A leader faces players spread in a fan formation. Well suited for kicking and passing skill drills.

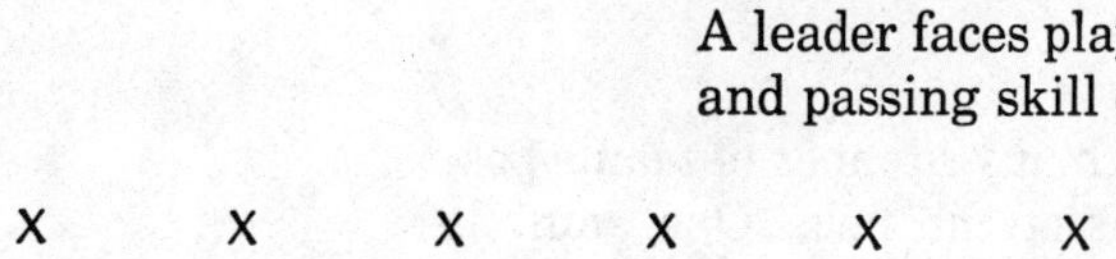

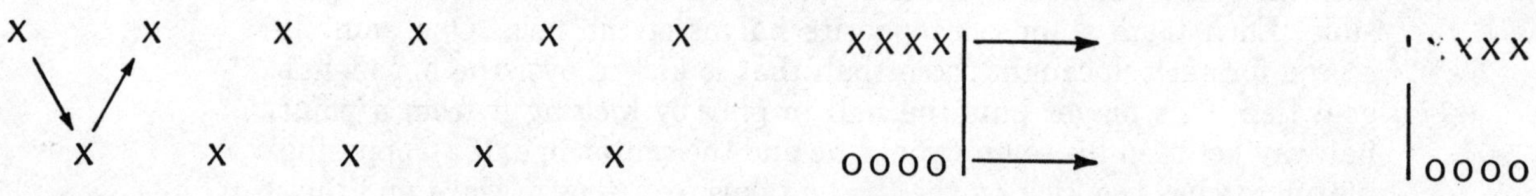

Diagram 11–7. Zig-Zag Formation

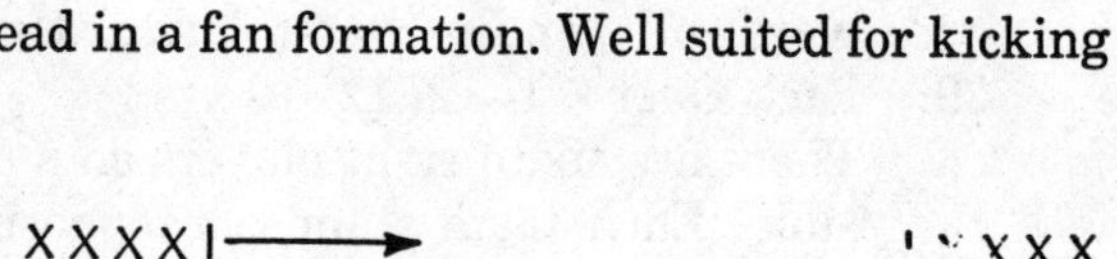

Diagram 11–8. Shuttle Formation

3. Zig-zag formation
Can be used for throwing and kicking skills. Two lines face each other. The ball is passed from the beginning of one line to the beginning of

1. Progress from simple to more complex relays and drills.

other line and continues down the lines, being passed consecutively back and forth, until reaching end player.

4. Circle formation
   To form when no areas are marked, all children join hands, and leader of the line walks around to join hands with last person in line. Circles are best for simple ball skill drills, games, and elementary dances.
5. Shuttle formation
   Especially good for passing, kicking, or hand-off skills. Two teams are formed on either side of two restraining lines, in line formation. When movement is involved, the first player performs skill and then goes to rear of opposite line. The opposite player then performs skill and shifts to the rear of the line he is facing, and so on.
6. Soccer dribble relay
   Dribble a soccer ball to a goal and back in basic relay or with obstacles added.
7. Softball throw relay
   Each team has a catcher on the goal line who throws to each team member in turn. The ball is thrown back to the catcher each time.
8. Basketball pass relay
   Two players work as partners for each team and pass the ball back and forth as they go to goal line and back.
9. Soccer dribble and pass relay
   Line formation. Player dribbles ball up to end line and continues dribbling back until reaching the kicking line. The player then kicks the ball back to the next person in line. The kicking line is approximately ten yards from the starting line. Play continues as in all basic relays.
10. Toe pick-up relay
    Teams are in shuttle formation, with a soccer ball. The first player kicks ball to opposite player. The receiving player traps the ball with foot and lifts the ball to hand by applying downward pressure on the ball and snapping foot back at the same time and then lifting with toe. The player then rolls the ball back to the opposite line.
11. Ball and stick relay
    Players are in line formation. Beginning player pushes ball with a stick to designated line and back to next player, who continues same progression.
12. Zig-zag volley relay
    Players are in zig-zag formation. Ball is volleyed back and forth, down the line and back. The first team to get the ball back to the starting player wins.
13. Volley relay
    Players are in line formation. Player begins with volleyball and volleys to a marked square on wall, then steps to the side. The next person keeps the ball up by volleying the rebound against the wall again. Relay continues until all members of one team have consecutively struck the ball against the wall.
14. Scatter formation
    A random type of formation. Students spread out anywhere on playing area, at least arms' distance apart to prevent collisions.
15. Opposing line formation
    Players spread out in two lines. Each player is directly across from another player.
16. Square formation
    Four people stand at corners. This formation may be used for passing

drills and simple games. A leader may stand in the center, throwing the ball to each player and can correct errors when she throws it back. Square may also be formed with four lines with a leader at each corner. This formation works well for simple relays.

17. V-corner formation
Leader stands facing her line. Players are numbered consecutively. When signal is given by leader, the first two members run in V pattern. Odd numbers go to the right; even-numbered players move to the left. This formation may be used for running and passing drills.

12

GEDDES PSYCHOMOTOR DEVELOPMENT PROGRAM (GPDP)
Young Adult Level Activities

From the following activities, select those that are indicated by the completed Psychomotor Individualized Educational Program (IEP) form. Emphasize the activities associated with competencies recorded as "Improve." Give minimal emphasis to activities related to competencies recorded as "Maintain." Modify the activities according to the student's functional age levels and information given in the chapters on handicapping conditions. No activities are described in this age range since it is assumed that teachers already know how to teach activities such as volleyball, square dance, swimming, and ball handling.[1]

1. The page numbers in parentheses following each performance competency statement refer to the GPI long and short forms.

YOUNG ADULT LEVEL ACTIVITIES (1)

Locomotion and Basic Movement
(If indicated, select additional activities from Intermediate Level)

RUNS (GPI pp. 81, 85)

RUNS IN PHYSICAL ACTIVITIES

Equipment: As indicated or items italicized.

1. Run in individual, dual, and team sports such as *fifty-yard dash, six-hundred-yard run-walk, basketball, soccer, badminton, bowling, tennis, field hockey, softball, speedball,* and *football.*
2. Run in rhythmic activities or dances such as Schottische, square dance, and creative dance.
3. Run in relays and drill formations such as rescue relay, line relay, file relay, around the bases, shuttle formation, and zig-zag formation. See activities 1, 5, 19, 35, 3, and 5 on pages 194, 197, and 201–202.
4. Other:____________________

Figure 12–1. Jump in individual and team sports (basketball lay-up shot).

JUMPS (GPI pp. 81, 85)

Jumps with and without equipment

Equipment: As indicated or items italicized.

1. Practice *standing broad jump.*
2. Compete with others in *standing broad jump.*
3. Practice *vertical jump.*
4. Compete with others in *vertical jump.*
5. Jump in individual and team sports such as *basketball, volleyball, track (hurdles), gymnastics (vaulting), softball* (catch fly ball), and *speedball* (jump ball).
6. Other:____________________

YOUNG ADULT LEVEL ACTIVITIES (2)

Aquatics

DOES STYLES OF SWIMMING (GPI pp. 82, 85)

Equipment: As indicated or items italicized

1. Practice front crawl, back crawl, elementary backstroke, breast stroke, sidestroke, and trudgeon crawl.
2. Compete with others in various styles of swimming.
3. Other:__________

DIVES (GPI pp. 82, 85)

Equipment: As indicated or items italicized.

1. Practice springboard diving such as running front dive, swan dive, front jackknife, and back dive.
2. Compete with others in various styles of diving.
3. Other:__________

DOES STUNTS (GPI pp. 82, 85)

Equipment: As indicated or items italicized.

1. Practice the dolphin, shark, single and double ballet leg, back somersault tuck, kip, and catalina.
2. Compete with others in synchronized swimming events.
3. Other:__________

Ball Handling
(If indicated, select additional activities from Intermediate Level)

Figure 12–2. Softball throw.

THROWS (GPI pp. 82, 85)

Equipment: As indicated or items italicized.

YOUNG ADULT LEVEL ACTIVITIES (3)

1. Play individual and team sports such as *basketball, bowling, softball, football,* and *speedball.*
2. Practice specific throwing skills such as softball throw, underhand pitch *(softball),* chest pass, two-hand underhand pass, bounce pass, overhead pass *(basketball),* forward pass, lateral pass *(football),* throw-in, forward pass *(speedball)* and roll ball *(bowling).*
3. Other:________________

Figure 12–3. Two hand catch of softball (chest high).

CATCHES (GPI pp. 83, 86)

Equipment: As indicated or items italicized.

1. Practice specific catching skills such as catching kick-up ball, throw-in ball, and forward pass *(speedball),* catching chest pass, two-hand underhand pass, bounce pass, overhead pass *(basketball),* softball throw, fly ball, ground ball *(softball),* forward pass, lateral pass, and punt kick *(football).*
2. Play individual and team sports such as speedball, *basketball, softball,* and *football.*
3. Other:________________

Figure 12–4. Kick stationary ball (soccer).

KICKS (GPI pp. 83, 86)

Equipment: As indicated or items italicized.

1. Practice specific kicking skills such as dribble, kick-off, kicking to teammate, punt, drop kick, goal kick *(soccer)*, place kick, punt *(football)*, and dribble, kick-up *(speedball)*
2. Play team sports such as *soccer, speedball,* and *football.*
3. Other:____________________

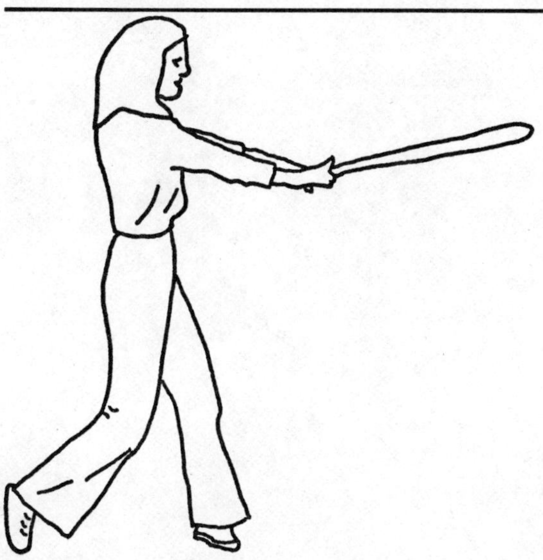

Figure 12–5. Bats pitched softball.

STRIKES (GPI pp. 83, 86)

Equipment: As indicated or items italicized.

1. Practice specific striking skills such as batting, bunting *(softball)*, serve, forehand, backhand *(tennis)*, overhead clear *(badminton)*, tee shot *(golf)*, overhand serve, volley *(volleyball)*, and heading ball *(soccer)*.
2. Play individual, dual, and team sports such as *softball, tennis, badminton, golf, volleyball,* and *soccer.*
3. Other:____________________

13

THE GPI AND THE GPDP APPROACH TO PERCEPTUAL MOTOR ACTIVITIES

Perceptual motor training programs stress motor activities designed to improve known or suspected perceptual deficits in children. Kephart (1960), Frostig (1966), Barsch (1965), Delacato (1959), Ayres (1964), Getman (1965), and other theorists have generated strong interest in this subject area since the late 1950s. Many of the perceptual motor programs originated in clinical environments, but it has become a well-established trend recently to employ these programs in educational situations. Educators, clinicians, therapists, medically affiliated professionals, and the lay public have become involved in the widespread use of perceptual motor training programs even though such programming is controversial.

Proponents of perceptual motor theory believe that selected movement experiences will improve the functional capacity of the visual, auditory, proprioceptive, and/or tactual modes of perception (Seefeldt 1972). The rationale behind perceptual motor training is that children need to move in certain ways through their environment to gain adequate sensory stimulation. This sensory input is interpreted, associated, and integrated cortically in relation to previous information gained by motor activity so that, ultimately, specific perceptions are developed. Conceptualization is a further refinement of these evolving perceptions. Some theorists (Kephart 1960; Barsch 1965) believed that the relationship between movement experiences and cognition was so strong that they proposed a rationale that other educators have termed a "motoric base to the intellect."

Overall the perceptual motor training trend has had a tremendous impact upon professional and educational fields. Increased activity has been observed in terms of federal funding of programs, research investigations, curricular expansion, professional conferences, educational media, and equipment.

The impetus of perceptual motor training has raised questions and concerns regarding the effectiveness of such training. And consensus has been lacking in relation to the nature and mechanisms of perceptual motor behavior. Therefore it is the purpose of this chapter to identify pertinent research perspectives obtained by a review of the literature and suggest an approach to perceptual motor activities as part of the Geddes Psychomotor Inventory (GPI) and the Geddes Psychomotor Development Program (GPDP).

RESEARCH PERSPECTIVES

The literature concerning the development of perception and/or cognition following treatment with remedial perceptual motor training programs and/or selected motor/physical activities reveals support both for and against this premise. Some studies (Ball and Edgar 1967; Ritz 1970) indicated that selected perceptual motor skills were significantly improved following treatment with perceptual motor activities; however, similar investigations (Eason 1973; Elmore 1973; Fisher 1971; Klanderman 1973; Ball and Wilsoncroft 1967; Geddes 1968) showed no significant changes in perceptual motor skills measured.

Other investigators, such as Oliver (1958), Corder (1965), Lowe (1966), and Gamsky and Lloyd (1971), have described positive increases in measures of academic achievement and/or in intelligence quotient following treatment programs of motor or physical skills. Conversely studies by researchers such as Robbins and Glass (1968), Buckland and Balow (1973), Solomon and Pangle (1966), and a follow-up study by Corder (1969) did not provide support for significant improvement in such measures following similar treatment. It should be noted that Oliver (1958) attributed increases in intelligence quotient and/or academic achievement to the positive relationship of successful performance in physical activity (with resultant enhanced self-concept) to improved classroom performance. Frequent misinterpretations of these studies suggested cause and effect rather than indirect relationships between physical activity and measures of intellectual function.

There is both empirical and theoretical support for the premise that there is a direct relationship between movement behavior normally observed in human growth and development and the stimulation of perceptual development (Wright 1969; Piaget 1952; Denhoff 1969; Kershner 1972). In particular, the first two years of a child's development are crucial if he is in need of additional enrichment through motor experiences.

To date, the extensive literature permits no definite conclusion regarding the effectiveness of perceptual motor programs. Information provided is inconclusive, confusing, conflicting, and sometimes not informative at all. In addition, many problems exist in this area of inquiry as a result of weak research designs, training programs that taught the test, uncontrolled Hawthorne effect, misinterpretation of data, and uncontrolled variables.

Major criticisms of the testing batteries include insufficient numbers of skills to be evaluated and nonvalidated test items. When one considers the large numbers of motor skills involved in human growth and development, the majority of perceptual motor batteries seem inadequate in scope since they employ small numbers of test items that measure only a few factors. Closer scrutiny of attributes measured by the test items need to be done. For example Geddes (1972) indicated that four of the six items in the Cratty (1966) battery loaded significantly on one factor alone during factor analysis procedures.

AN IMPLICATION FOR THE FUTURE

Although the situation at the present time is such that we do not know exactly the effects of perceptual motor training or even the validity of perceptual motor testing batteries, numerous people enthusiastically are providing these testing and training programs based upon partial research support and subjective evaluations.

It remains to be seen whether perceptual motor training will retain its influence in the years to come, or whether the views of dissenters based upon critical reviews of the literature (Hammill 1972; Goodman and Hammill 1973; Mann

1971) will lessen its impact. Presumably, however, unless improved designs for investigating the effects of perceptual motor training are employed, no definitive conclusion will be forthcoming in the near future. Therefore practitioners are left without a confident answer to the question of what approach to use in attempting to influence the perceptual motor development of children in their programs.

One answer to this question would be to recognize that a perceptual motor skill is, in reality, a psychomotor skill, which is a task observed in the psychomotor domain in human growth and development. Psychomotor behavior is considered to be voluntary, purposeful, and observable movement behavior that is the result of a holistic integration of sensory, perceptual, mental and motor components. Such a holistic conception of the movement behavior of the human organism does not support an artificial analysis that would separate mental processes and motor performance.

If the viewpoint is taken that a perceptual motor skill is a synonym for psychomotor skill, then the large body of knowledge available in the literature on psychomotor performance learning would be applicable to the program level. Psychomotor literature contains information on such aspects as motor skill and movement pattern development; learning theories and concepts; information processing; conditions for learning; motor abilities; arousal levels and motivation; analysis of motor skills; motor control; methods and processes for instruction; and retention and transfer of learning (Singer 1972; Marteniuk 1976; Stallings 1973; Cratty 1973; Schmidt 1975).

Factors of concern in the psychomotor domain are described by authors such as Fleishman (1964) and Guilford (1958), while psychomotor developmental milestones are presented in a variety of publications (Gessel and Ilg 1946; Frankenburg, Dodds, and Fandal 1970; Espenschade and Eckert 1967). In addition, competencies such as agility, balance, eye-hand coordination, spatial orientation, laterality, and motor planning all are described in the psychomotor literature (Singer 1972).

One example of the application of psychomotor literature to the program level would be as an answer to the question of whether there is a transfer of learning as proposed by Kephart (1960) in his concept of generalization. Psychomotor skills are considered to be specific in nature. Therefore if a child walks forward in a particular manner on a balance beam, then that specific balance skill is being practiced for development. We cannot assume that this skill will generalize or transfer to other areas of learning.

Thus the implication for the future is to stress the psychomotor development of children by utilizing the body of knowledge in psychomotor performance and learning. Such a program approach would contribute to total human development in terms of the sensory, perceptual, mental, and motor components of movement behavior. This is the approach taken in the Geddes Psychomotor Inventory (GPI) and the Geddes Psychomotor Development Program (GPDP), with the exception that activities highly relevant to specific perceptual abilities and body awareness skills are identified in the Early Childhood and Primary-Levels.

REFERENCES

Ayres, Jean. "Tactile Functions, Their Relation to Hyperactive and Perceptual-Motor Behavior." *American Journal of Occupational Therapy* 6 (1964): 6–11.

Ball, T. S., and Edgar C. L. "The Effectiveness of Sensory-Motor Training in Promoting Generalized Body Image Development." *Journal of Special Education* 4 (1967): 387–395.

Ball, T. S., and Wilsoncroft, W. E. "Perceptual-Motor Deficits and the Phi Phenomenon." *American Journal of Mental Deficiency* 3 (1967): 797–800.

Barsch, R. H. *A Movigenic Curriculum.* Madison, Wis.: State Department of Public Instruction, 1965.

Buckland, P., and Balow, B. "Effect of Visual Perceptual Training on Reading Achievement." *Exceptional Children* 39 (1973): 299–304.

Corder, W. O. *Effect of Physical Education on the Intellectual, Physical, and Social Development of Educable Mentally Retarded Boys.* Education Specialist Project, Nashville, George Peabody College, 1965.

———. *"Effects of Physical Education on the Psycho-physical Development of Educable Mentally Retarded Girls."* Ph.D. dissertation, University of Virginia, 1969.

Cratty, Bryant J. *The Perceptual-Motor Attributes of Mentally Retarded Children and Youth.* Los Angeles: Mental Retardation Services Board of Los Angeles County, 1966.

———. *Movement Behavior and Motor Learning.* Philadelphia: Lea & Febiger, 1967.

Delacato, Carl H. *The Treatment and Prevention of Reading Problems.* Springfield, Ill.: Charles C Thomas, 1959.

Denhoff, Eric. "Motor Development as a Function of Perception." In *Perceptual-Motor Foundations: A Multidisciplinary Concern: Proceedings of the Perceptual-Motor Symposium,* pp. 49–68. Washington, D.C.: AAHPER, 1969.

Eason, J. E. "The Comparison of the Effects of Two Programs of Physical Activity on Perceptual-Motor Development and Primary Mental Abilities of Preschool Aged Children." *Dissertation Abstracts* 33 (1973): 2147-A.

Elmore, W. R. "Effects of Training Procedures on Visual Perceptual Skills of Disadvantaged Youngsters." *Dissertation Abstracts* 33 (1973): 4979-A.

Espenschade, Anna S., and Eckert, Helen M. *Motor Development.* Columbus: Charles E. Merrill Books, 1967.

Fisher, K. I. "Effects of Perceptual-Motor Training on the Educable Mentally Retarded." *Exceptional Children* 38 (1971): 264–266.

Fleishman, Edwin A. *The Structure and Measurement of Physical Fitness.* Englewood Cliffs, N.J.: Prentice-Hall, 1964.

Frankenburg, W. K.; Dodds, J. B.; and Fandall, A. W. *Denver Developmental Screening Test Manual.* Denver: University of Colorado Medical Center, 1970.

Frostig, Marianne; Miller, A. M.; and Horne, D. *The Developmental Program of Visual Perception: Beginning Pictures and Patterns.* Chicago: Follett, 1966.

Gamsky, N. R., and Lloyd, F. W. "A Longitudinal Study of Visual Training and Reading Achievement." *Journal of Educational Research* 64 (1971): 451–454.

Geddes, Dolores M. "Effects of Mobility Patterning Techniques upon Selected Motor Skills of Primary School Educable Mentally Retarded Children." *Research Quarterly* 39 (1968): 953–957.

———. "Factor Analytic Study of Perceptual-Motor Attributes as Measured by Two Test Batteries." *Perceptual and Motor Skills* 34 (1972): 227–230.

Gessell, A., and Ilg, F. L. *The Child from Five to Ten.* New York: Harper & Row, 1946.

Getman, G. N. "The Visuomotor Complex in the Acquisition of Learning Skills." In J. Hellmuth, *Learning Disorders,* I: 49–76. Seattle: Special Child Publications, 1965.

Goodman, Libby, and Hammill, Donald. "The Effectiveness of the Kephart-Getman Activities in Developing Perceptual Motor and Cognitive Skill." *Focus on Exceptional Children* 4 (1973): 1–9.

Guilford, J. P. "A System of Psychomotor Abilities." *American Journal of Psychology* 71 (1958): 164.

Hammill, Donald. "Training Visual Perceptual Processes. *Journal of Learning Disabilities* 5 (1972): 552–559.

Kephart, Newell C. *The Slow Learner in the Classroom.* Columbus, Ohio: Charles E. Merrill Books, 1960.

Kershner, John R. *Relationship of Motor Development to Visual-Spatial Cognitive Growth.* Toronto: Ontario Institute for Studies in Education and University of Toronto, 1972.

Klanderman, J. W. "A Study of the Effects of a Kindergarten Perceptual-Motor Development Program." *Dissertation Abstracts* 33 (1973): 1023-A

Lowe, Benjamin. "Effects of Physical Education on the Cognitive Functioning and Physical Development of Educationally Subnormal Boys." Ph.D. dissertation, University of Birmingham, 1966.

Mann, Lester. "Perceptual Training Revisited: The Training of Nothing at All." *Rehabilitation Literature* 32 (1971): 322–335.

Marteniuk, Ronald G. *Information Processing in Motor Skills.* New York: Holt, Rinehart and Winston, 1976.

Oliver, J. N. "The Effect of Physical Conditioning Exercises and Activities on the Mental Characteristics of Educationally Subnormal Boys." *British Journal of Educational Psychology* 28 (1958): 155–165.

Piaget, Jean. *The Origins of Intelligence in Children.* New York: International Universities Press, 1952.

Ritz, W. C. "The Effect of Two Instructional Programs on the Attainment of Reading Readiness, Visual Perception, and Science Skills of Kindergarten Children." *Dissertation Abstracts* 30 (1970): 1082-A.

Robbins, M. P., and Glass, G. V. "The Doman-Delacato Rationale: A Critical Analysis." In J. Hellmuth, ed., *Educational Therapy.* Seattle: Special Child, Vol. II, 1968.

Schmidt, Richard A. *Motor Skills.* New York: Harper & Row, 1975.

Seefeldt, V. "Substantive Issues in Perceptual Motor Development." Paper presented at a symposium on research methodology in perceptual-motor development, May 12–13, 1972, at Springfield College, Springfield, Massachusetts.

Singer, Robert N., ed. *The Psychomotor Domain: Movement Behavior.* Philadelphia: Lea & Febiger, 1972.

Solomon, Amiel H., and Pangle, Roy V. *"The Effects of a Structured Physical Education Program on Physical, Intellectual, and Self-Concept Development of Educable Retarded Boys.* Behavioral Science Monograph No. 4. Nashville, Tenn.: George Peabody College, Institute on Mental Retardation and Intellectual Development, 1966.

Stallings, Loretta M. *Motor Skills—Development and Learning.* Dubuque: Wm. C. Brown Co., Publishers, 1973.

Wright, Logan. "Highlights of Human Development, Birth to Age Eleven." In *Perceptual-Motor Foundations: A Multidisciplinary Concern: Proceedings of the Perceptual-Motor Symposium,* pp. 1–22. Washington, D.C.: AAHPER, 1969.

14

IEP FORMS FOR ADAPTED PHYSICAL EDUCATION

This chapter presents copies of the forms that are employed by Office of the Los Angeles County Superintendent of Schools, Division of Special Education and Special Schools, Adapted Physical Education Program.[1] The forms, letters, and procedures that have been utilized by the Adapted Physical Education Program were designed to be consistent with both Public Law 94–142 and recently revised California Administrative Code, Title 5 Regulations. The forms were developed prior to the enactment, in 1980, of California Senate Bill 1870 which is concerned with special education programs in that state.

*The forms that are reproduced in this chapter are reprinted by permission of the Office of the Los Angeles County Superintendent of Schools.

1. Appreciation is expressed to G. Robert Roice, consultant, Adapted Physical Education, for assistance in the inclusion of these materials.

RECOMMENDATION FOR SCREENING FORM

OFFICE OF THE LOS ANGELES COUNTY SUPERINTENDENT OF SCHOOLS

ADAPTED PHYSICAL EDUCATION PROGRAM

RECOMMENDATION
FOR SCREENING

Pupil's Name ______________________ Birthdate ____________

Some pupils in regular classes find it difficult, if not impossible, to safely and successfully participate in regular physical education. This may be due to low fitness, poor coordination, sensory problems, orthopedic conditions, low emotional tolerance, language disabilities, etc.

In recommending this pupil, please consider the above areas and provide us with your impressions of the child's level of function and the reason(s) for your recommendation.

By ____________________
name and position

School ____________________

Date ____________________

Form No. 301-544
Rev. 7/78
GRR:vb

This form is used whenever a pupil is suspected of being eligible for adapted physical education. It is to be used as an aid for physical education teachers in locating potentially eligible students.

PROGRAM DESCRIPTION AND PERMISSION FOR ASSESSMENT

OFFICE OF THE LOS ANGELES COUNTY SUPERINTENDENT OF SCHOOLS

DIVISION OF SPECIAL EDUCATION

ADAPTED PHYSICAL EDUCATION PROGRAM DESCRIPTION
and
PERMISSION FOR ASSESSMENT

Re:____________________________

Dear Parent,

We are pleased to inform you that classes in Adapted Physical Education are being offered at your school. Small classes such as these provide an opportunity for more individual physical education, taught by a trained adapted physical education specialist.

Class instruction is designed to aid the student in increasing his efficiency in the areas of movement, coordination, and the realization of physical potential. This may be achieved through corrective work according to specific physical needs; movement education related to general language development, behavior management, or adaptation of games and activities.

Your child has been referred to us and may be eligible to participate in this specialized physical education program. Admission to the Adapted Physical Education class is dependent upon the recommendation of an Eligibility and Planning Committee. In order to determine eligibility and specific educational needs, it will be necessary to conduct an assessment. This assessment will be done by appropriately qualified staff in the area of adapted physical education. The assessment may include pupil observation in a group setting; a review of any reports you have authorized us to request, or that already exist in current school records; or the use of specific tests designed to measure how well an individual coordinates body movements in both small and large muscle activities.

We believe that you, as a parent, will consider this a real opportunity for your child, and can aid us in qualifying your child by granting permission for our staff to conduct the assessment described above.

Following the collection of this information, an Eligibility and Planning Committee will meet to consider the appropriate physical eduction placement for your child. You will be notified of the time and place of the committee meeting and invited to attend. No placement will be made without your permission.

If we can provide you with any additional information, please feel free to contact our physical education specialist.

If you do not wish your child considered for Adapted Physical Education, please check here. ☐

____________________________ ____________________________

Physical Education Specialist | Parent Signature

____________________________ ____________________________

School, Address, Telephone | Date

PLEASE SIGN AND RETURN WHITE COPY TO YOUR SCHOOL

FORM NO. 301-546 DISTRIBUTION: WHITE-Site; YELLOW-Parent
Rev. 7/79

This letter is used to notify parents that their child may be eligible for adapted physical education. The letter describes the program under consideration and requests permission from the parent to gain assessment data by review of existing medical health records or conducting motor assessment. The parent has the right to stop all consideration at this point by checking the appropriate box. The white copy of the form must be returned before assessment data can be collected.

OFFICE OF THE LOS ANGELES COUNTY SUPERINTENDENT OF SCHOOLS

DIVISION OF SPECIAL EDUCATION

PROGRAM DESCRIPTION

ADAPTED PHYSICAL EDUCATION

Adapted Physical Education is a program of developmental activities, games, sports, and rhythms suited to the interests, strengths, and weaknesses of students possessing movement problems who cannot safely and successfully participate in the regular Physical Education program.

We are pleased to be able to provide this specialized instruction which is designed to work with students in the areas of movement and coordination and to assist them to realize their full physical potential. This may be achieved through:

1. **The development of perceptual motor skills, including coordination training.**
2. **The improvement of physical fitness.**
3. **Development of a positive self-image and social skills.**
4. **Increased insterest in individual and group recreational activities.**
5. **The enhancement of language and cognitive development.**

The maximum size of the adapted physical education class is 20 students. The classes are taught by physical education specialists who are well-trained in the functional basis of movement, knowledge of growth and development, and the improvement of fitness. Based upon appropriate assessment, they will determine the individual needs of each student, and develop an individualized plan of action for them.

Favor de ver el reverso para la traduccion en español.

Form No. 301-033
8/78

Program description provided parents regarding the type of Adapted Physical Education Program their child would receive.

OFFICE OF THE LOS ANGELES COUNTY SUPERINTENDENT OF SCHOOLS

DIVISION OF SPECIAL EDUCATION

NOTIFICATION OF APPEAL PROCEDURES

This report of the Program Planning Committee contains decisions regarding your pupil's special education needs. As the parent of this pupil, you have the right to use the following procedures if you disagree with the Committee's decision or recommendations. You also have the right to seek civil action.

These procedures may also be used if you disagree with pupil assessment. In such cases, you may obtain independent assessment of the pupil. Resources for both independent pupil assessment and legal services will be provided upon request. Results of such assessment may be made part of the pupil record.

We welcome the opportunity to discuss any concern you have regarding the education of this pupil. You may contact the school, or area office for discussion. For information, call the Admissions Office (213/922-6248). These procedures may be terminated at any step at which the problem is solved.

PROCEDURE FOR RESOLVING DIFFERENCES REGARDING IDENTIFICATION, ASSESSMENT OR PLACEMENT

1. Inform the Administrator (Principal) of Program Planning Committee of your concern. If the problem cannot be solved at the school level, go on to Step 2.

2. Notify the Area Administrator in writing of your request to appeal. (Contact your school or Admissions Office for address). During the appeal process, the pupil remains in current placement except by mutual consent, or if pupil presents a danger to self or others.

3. The Superintendent's Designee, Support Services, will be informed of your request immediately.

4. The Area Administrator will begin informal review of your concern within ten (10) school days. Your Area Psychologist and other appropriate personnel will be included. You will be notified in advance, in writing, of this conference, which will be arranged at a convenient time.

5. Within five (5) school days after the informal review, a written report, including recommendations, will be sent to you, your school district, the County central office, and the school Program Planning Committee. If you disagree with these recommendations, inform the Area Administrator that you wish to continue to Step 6.

6. The Assistant Superintendent, Administration of School Operations, will appoint a formal hearing panel as required by California Administrative Code, Title 5. You will be sent the full text of these regulations.

7. Further appeal, if required, is directed to the Superintendent of Public Instruction, State Department of Education.

NOTE TO PARENTS: If you have any questions about the above or need further information, please contact the school principal.

Form No. 301-519
Rev. 6/79

The notification of appeal procedures must be made available to the parent prior to final consideration of pupil placement. The procedures detail the steps, both formal and informal, that the parent may wish to pursue if she or he disagrees with the decision of the committee. These rights are also printed on the back of the IEP form (301-521).

GEDDES PSYCHOMOTOR DEVELOPMENT PROGRAM (GPDP)

PROGRAM PLANNING CONFERENCE REPORT/INDIVIDUAL EDUCATION PLAN

OFFICE OF THE LOS ANGELES COUNTY SUPERINTENDENT OF SCHOOLS
DIVISION OF SPECIAL EDUCATION
ELIGIBILITY AND PLANNING CONFERENCE REPORT/ INDIVIDUAL EDUCATIONAL PLAN

☐ Initial IEP/Program Change
☐ Review of IEP (date) ____________
☐ Supplementary Service(s)
☐ Triannual IEP
☐ LES ☐ NES (as applicable)

NAME		DISTRICT	DATE
BIRTHDATE	PRINCIPAL ADMINISTRATIVE UNIT	SCHOOL GRADE OR LEVEL PLACEMENT	

After discussing educational alternatives, the Eligibility and Planning Committee makes the following recommendations:

I. EDUCATIONAL ALTERNATIVE

☐ Return to district for placement
☐ Special day class: Specify County *program* and *school*: ____________
  ☐ Transfer from parallel program: From ____________
  ☐ Placement changed from one county-operated program to another, indicate:
  from ____________ to ____________
  ☐ Extent of participation in regular class activities or with other regular class pupils: ____________
☐ Individual instruction: (Describe) ____________
☐ Other: (Specify) ____________

DATE OF ENROLLMENT *	PROJECTED DURATION OF PLACEMENT	DATE OF REVIEW OF EDUCATIONAL PLAN
LAST DATE OF ENROLLMENT	REASON FOR TERMINATION (INCLUDE PLACEMENT RECOMMENDATIONS AS APPPOPRIATE)	

*II OTHER SPECIAL EDUCATION SERVICES to be provided by County *Eligibility has been determined:*

☐ Adapted Physical Education . . . . From ____________ To ____________
☐ Remedial Language/Speech/Hearing . . . . . . From ____________ To ____________
  Estimate frequency of service ____________
☐ ____________ From ____________ To ____________
☐ ____________ From ____________ To ____________
☐ ____________ From ____________ To ____________
☐ ____________ From ____________ To ____________

III. JUSTIFICATION FOR EDUCATIONAL ALTERNATIVE(S) AND SERVICE(S) SELECTED. *Include a summary of handicapping condition(s), list alternatives discussed and rejected.*

IV. GENERAL COMMENTS. *Include specific alternative means for a secondary pupil to meet graduation proficiency standards. Include provisions for return to regular education and career education as appropriate.*

**If implementation not within 20 days justify and estimate implementation date under "Comments".*

Form No 301 521 (1 of 3) Rev. 9/79 DISTRIBUTION First Copy · Central Office; Second Copy District; Third Copy Site; Fourth Copy · Parent

Public Law 94-142 requires that a written Individual Education Program (IEP) be developed or revised for each child who is receiving or is eligible to receive special education services. This multipage document serves as the IEP for children receiving services, including adapted physical education. The form is completed at the eligibility and planning conference and should be signed by all required members.

The physical education component of the IEP, including present functioning level, annual goals, and short-term objectives, is to be completed on form 301-549. This takes the place of page 2 (301-521), which is used by classroom teachers.

IEP, PAGE 2

OFFICE OF THE LOS ANGELES COUNTY SUPERINTENDENT OF SCHOOLS
DIVISION OF SPECIAL EDUCATION

(Use additional sheets as needed)

INDIVIDUAL EDUCATIONAL PLAN

NAME OF PUPIL	BIRTHDATE	DATE

NOTE LEVELS OF EDUCATIONAL PERFORMANCE IN AREAS RELATING TO SPECIAL NEEDS. SUCH DATA SHOULD INCLUDE STRENGTHS AND WEAKNESSES (i.e., ACADEMIC, SOCIAL/ADAPTIVE, PSYCHO-MOTOR, PRE-VOCATIONAL, SELF-HELP, LANGUAGE, INTELLECTUAL, MEDICAL, LES, NES)	GOAL NUMBER	LIST ANNUAL GOALS AND SHORT TERM OBJECTIVES INCLUDE MEASUREMENT CRITERIA AND RELATE TO PERFORMANCE LEVELS	SERVICE PROVIDED BY (USE SOURCE CODE)
		GOAL .... OBJECTIVE(S)	
		GOAL .... OBJECTIVE(S)	
		GOAL .... OBJECTIVE(S)	

DIRECTIONS: Under Column 1 headings indicate (1) Examiner/Source; (2) Assessment Date (where applicable); (3) Data supporting functional descriptions/strengths and weaknesses. Where appropriate, include information from the classroom observation and parent input.*

*SOURCE ABBREVIATION CODE:
Pa = Parent
A = Administrator
Au = Audiologist
LSS = Language/Speech Specialist
PS = Program Specialist
Outside = Agency/Medical Report
Psyc. = Psychologist
APE = Adapted Physical Education
T = Teacher
Nu = School Nurse
SDi. = District

NOTE: A pupil's individual program includes all areas of the curriculum appropriate to his/her level(s) of functioning. The above goals and objectives are written in priority areas of instruction to ameliorate the effects of the handicapping condition(s).

Form No. 301-521 (2 of 3)
Rev. 9/79

DISTRIBUTION: First Copy - Central Office; Second Copy - District; Third Copy - Site; Fourth Copy - Parent

This form is used by classroom teachers to specify the levels of function, annual goals, and short-term objectives. It may be used by adapted physical education staff for teacher-written objectives; however, form 301-549 is usually used for these objectives.

IEP, PAGE 3

OFFICE OF THE LOS ANGELES COUNTY SUPERINTENDENT OF SCHOOLS
DIVISION OF SPECIAL EDUCATION

ELIGIBILITY AND PLANNING CONFERENCE REPORT – INDIVIDUAL EDUCATIONAL PLAN

NAME	BIRTHDATE	DATE

V. It is the professional judgment of this committee that recommendations are based on adequate assessment data and are appropriate to the implementation of the Individual Educational Plan. For enrolled pupils, the undersigned assume responsibility for implementation and monitoring of the individual pupil's plan as specified.

ADMINISTRATOR**	DATE	SCHOOL NURSE	DATE
SPECIAL EDUCATION TEACHER	DATE	PROGRAM SPECIALIST	DATE
SCHOOL PSYCHOLOGIST	DATE	AUDIOLOGIST/PHYSICIAN/OTHER	DATE
LANGUAGE AND SPEECH SPECIALIST	DATE	DISTRICT REPRESENTATIVE	DATE
INTERPRETER/OTHER	DATE	OTHER (SPECIFY)	DATE
TEACHER SPECIALIST (SPECIFY)	DATE	OTHER (SPECIFY)	DATE

VI. PARENT/PUPIL PARTICIPATION
RIGHTS/NOTIFICATIONS

CHECK BELOW TO VERIFY THAT PARENT HAS BEEN GIVEN OR WILL BE SENT THE FOLLOWING:

- ☐ INDIVIDUAL EDUCATIONAL PLAN/APPEAL PROCEDURES (SEE REVERSE SIDE OF THIS FORM)
- ☐ PARENT RIGHTS AND PROCEDURAL SAFEGUARDS SIGNED COPY TO BE IN PUPIL FILE (ANNUAL NOTICE)
- ☐ MEETING HELD AT PARENT'S REQUEST WITHOUT ADVANCE WRITTEN NOTICE

Signature of parent, legal guardian or person acting as parent indicates participation, not necessarily agreement.

SIGNATURE OF PARENT, LEGAL GUARDIAN OR PERSON ACTING AS PARENT DATE	SIGNATURE OF PUPIL DATE
THE FOLLOWING DOCUMENTS EFFORTS TO CONTACT PARENTS. (SPECIFY DATES, PERSON(S) MAKING CONTACT, COMMENTS.)	

DISSENTING MEMBER: PRINT NAME, ASTERISK AND ATTACH RATIONALE INCLUDING SPECIFIC RECOMMENDATIONS.
**MUST BE IN COMPLIANCE WITH CAC TITLE 5 AND EDUCATION CODE.

I, the undersigned parent, legal guardian or person acting as parent give permission for placement/service(s) as outlined on Page 1.

SIGNATURE OF PARENT, LEGAL GUARDIAN OR PERSON ACTING AS PARENT	DATE

OTHER AGENCY SERVICES ARE TO BE PROVIDED AS NOTED BELOW

SERVICES	DATE		AGENCY	SIGNATURE OF AGENCY REPRESENTATIVE
	FROM	TO		

COMMENTS REGARDING ABOVE SERVICE(S)

Form No. 301-521 (3 of 3) Rev. 9/79 DISTRIBUTION: First Copy - Central Office; Second Copy - District; Third Copy - Site; Fourth Copy - Parent

This is the signature page of the IEP. A minimum eligibility and planning committee of teacher, administrator, parent, and pupil (if appropriate) must sign.

ADAPTED PHYSICAL EDUCATION INDIVIDUAL EDUCATION PLAN

OFFICE OF THE LOS ANGELES COUNTY SUPERINTENDENT OF SCHOOLS
DIVISION OF SPECIAL EDUCATION

PHYSICAL EDUCATION - INDIVIDUAL EDUCATIONAL PLAN
PART I

PUPIL	BIRTHDATE	DATE

Present Levels of Educational Performance:

Annual Goal(s): Select, modify, or write annual goal(s). Criteria for evaluating the achievement of selected goals will be based upon the pupils performance on identified short-term instructional objectives. Specific objectives related to goals are attached.

_____ C.10 The pupil, given a series of developmental tasks and sensory motor activities, will demonstrate use of the body and its parts, sensory modalities and space concepts.

_____ C.11 The pupil, given a series of developmental tasks in gross motor activities, will demonstrate ability to coordinate the body and its parts performing basic body control and locomotor skills.

_____ C.12 The pupil, given a series of developmental tasks in fine motor activities, will demonstrate ability to coordinate the body and its parts performing basic manipulative skills

_____ C.20 The pupil will develop efficient and effective motor skills; will understand the principles involved in those skills; and will develop an appreciation for the aesthetic quality of movement.

_____ C.21 The pupil will develop and maintain the best possible level of performance, understanding and appreciation for physical fitness to meet the demands of wholesome living and emergency situations.

_____ C.22 The pupil will develop a positive self-image, including awareness and understanding of the performance of one's body, the use of the body as an important means of expression; and as an instrument for self-realization.

_____ C.23 The pupil will develop socially desirable behavior involving movement and interaction with others, including enjoyment, sharing, group membership and leadership.

_____ C.24 The pupil will develop interest and proficiency in using the skill essential to successful participation in worthwhile recreation activities.

_____ Other

_____ Other

DISTRIBUTION (1) Central Office; (2) P E Teacher, (3) Classroom Teacher Office File; (4) Parent
FORM 30' 540 : Rev 9 79

This form is used by the physical education teacher in developing the student's IEP. It is designed to be used in conjunction with the IEP, part 1 (form 301-521), pages 1 and 3. This form is used to delineate the present levels of performance, annual psychomotor and physical education goals, and the specific learner objectives (pages 1–5).

For teacher-written objectives, form 301-521, page 2, may be used.

ADAPTED PHYSICAL EDUCATION INDIVIDUAL EDUCATIONAL PLAN, PART II: SHORT-TERM INSTRUCTIONAL OBJECTIVES

OFFICE OF THE LOS ANGELES COUNTY SUPERINTENDENT OF SCHOOLS
DIVISION OF SPECIAL EDUCATION
ADAPTED PHYSICAL EDUCATION — INDIVIDUAL EDUCATIONAL PLAN
PART II
SHORT TERM INSTRUCTIONAL OBJECTIVES

PUPIL ______________________

____

Circle the number of the objectives which are in progress. Enter each date (Mo./Da./Yr.) the objective was tested and circle date if pupil passed. Underline end of year objective.

THE PUPIL WILL:		DATE	DATE	DATE	COMMENTS
12.2.19	Put 3 pegs (¼") in pegboard in 2 minutes.				
12.2.20	Catch 8½" ball with straight arm, palms up, tossed from 5', 3 out of 5 times.				
12.2.21	Hold shoe lace in one hand & string 7 large beads (½" diam.) with other hand, one at a time in 2 minutes.				
12.2.22	Lace shoe through 3 pairs of eyes, once.				
12.2.23	Catch 16" playground ball bounced chest high, 8-10' away, 4 out of 5 times.				
12.2.24	Catch 8½" playground ball, 8-10' away, arms bent, 3 out of 5 times.				
12.2.25	Throw 8½" playground ball, 12 feet, using overhand motion, with weight shift.				
12.2.26	Throw 8½" playground ball, 8 feet with both hands (push throw).				
12.2.27	Draw a crude square, 3 out of 3 times.				
STAGE III					
12.3.1	Catch 8½" ball from 15 feet away with 2 hands, 3 out of 3 times.				
12.3.2	Kick 8½" ball, rolled from 10', in direction of thrower, 3 out of 5 times.				

THE PUPIL WILL:		DATE	DATE	DATE	COMMENTS
12.3.3	Strike a tennis ball (suspended from string, waist high in front of pupil) with hand, sidearm swing.				
12.3.4	Bounce and catch 8½" ball on first bounce with 2 hands.				
12.3.5	Drop tennis ball with one hand and catches it with 2 hands, 3 out of 5 times.				
12.3.6	Throw softball at target (3' above ground and 15' away) using overhand throw, hits target 3 out of 5 times				
12.3.7	Draw a recognizable diamond shape from picture of diamond.				
12.3.8	Catch tennis ball from distance of 8' away with 2 hands, 3 out of 5 times.				
12:3.9	Touch finger of one hand, with thumb, in order and without hesitation, each hand, both directions, once.				
12.3.10	Bounce 8½" ball with one hand, tapping the ball on each bounce, 4 consecutive bounces.				
12.3.11	Dribble 8½" ball forward 20 yards with inside of feet, 3 kicks each foot in straight line				
12.3.12	Catch tennis ball in one hand from distance of 8 feet, 6 out of 10 times.				
12.3.13	Throw a softball, 50 feet.				

RECOMMENDATIONS & COMMENTS:

SAMPLE PAGE

FORM NO. 301-549-6 Rev 9/79 DISTRIBUTION: (1) Central Office; (2) P.E. Teacher; (3) Classroom Teacher/Office File; (4) Parent

Short-term instructional objectives for students enrolled in adapted physical education are usually completed on form 301-549, 2 through 6. These forms provide sequenced fine- and gross-motor objectives that can be selected or modified to meet the needs of the pupil.

Teachers wishing to write their own objectives may do so on form 301-521-2.

The objectives set for the pupil should reflect the needed intermediate steps to be taken between the present level of function and annual goals stated on form 301-549-1.

ASSESSMENT PLAN

OFFICE OF THE LOS ANGELES COUNTY SUPERINTENDENT OF SCHOOLS
DIVISION OF SPECIAL EDUCATION

ASSESSMENT PLAN

PLEASE SIGN AND RETURN SECOND COPY TO SCHOOL

Pupil Name ______________________ Birthdate ____________ Date ____________

Assessment will be done by appropriately qualified staff members in the areas checked below. The assessment may include pupil observation in a group setting and may include an interview with you and a review of any reports you have authorized us to request or that already exist in current school records. The purpose of this evaluation is to determine individual educational needs and may result in a recommendation for special education placement or services.

____ **ACADEMIC/PREACADEMIC ACHIEVEMENT**

Purpose: These tests measure current reading, spelling and arithmetic skills or skills such as matching or sorting. Tests may include, but are not limited to:

Peabody Individual Achievement Test, KeyMath Diagnostic Test, Spache Diagnostic Reading Scales, Developmental Scales, Wide Range Achievement Test.

____ **SOCIAL/ADAPTIVE BEHAVIOR**

Purpose: These scales of development help to tell what an individual can do independently and how (s)he gets along with other people. They may include, but are not limited to:

Adaptive Behavior Scale, Fairview Self-Help Scale, Vineland Test Of Social Maturity, Pre-School Attainment Record, Burke's Behavior Rating Scale.

____ **PSYCHO-MOTOR DEVELOPMENT**

Purpose: Instruments in this area measure how well an individual coordinates body movements in both small and large muscle activities. They may also measure visual perceptual skills. Assessment tools may include, but are not limited to:

Frostig Developmental Test Of Visual Perception, Bender-Gestalt Visual Motor Integration Test, Developmental Scales, Purdue Perceptual Motor Inventory.

____ **LANGUAGE/SPEECH/COMMUNICATION DEVELOPMENT**

Purpose: These tests measure the individual's ability to understand, relate to and use language and speech clearly and appropriately. They may include, but are not limited to:

Illinois Test Of Psycholinguistic Ability, Peabody Picture Vocabulary Test, Northwestern Syntax Screening Test, Language Samples, Fisher Logemann Articulation Test, Language Developmental Scales.

____ **INTELLECTUAL DEVELOPMENT**

Purpose: These tests measure how well an individual remembers what (s)he has seen and heard, how well (s)he can use that information and how (s)he solves problems. They also reflect learning rate and assist in predicting how well (s)he will do in school. Verbal and performance instruments are used, as are appropriate. Tests may include, but are not limited to:

Cattell Intelligence Scale, Stanford Binet Intelligence Scale, Wechsler Tests Of Intelligence, Leiter International Performance Scale, Merrill-Palmer Scale.

____ **AUDIOLOGICAL ASSESSMENT**

Purpose These instruments measure the nature and degree of possible hearing loss. Tests may include measures of how well an individual hears, understands and listens to speech. On-going assessment of adequacy of hearing aids and monitoring of hearing levels is indicated for some individuals. Tests may include, but are not limited to:

Air and bone conduction pure-tone audiometry, speech awareness, reception, discrimination tests, impedance audiometry, and visual inspection of the external ear.

____ **OTHER:** Includes Vocational, Medical or special provision to be made for a NES/LES pupil.

The following professional(s) will be involved in the individual assessment outlined above:

____ Adapted Physical Education Teacher; ____ Audiologist; ____ Nurse; ____ Program Specialist;

____ Psychologist; ____ Language/Speech Specialist; ____ Teacher

PARENTAL CONSENT FOR PUPIL ASSESSMENT

If pupil speaks other than English at home, please indicate language ______________________

I authorize the use of a suitable interpreter or pre-recorded tests in individual's primary language as appropriate.

I have received a Notice Of Intent to conduct pupil assessment and proposed Assessment Plan, and understand its purpose. The box checked below indicates my decision.

☐ Yes, I give permission to conduct the assessment as described.

☐ No, permission is denied.

____
Parent/Legal Guardian/Adult Pupil/Person Acting As Parent (Specify)

PLEASE SIGN AND RETURN SECOND COPY TO SCHOOL

____
(Date)

OFFICE USE

____
Date Rec'd at School

Form 301-552
Revised 9/79

Distribution: First Copy - Parent; Second Copy - Site; Third Copy - Site (Temporary Copy)

This form is used whenever there is a need for formal psychomotor assessment data to determine the appropriate physical education setting. It is routinely used in county-operated programs for students referred by districts for special day class consideration. If the pupil is to be considered for adapted physical education in addition to special day class, this form is used and the "psychomotor" area and the "APE" teacher box is checked. Program Description Adapted Physical Education should also be sent when using this form.

Appendix A

LISTING OF PSYCHOMOTOR ASSESSMENT ITEMS AND BATTERIES

Items or batteries designed to assess psychomotor skills for special populations and nonhandicapped populations are listed here. Special population test reference categories are provided for mental retardation, learning disabilities, and emotional and behavioral disabilities. Perceptual motor tests for special and nonhandicapped persons are combined in a category for motor ability, motor educability, sport skills, and perceptual motor skills since there was much redundancy among these psychomotor areas. Since many of the assessment criteria for nonhandicapped persons can be used with individuals who have mild to moderate disabilities, those references are given in categories of kinesthesia, physical fitness, and posture. It depends upon the person being evaluated whether one of the tests should be selected, obtained, and administered either in the form originally provided or in modified form.

The source for obtaining such materials is indicated following the listing. For example, in section 1, "Mental Retardation," number 15, the "Special Fitness Test Manual for the Mildly Mentally Retarded" listing, is followed by "(1:43) (5:32)." This indicates that this test is described in reference 1 on page 43 and in reference 5 on page 32 in the listing of references at the end of Appendix A. If a source is known for obtaining the testing materials directly, this is given. Example: (order from: AAHPERD, 1900 Association Drive, Reston, Virginia 22091).

MENTAL RETARDATION

1. Adapted Minnesota Manipulative Test. (31:25)
2. Basic Motor Abilities Test for Retardates (JFRC). (5:36) (order from: National Children's Center, Jewish Foundation for Retarded Children, 6200 Second Street, N.W., Washington, D.C. 20011.)
3. Centennial Athletic Programme Testing Program. (5:26) (order from: Canadian Association for Retarded Children, 4700 Deele Street, Downsview, Toronto, Canada.)

4. Evaluation Test for TMR Children. (5:81) (order from: University of Northern Colorado, Department of Special Education, Greeley, Colorado 80631.)
5. Florida State University Diagnostic Battery of Recreative Functioning for the Trainable Mentally Retarded. (5:68) (order from: Department of Recreation, Florida State University, Tallahassee, Florida 32306.)
6. Modification of Buttonwood Farms Physical Fitness Tests. (36:49–51;275)
7. Modified Burpee Test. (18:345)
8. Modified Physical Fitness Index (PFI). (36:51–56)
9. Motor Developmental Activities for the Mentally Retarded. (5:46) (order from: College of Education, University of South Florida, Tampa, Florida 33620.)
10. Motor Fitness Test for the Moderately Mentally Retarded. (order from: AAHPERD, 1900 Association Drive, Reston, Virginia, 22091.)
11. Perceptual-Motor Attributes of Mentally Retarded and Educationally Handicapped Children and Data Collection Sheets. (5:55) (order from: Education Branch, Los Angeles City Schools, 450 North Grand Avenue, Los Angeles, California 90012.)
12. Physical Fitness for the Mentally Retarded. (5:29) (order from: Metropolitan Toronto Association for Retarded Children, 186 Beverly Street, Toronto 2B, Ontario, Canada.)
13. Physical Fitness Test Battery for Mentally Retarded Children. (5:29) (order from: School of Physical Education, University of Connecticut Storrs, Connecticut 06268.)
14. Sensory-Motor Training of the Profoundly Retarded. (5:83)
15. Special Fitness Test Manual for the Mildly Mentally Retarded. (1:43) (5:32) (order from: AAHPERD, 1900 Association Drive, Reston, Virginia.)
16. Teaching Research Motor Development Scale for Moderately and Severely Retarded Children. (5:53) (order from: Charles C Thomas Publisher, Springfield, Illinois 62717.)
17. TMR Performance Profile. (5:79) (order from: Reporting Service for Exceptional Children, 563 Westview Avenue, Ridgefield, New Jersey 07657.)

LEARNING DISABILITIES

1. Auditory Discrimination Test. (2:81) (37:37)
2. Ayres Space Test. (2:11;13;81)
3. Bender-Gestalt Visual-Motor Test. (2:82) (30:175–78) (31:144) (37:28)
4. Benton Finger Identification Test. (14:142)
5. Berges & Lezine Body Awareness Test. (14:138)
6. Cratty Body Image Rating Scale. (14:139)
7. Dayton Sensory Motor Awareness Survey. (2:111) (7:363)
8. Developmental Test of Visual-Motor Integration (VMI) (2:84) (5:67) (order from Follett Educational Corporation, 1018 West Washington Boulevard, Chicago, Illinois 60607.)
9. Embedded Figures Test. (30:82)
10. Figure-Ground Test. (36:93–95)
11. Frostig Developmental Test of Visual Perception. (2:23–7;92;111) (4:68) (5:59) (6:39) (30:190–94) (37:37) (order from: Consulting Psychologist Press, 577 College Avenue, Palo Alto, California 94360.)
12. Functional Neurological Evaluation. (5:70) (order from: Dallas Academy, Oak Lawn Avenue, Dallas, Texas 75219.)

13. Geometric Form Completion Test. (36:93;285)
14. Gibson Spiral Maze Test. (6:39) (30:82;89;155;183–86)
15. Goodenough-Harris Drawing Test (DAP). (6:38) (30:140) (37:25–29)
16. Hamm-Marburg Body Coordination Test for Children. (6:37)
17. Hiskey-Nebraska Test of Learning Aptitude. (37:35–7)
18. Ilg & Ames Modified Draw-a-Person Test. (14:135)
19. Individual Motor Achievement Guided Education (IMAGE). (5:48) (order from: Devereu Foundation Press, Devon, Pennsylvania 19333.)
20. Kindergarten Auditory Screening Test. (5:49) (order from: Follett Educational Corporation, 1018 West Washington Boulevard, Chicago, Illinois 60607.)
21. Memory-for-Designs Test (MFD). (2:93) (37:27) (30:82;89;178–80)
22. Minnesota Percepto-Diagnostic Test. (37:167)
23. Motor Impersistence Test. (30:83;89)
24. Motor-Free Visual Perception Test (MVPT). (5:54) (order from: Academic Therapy Publications, 1539 Fourth Street, San Rafael, California 94901.)
25. Perceptual Rating Survey Scale. (2:111) (37:167)
26. Perceptual Test Battery. (5:45) (order from: Department of Education of the University of Chicago, 5801 Ellis Avenue, Chicago, Illinois 60637.)
27. Psychoeducational Inventory of Basic Learning. (2:101) (5:47) (order from: Fearon Publishers, 6 Davis Drive, Belmont, California 94002.)
28. Purdue Perceptual-Motor Survey. (2:32;102) (4:67–9) (5:62) (6:40) (20:261) (38:25;34) (order from: Charles E. Merrill Publishing Co., 1300 Alum Creek Drive, Columbus, Ohio 43216.)
29. Robbins Speech Sound Discrimination and Verbal Imagery Type Tests. (2:103)
30. Sound Discrimination Set. (2:104)
31. Southern California Figure-Ground Visual Perception Test. (2:104)
32. Southern California Kinesthesia & Tactile Perception Test. (2:104)
33. Southern California Sensory Integration Tests. (6:41)
34. Tactile Discrimination Set. (2:106)
35. Three-D Test for Visualization Skill. (5:56) (order from: Academic Therapy Publications, 1539 Fourth Street, San Rafel, California 94901.)
36. Valett Developmental Survey of Basic Learning Ability. (2:107) (order from: Consulting Psychologists Press, 577 College Avenue, Palo Alto, California 94306.)
37. Varied Shapes and Forms Set. (2:107)
38. Weight Discrimination Set. (2:109)
39. Wepman Test of Auditory Discrimination. (37:25)

EMOTIONAL AND BEHAVIORAL DISABILITIES

1. Basic Motor Fitness Test for Emotionally Disturbed Children. (36:40–47)
2. Modification of Buttonwood Farms Physical Fitness Tests. (36:49–51;275)

MOTOR ABILITY, MOTOR EDUCABILITY, SPORT SKILLS, AND PERCEPTUAL MOTOR SKILLS (NONHANDICAPPED AND SPECIAL POPULATIONS)

1. Adams Sport-Type Test of Motor Educability. (10:336) (11:239) (38:270)
2. Adapted Minnesota Manipulative Test. (31:25)
3. Auditory Discrimination Test. (2:81) (37:37)
4. Ayres Southern California Perceptual Motor Test. (2:13)

5. Ayres Space Test. (2:11;13;81)
6. Badge Test. (28:193–95)
7. Barrow Motor Ability Test. (7:157–60) (10:275) (11:237) (21:40–4) (26:135–37) (38:262)
8. Basic Concept Inventory. (2:87) (5:66) (order from: Follett Educational Corporation, 1018 West Washington Boulevard, Chicago, Illinois 60607.)
9. Basic Motor Ability Tests (BMAT). (6:79–88)
10. Basic Motor Fitness. (5:64) (order from: Department of Physical Education, Temple University, Philadelphia, Pennsylvania 19122.)
11. Basketball Throw for Distance Test. (21:34) (34:346) (38:263)
12. Basketball Wall Pass Test. (34:364)
13. Bender-Gestalt Visual-Motor Test. (2:82) (30:175–78) (31:144) (37:28)
14. Benton Finger Identification Test. (14:142)
15. Benton Revised Visual Retention Test (37:166)
16. Berges & Lezine Body Awareness Test. (14:138)
17. Brace Test of Motor Ability. (3:60;101) (6:34) (28:85–90)
18. Broad Jump Test. (34:387)
19. Bruininks-Oseretsky Test of Motor Proficiency. (9) (order from: American Guidance Service, Publisher's Building, Circle Pines, Minnesota 55014.)
20. California Achievement Tests. (37:38)
21. Carpenter Mat Tests. (3:103) (28:99–100)
22. Carpenter-Stansbury Test. (10:273) (11:235) (38:260)
23. Carpenter Stunt Tests for the First Three Grades. (28:91)
24. Collins-Howe Test of Accurate Lunging. (28:102)
25. Cozens Athletic Ability Test. (3:60;103) (10:275) (11:236–37) (26:137–40) (38:257)
26. Cratty Body Image Rating Scale. (14:139)
27. Cratty Six-Category Gross Motor Test. (13:191–204)
28. Dash (4-second). (34:349) (38:263)
29. Dayton Sensory Motor Awareness Survey. (2:111) (7:363)
30. DeOreo Fundamental Motor Skills Inventory (DFMSI). (32:181–84)
31. Developmental Test of Visual-Motor Integration (VMI). (2:84) (5:67) (order from: Follett Educational Corporation, 1018 West Washington Boulevard, Chicago, Illinois 60607.)
32. Doman-Delacato Developmental Mobility Scale. (5:63) (order from: Rehabilitation Center at Philadelphia, 8801 Stenton Avenue, Philadelphia, Pennsylvania 19063.)
33. Early Detection Inventory (EDI) (5:61) (order from: Follett Educational Corporation, 1018 West Washington Boulevard, Chicago, Illinois 60607.)
34. Embedded Figures Test. (30:82)
35. Emory University Test. (10:276)
36. Evanston Early Identification Scale. (2:88) (5:66) (order from: Follett Educational Corporation, 1018 West Washington Boulevard, Chicago, Illinois 60607.)
37. Figure-Ground Test. (36:93–95)
38. Frostig Developmental Test of Visual Perception. (2:23–7;92;111) (4:68) (5:59) (6:39) (30:190–94) (37:37) (order from: Consulting Psychologists Press, College Avenue, Palo Alto, California 94360.)
39. Frostig Movement Skills Test Battery. (6:37)
40. Functional Neurological Evaluation. (5:70) (order from: Dallas Academy, Oak Lawn Avenue, Dallas, Texas 75219.)

41. Geometric Form Completion Test. (36:93;185)
42. Gibson Spiral Maze Test. (6:39) (30:82;89;155;183–86)
43. Goodenough-Harris Drawing Test (DAP). (6:38) (30:140) (37:25–29)
44. Hamm-Marburg Body Coordination Test for Children. (6:37)
45. Hill Test. (28:86–91)
46. Hiskey-Nebraska Test of Learning Aptitude. (37:35–7)
47. Howard-Dohlman Test. (28:237–38)
48. Hughes Basic Gross Motor Assessment (BGMA). (5:69) (order from: Office of Special Education, Denver Public Schools, Denver, Colorado 80203.)
49. Humiston Motor Ability Test. (3:63;122) (10:272) (11:234)
50. Ilg & Ames Modified Draw-a-Person Test. (14:135)
51. Illinois Test of Psycholinguistic Abilities (ITPA). (37:25;31–34)
52. Individual Motor Achievement Guided Education (IMAGE). (5:48) (order from: Devereu Foundation Press, Devon, Pennsylvania 19333.)
53. Iowa-Brace Test. (3:118) (10:277) (11:237–38) (26:150–54) (28:85–90) (38:265–68)
54. Johnson Fundamental Skills Test. (7:160–68)
55. Johnson Test of Motor Educability. (3:61;120) (26:154–58) (28:95–98) (38:268)
56. Kindergarten Auditory Screening Test. (5:49) (order from: Follett Educational Corporation, 1018 West Washington Boulevard, Chicago, Illinois 60607.)
57. Koerth Pursuitmeter Test. (28:103)
58. Larson Motor Ability Test. (3:63;122) (10:272) (11:234) (26:140) (28:221) (38:259)
59. Lincoln-Oseretsky Test. (6:36) (14:189;268) (30:81;155;167–70) (32:169–71) (37:167)
60. McCloy's Motor Ability and Capacity Test. (3:61) (10:270–72) (11:232–34) (26:145–48) (28:115–26;321) (38:256)
61. Meeting Street School Screening Test (MSSST). (5:78) (order from: Meeting Street School, 333 Grotto Avenue, Providence, Rhode Island 02906.)
62. Memory-for-Designs Test (MFD). (2:93) (30:82;89;178–80) (37:27)
63. Metheny-Johnson Test. (3:61;126) (10:46;278–80) (11:238) (17:172) (26:158) (28:98–99) (38:269)
64. Miles Pursuitmeter Test. (28:103)
65. Miles Pursuit-pendulum Test. (28:103)
66. Minnesota Percepto-Diagnostic Test. (37:167)
67. Minnesota Rate of Manipulation Test (MROMT). (6:39) (26:48) (30:82;155;182–83)
68. Minnetonka Physical Performance Readiness Test. (2:111)
69. Morrison Test of Basic Sport Skills for College Women. (7:169–79)
70. Motor Aids to Perceptual Training—Observation Checklists. (2:95)
71. Motor Developmental Activities for the Mentally Retarded. (5:46) (order from: College of Education, University of South Florida, Tampa, Florida 33620.)
72. Move-Grow-Learn Movement Skills Survey. (2:96) (5:51) (order from: Follett Educational Corporation, 1018 West Washington Boulevard, Chicago, Illinois 60607.)
73. Movement Pattern Checklist. (2:97) (5:51) (20:153–70) (order from: Department of Physical Education, University of Illinois, Urbana, Illinois 61801.)
74. Movement Pattern Checklist—Short Form. (20:173–77)

75. Movigenic Curriculum. (2:15) (5:50) (order from: Bureau for Handicapped Children, State Department of Public Instruction, Madison, Wisconsin 53706.)
76. Motor-Free Visual Perception Test (MVPT). (5:54) (order from: Academic Therapy Publications, 1539 Fourth Street, San Rafael, California 94901.)
77. Newton Motor Ability for High School Girls. (10:274) (11:235)
78. Oberlin College Test. (26:144) (38:256)
79. Obstacle Race Test. (21:33) (34:344 46;387) (38:263)
80. Ohio State University Scale of Intra-Gross Motor Assessment (OSU Sigma). (32:178–81)
81. Oseretsky Tests of Motor Proficiency. (2:98) (4:68) (5:59) (6:35) (14:161) (30:82;155;159–67)
82. Perceptual Test Battery. (5:45) (order from: University of Chicago Press with the Department of Education of the University of Chicago, 5801 Ellis Avenue, Chicago, Illinois 60637.)
83. Physical Ability Rating Scale. (5:46) (order from: Orrin Marx, University Hospital School, Iowa City, Iowa 52240.)
84. Pontiac Kindergarten Perceptual-Motor Screening Test. (2:111)
85. Project Genesis Perceptual-Motor Screening. (2:111)
86. Psychoeducational Inventory of Basic Learning. (2:101) (5:47) (order from: Fearon Publishers, 6 Davis Drive, Belmont, California 94002.)
87. Purdue Pegboard Test. (30:25) (31:48)
88. Purdue Perceptual-Motor Survey (2:32;102) (4:67–9) (5:62) (6:40) (20:261) (37:25;34) (order from: Charles E. Merrill Publishing Co., 1300 Alum Creek Drive, Columbus, Ohio 43216.)
89. Rail-Walking Test for Boys and Girls. (2:102) (5:68) (31:29;48)
90. Roach/Kephart's Visual Achievement Forms. (36:69–75)
91. Robbins Speech Sound Discrimination and Verbal Imagery Type Tests. (2:103)
92. Rodger's Motor Ability Test. (28:223)
93. Sandbag Throw Test. (34:361)
94. Scott-French Motor Ability Test. (3:134) (7:180–89) (26:132–35) (28:223) (34:344–63) (38:263)
95. Scott's 3-Item Test. (21:33–39)
96. Scott Obstacle Course. (28:216)
97. Shuttle Race Test. (18:339) (34:259)
98. Sigma Delta Psi Test. (10:265) (26:144) (28:217)
99. Soccer Wall Volley Test. (34:371)
100. Sound Discrimination Set. (2:104)
101. Southern California Figure-Ground Visual Perception Test. (2:104)
102. Southern California Kinesthesia & Tactile Perception Tests. (2:104)
103. Southern California Motor Accuracy Test. (2:13;104)
104. Southern California Perceptual-Motor Tests. (2:105)
105. Southern California Sensory Integration Tests. (6:41)
106. Standing Broad Jump Test. (10:282) (11:243) (14:206) (18:338) (19:49) (21:35;40) (29:68) (31:18;142) (34:347;368) (38:253)
107. Stork Stand Test. (31:28) (34:389)
108. Stott's Test of Motor Impairment for Children. (6:36) (14:268) (30:65;82;89;155;171–74)
109. Tactile Discrimination Set. (2:106)
110. Target-throwing Tests. (28:102)
111. Test of Handedness for Athletics. (28:233–36)

112. Texas Physical Fitness-Motor Ability Test. (order from: Governor's Commission on Physical Fitness, 4200 North Lamar, Suite 101, Austin, Texas 78756.)
113. Vertical Jump Test. (3:42) (10:280–82) (11:240) (14:205) (18:337) (19:48) (28:67–71) (29:68) (31:18) (34:367) (38:253)
114. Vineland Adaptation of Oseretsky Test. (30:155;170–71)
115. Volleyball Wall Volley Test. (34:366)
116. Wall Pass Test. (34:348) (38:264)
117. Waterbury Obstacle Race Test. (28:215)
118. Wear Multiple-Obstacle Course. (28:215)
119. Wendler Test for Catching a Fly Ball. (28:102)
120. Wendler Test for Fielding Ground Balls. (28:100)
121. Wendler Test for Throwing a Soccer Ball. (28:101)
122. Wendler Test for Throwing a Softball. (28:101)

KINESTHESIA (NONHANDICAPPED POPULATIONS)

1. The Phillips Test of Kinesthesis. (28:112)
2. The Scott Test of Kinesthesis. (34:391–96) (38:250)
3. The Wiebe Test of Kinesthesis. (28:113) (38:250)
4. The Young Test of Kinesthesis. (28:112)

PHYSICAL FITNESS (NONHANDICAPPED POPULATIONS)

General

1. AAHPERD Youth Fitness Tests. (1:43) (7:191–206) (10:210) (11:179–80) (17:226) (18:343) (19:150) (21:14–32) (31:141) (38:161–64) (order from: AAHPERD, 1900 Association Drive, Reston, Virginia 22091.)
2. AAU Jr. Olympics Physical Fitness Test. (10:220) (38:177)
3. AAU Physical Fitness and Proficiency Test. (5:37) (order from: National AAU Office, Attention: Physical Fitness Program, 3400 West Eighty-sixth Street, Indianapolis, Indiana 46268)
4. Anderson-McCloy Physical Efficiency Test. (28:164)
5. Armed Forces Motor Fitness Tests. (3:54) (10:212–18) (11:184)
   a. Army Physical Fitness Test. (3:54) (10:215–16) (11:186) (26:116–19) (38:107)
   b. Marine Corps Physical Readiness Test. (10:217) (11:184) (28:181)
   c. Navy Standard Physical Fitness Test. (3:54) (10:213–15) (11:185) (26:119) (38:181)
   d. United States Military Academy Physical Efficiency Test. (10:216) (38:182)
   e. USAF Physical Fitness Test. (10:215) (11:185) (26:116–19) (38:179)
   f. U.S. Coast Guard Academy Fitness Test. (10:216) (11:185)
6. CAHPER Fitness Performance Test (Canadian). (10:221)
7. California Physical Performance Tests. (10:208–10) (11:178) (12:100) (38:166)
8. Carpenter Physical Efficiency Test. (28:164)
9. DGWS Tests. (26:112–16)
10. Elder Motor Fitness Test. (10:219) (11:188)
11. Fleishman Basic Fitness Test. (10:221) (11:189) (18:343) (19:135; 161–76)

12. Glover Physical Fitness Items for Primary Grade Children. (7:211–16) (11:183)
13. Indiana Motor Fitness Test. (3:43) (10:46;220) (11:188) (12:100) (17:172) (26:95–100) (38:172–75)
14. Minnesota Physical Efficiency Test. (38:175)
15. Mr. Peanut's Guide to Physical Fitness. (5:31) (order from: Standard Brands Education Service, P.O. Box 2695, Grand Central Station, New York, New York 10017.)
16. New York State Physical Fitness Test. (7:228–48) (10:219) (11:182) (12:100) (38:164–66)
17. North Carolina Fitness Test. (7:249–55) (11:189) (12:100)
18. NSWA Physical Performance Test. (10:212) (11:181) (38:176)
19. Oregon Motor Fitness Test. (10:46;203–08) (11:174–77) (12:100) (38: 171–72)
20. Oregon Simplification of the PFI. (10:166–69) (11:142) (12:90) (26:76) (38:144)
21. PCPFS Screening Test. (10:211) (11:181)
22. Peabody Test of Physical Fitness. (5:35) (order from: Institute on School Learning and Individual Differences, George Peabody College for Teachers, Nashville, Tennessee 37203.)
23. Phillip's JCR Test. (10:219) (11:188) (26:110–12) (28:220) (38:176)
24. Purdue University Motor Fitness Test. (10:221) (11:189)
25. AAHPERD Youth Fitness Test. (10:210) (26:94;106–10) (order from: AAHPERD, 1900 Association Drive, Reston, Virginia 22091.)
26. Roger's Physical Fitness Index (PFI). 3:130) (10:46;145–66) 11:126–42) (12:90) (17:172) (18:343) 26:62–77;141) (38:126;141–44)
27. Schaffer Girl's Motor Fitness Test. (10:221)
28. Stansbury Physical Efficiency Test. (28:164)
29. Texas Physical Fitness-Motor Ability Test. (order from: Governor's Commission on Physical Fitness, 4200 North Lamar, Suite 101, Austin, Texas 78756.)
30. Tulsa Elementary Physical Fitness Test. (10:220)
31. University of California Physical Efficiency Test. (28:17–19)
32. University of Florida Motor Fitness Test. (38:168)
33. University of Illinois Motor Fitness Test. (3:56) (10:218) (11:187) (28:224) (38:169–71)
34. University of Maryland Motor Fitness Test. (38:168)
35. Washington Elementary School Physical Fitness Test. (38:175)
36. Washington Motor Fitness Test. (10:220) (11:188) (12:100)
37. Yale University Physical Fitness Test. (38:168)

Strength

1. Cable-Tension Strength Test. (10:141–42;171–73) (11:123) (12:100; 107–25) (26:77–80) (38:147–50)
2. Clarke Test. (12:101) (28:154) (38:127)
3. Dynamometer. (18:335) (19:46–7) (26:60) (31:16)
4. Flexed Arm Hang Test. (19:50) (29:68) (31:141)
5. Hanging Test. (34:297)
6. Intercollegiate Strength Test. (28:128;321)
7. Kellogg Strength Test. (3:35) (28:154)
8. Kraus-Weber Test of Minimum Muscular Fitness. (10:47;173–78) (11:147–50) (12:98) (18:342) (26:80–90) (27:186–91) (38:150–56)

9. Larson Muscular Strength Test. (3:43;121) (26:141) (38:146)
10. Lookabaugh Potential-strength Score. (28:148)
11. Manuometer. (18:334) (26:60–1)
12. Martin Test. (3:34) (28:155–60)
13. McCloy's Athletic Strength Index. (3:38;124) (10:98;170) (11:145) (28:141–43)
14. McCloy's Pure Strength Index. (3:38) (10:170) (11:145) (28:143)
15. McCloy's Strength Index Revision. (3:38) (10:169) (11:144)
16. McCloy's Strength Test. (28:129–41;321)
17. Modified Pull-up Test. (21:11)
18. Modified Push-up Test. (21:9)
19. Oregon Cable-Tension Strength Batteries. (12:125)
20. Pull-up on Horizontal Bar Test. (18:335) (19:51) (21:11) (28:150;168) (29:70) (34:295)
21. Push and Pull Test. (28:151–52) (34:291)
22. Push-up on Knees Test. (28:170) (34:292)
23. Rocker Test. (34:301)
24. Roger's Strength Index. (3:36;131) (10:145;266–70) (11:127;135) (12:90) (26:62;141–44) (38:126;131–40;255)
25. Roger's Strength Test. (17:149) (28:128;321)
26. Sit-up Test. (10:222) (18:337) (19:44) (28:171) (29:71) (31:20;141) (34:299)
27. Vertical Pull with Dynanometer Test. (34:288)
28. Vertical Pull with Spring Scale Test. (34:290)

Endurance

1. Amplitude-Puls-Frequenz Test (APF). (29:107)
2. Army Test of Endurance. (28:177)
3. Åstrand-Rhyming Step Test. (10:193) (12:94–6) (29:109)
4. Balke Fifteen-minute Run Test. (10:193) (12:94–6) (29:109)
5. Balke Treadmill Test. (11:166) (26:190) (29:108)
6. Barringer Test. (28:301–02)
7. Bicycle Ergometer (PWC). (29:107)
8. Branch Energy Index. (10:181) (11:153) (26:191) (28:310) (38:109)
9. Breath-holding Test. (3:7) (28:238–39) (38:108)
10. Burger Test. (26:192)
11. Carlson's Fatigue Curve Test. (26:192–94) (28:182) (38:112–13)
12. Clarke Modification of the Harvard Step Test. (10:190) (28:304)
13. Cooper's Aerobics Test. (7:207–11) (11:171) (12:98) (29:84)
14. Crampton's Blood Ptosis Test (10:180) (11:153) (26:194–96) (28:291) (38:111–12)
15. Drop-off Index. (10:200) (38:158)
16. Endurance Running Tests. (11:170–72) (26:148) (38:158)
17. Flarimeter Test. (28:298)
18. Foster's Test. (26:196) (38:110)
19. Gallagher and Brouha Test. (11:161) (26:197–201)
20. Harvard Step-up Test. (7:217–27) (10:188–89) (11:158) (12:92) (21:13–15) (26:201–03) (28:303–04) (29:100) (38:117–20)
21. Heartometer. (11:156) (38:110)
22. Iowa High School Test of Endurance. (28:178)
23. Martinet Test. (28:297–98)
24. McCloy's Cardiovascular Rating of "Present Health." (18:342) (28:294) (38:107)

25. McCloy's Endurance Ratio. (18:342) (38:157)
26. McCurdy-Larson Organic Efficiency Test. (3:10;125) (10:110;184) (11:155) (28:305) (38:114)
27. Navy Test of Endurance. (28:178)
28. Ohio State University Step Test. (11:165)
29. Patterson's Modified Step Test Apparatus. (10:193) (11:164)
30. PCPFS Test (Recovery Index Test). (11:162)
31. Queens College Step Test. (11:160)
32. Schneider Physical Efficienty Index. (3:5–6;132) (10:182–84) (11:154) (26:204) (28:292–94) (38:115–16)
33. Shuttle Run Test. (19:51) (28:183) (31:142)
34. Six-hundred Yard Run-Walk Test. (11:170) (12:97) (29:85)
35. Skubic and Hodgkins Cardiovascular Efficiency Test. (10:190) (11:160)
36. Triple Lap Test. (34:305)
37. Tuttle Pulse-Ratio Test. (3:9;136) (10:185–87) (11:157) (12:92) (26:205–07) (28:299–303) (38:120–21)

Flexibility

1. Elgon (electrogoniometer by Karpovich) (10:139) (11:121)
2. Fleishman's Twist and Touch Test. (18:341) (19:78)
3. Fleishman's Test for Dynamic Flexibility. (18:341) (19:79)
4. Goniometer Test. (3:50) (10:137) (11:121) (12:106;128) (28:228) (36:83) (38:273)
5. Kraus-Weber Floor-Touch Test. (10:140) (11:123) (12:128;131) (38:272)
6. Leighton Flexometer Test. (3:50;123) (10:138) (11:121) (26:269–75) (27:199–208) (28:228) (29:126–40) (36:83–5) (38:275)
7. Modification of Cureton Tests of Flexibility. (28:226–27)
8. Opposite Arms across Back Test. (34:318)
9. Protractor Test. (36:83) (38:273)
10. Reach across the Chest and Down Test. (34:319)
11. Reach down the Back Test. (34:318)
12. Scott and French Test. (3:50) (10:139) (11:122) (12:129) (28:227)
13. Sitting, Bending, and Reach Test. (34:313–15)
14. Spinal Extension Test. (34:316)
15. Standing, Bending, and Reach Test. (34:311)
16. Wells-Dillon Sit and Reach Test. (10:140) (11:122) (12:129) (26:275) (27:208) (28:227) (38:273)
17. Wing Lifts Test. (34:316)

Agility

1. Auto-tire Test. (28:81)
2. Burpee Test. (38:250)
3. Cable Jump Test. (14:214)
4. Dodging Run Test. (28:80)
5. Figure Eight Test. (34:311)
6. Forty-yard Maze Run Test. (28:79)
7. Loop-the-Loop Run Test. (28:79)
8. Obstacle Race Test. (34:310)
9. Right-Boomerang Run Test. (28:78)
10. Shuttle Race Test. (19:83) (28:206–07) (34:310)

11. Sidestep Test. (28:80)
12. Squat Thrust Test. (28:75–8)
13. Thirty-foot Shuttle Run Test. (28:80)
14. Zigzag Run Test. (28:80)

Balance

1. Balance Beam Test of Static Balance. (14:202–03) (18:339) (28:104)
2. Balance on a Stick Test. (17:165) (34:322)
3. Bass Stick Tests of Static Balance. (28:104)
4. Bass Test of Dynamic Balance. (18:340) (28:106)
5. Collins-Howe Test of Static Balance. (28:105)
6. Reynolds Static Balance Test. (38:249)
7. Sideward Leap Test. (34:320–22)
8. Springfield Beam-Walking Test of Static Balance. (28:104)
9. Stork Stand. (18:339)

Posture (Nonhandicapped Populations)

Postural deviations

1. Bancroft's Straight Line Test. (10:116–17) (11:101)
2. Bancroft's Triple Line Test. (27:155)
3. Bancroft's Triple Posture Test. (10:117) (11:101–03) (28:257)
4. Brownell's Scale of Silhouettes. (10:117) (26:238) (27:157) (28:261) (38:199)
5. Buhl-Morril Posturemeter. (10:117) (11:103)
6. Center of Gravity Test. (3:113) (10:130) (11:114) (12:132) (26:251–53) (27:172) (28:270)
7. Children's Bureau Posture Chart. (28:261–62)
8. Christenson's Technique of Evaluating Silhouettes. (26:239) (27:159)
9. Clarke-Shay Scoliometer. (3:26) (38:209)
10. Crampton Wall Test. (27:155)
11. Crampton's Work-a-Day Test. (10:117) (11:103)
12. Crook's Scale of Silhouettes. (10:117) (26:238) (27:158) (28:262;265)
13. Cureton's Posture Measurement. (3:25) (10:124) (11:109) (36:60)
14. Cureton-Gunby Conformateur. (3:107) (26:241) (27:160) (38:200)
15. Denniston's Double-Pole Posture Test. (10:117) (11:103)
16. Gray Posture Standards. (28:262)
17. Harvard Posture Charts. (11:101)
18. Howland Alignometer. (10:130) (11:114) (26:248–51) (27:170) (36:181) (38:204)
19. Hubbard's Silhouette Technique. (26:239) (27:158) (38:199)
20. Iowa Posture Test. (7:358–62) (10:118) (11:103) (12:132) (28:257–61) (36:61)
21. Korb's Technique of Recording Silhouettes. (26:240) (27:158)
22. Kraus-Weber Refined Posture Test. (26:259–62) (27:182) (38:209)
23. Lowman's Test. (27:155)
24. Massey's Posture Technique. (3:25) (10:129) (11:114) (26:247) (27:168) (28:268–69) (38:208)
25. New York State Posture Rating Test. (7:363) (10:119–23) (11:104–07) (12:132) (18:312–13) (21:45–50) (36:61–5;176) (38:205–07)

26. Phelps, Kiphuth, and Goff Posture Appraisal. (10:118) (11:103) (12:132)
27. Scoliometer. (10:131–33) (11:115) (12:132)
28. Springfield Posture Measurements. (28:268)
29. Washington State College Screening Test. (26:253–55) (27:175)
30. Woodruff Body Alignment Posture Test. (10:123) (11:107) (12:132) (38:204)

Foot problems

1. Clarke's Footprint Angle. (3:26) (10:136) (11:118) (12:132) (26:264–65) (27:193–95) (28:271–72) (38:211)
2. Iowa Foot Mechanics Test. (10:135) (11:117) (12:132)
3. Kelly Foot Pain Test. (3:27) (10:134) (11:117) (12:132) (38:210)
4. Pedorule. (11:120) (12:132) (26:265) (27:195–96) (28:271;274) (38:212)
5. Truslow's Foot Ratio. (26:267) (27:197–98)

REFERENCES

1. AAHPER. *Adapted Physical Education Guidelines: Theory and Practice for the Seventies and Eighties.* Washington, D.C.: The Alliance, 1976.
2. ———. *Annotated Bibliography on Perceptual-Motor Development.* Washington, D.C.: The Alliance, 1973.
3. ———. *Measurement and Evaluation Materials in Health, Physical Education, and Recreation.* Washington, D.C.: The Alliance, 1950.
4. ———. *Physical Education and Recreation for Impaired, Disabled and Handicapped Individuals . . . Past, Present, and Future.* Washington, D.C.: The Alliance, 1975.
5. ———. *Testing for Impaired, Disabled, and Handicapped Individuals.* Washington, D.C.: The Alliance, 1978.
6. Arnheim, Daniel D., and Sinclair, William A. *The Clumsy Child: A Program of Motor Therapy.* Saint Louis: C. V. Mosby Company, 1975.
7. Barrow, Harold M., and McGee, Rosemary. *A Practical Approach to Measurement in Physical Education.* 2d ed. Philadelphia: Lea & Febiger, 1971.
8. Brazelton, T. B. *Neonatal Behavioral Assessment Scale.* Clinics in Developmental Medicine, No. 50. London: National Spastic Society, 1973.
9. Bruininks, Robert H. *The Bruininks-Oseretsky Test of Motor Proficiency.* Circle Pines, Minn.: American Guidance Service, n.d. (order from: Publisher's Building—A.G.S., Circle Pines, Minnesota 55014.)
10. Clarke, H. Harrison. *Application of Measurement to Health and Physical Education.* 4th ed. Englewood Cliffs, N.J.: Prentice-Hall, 1967.
11. ———. *Application of Measurement to Health and Physical Education.* 5th ed. Englewood Cliffs, N.J.: Prentice-Hall, 1976.
12. Clarke, H. Harrison, and Clarke, David H. *Developmental and Adapted Physical Education.* 2d ed. Englewood Cliffs, N.J. : Prentice-Hall, 1978.
13. Cratty, Bryant J., ed. *Motor Activity and the Education of Retardates.* Philadelphia: Lea & Febiger, 1969.
14. Cratty, Bryant J. *Perceptual and Motor Development in Infants and Children.* 2d ed. Englewood Cliffs, N.J.: Prentice-Hall, 1979.
15. Egan, D. F.; Illingworth, R. S.; and MacKeith, R. C. *Developmental Screening 0–5 Years. Clinics in Developmental Medicine,* No. 30. London: National Spastic Society, 1969.
16. El Paso Rehabilitation Center. *Comprehensive Developmental Evaluation Chart.* El Paso, Tex.: El Paso Rehabilitation Center, 1975. (order from: 2630 Richmond, El Paso, Texas 79930.)
17. Espenschade, Anna S., and Eckert, Helen M. *Motor Development.* Columbus, Ohio: Charles E. Merrill Books, 1967.
18. Fait, Hollis F. *Special Physical Education: Adapted, Corrective, Developmental.* Philadelphia: W. B. Saunders Co., 1966.

19. Fleishman, Edwin A. *The Structure and Measurement of Physical Fitness.* Englewood Cliffs, N.J.: Prentice-Hall, 1964.
20. Godfrey, Barbara B., and Kephart, Newell C. *Movement Patterns and Motor Education.* New York: Appleton-Century-Crofts, 1969.
21. Haskins, Mary Jane. *Evaluation in Physical Education.* Dubuque, Iowa: Wm. C. Brown Company Publishers, 1971.
22. Illingworth, R. S. *An Introduction to Developmental Assessment in the First Year. Clinics in Developmental Medicine,* No. 3. London: National Spastic Society, 1962.
23. ———. *Basic Developmental Screening 0–2 Years.* Oxford: Blackwell Scientific Publications, 1973.
24. Koontz, Charles W. *Koontz Child Developmental Program: Training Activities for the First 48 Months.* Los Angeles: Western Psychological Services, 1974. (order from: 12031 Wilshire Boulevard, Los Angeles, Calif. 90025.)
25. Marx, Orrin H., and Healy, Alfred. *Physical Ability Rating Scale.* Iowa City: University of Iowa, University Hospital School, 1971.
26. Mathews, Donald K., ed. *Measurement in Physical Education.* 2d ed. Philadelphia: Wm. B. Saunders Co., 1963.
27. Mathews, Donald K.; Kruse, Robert; and Shaw, Virginia. *The Science of Physical Education for Handicapped Children.* New York: Harper & Brothers, 1962.
28. McCloy, Charles Harold, and Young, Norma Dorothy. *Tests and Measurements in Health and Physical Education.* 3d ed. New York: Appleton-Century-Crofts, 1954.
29. Montoye, Henry J. *An Introduction to Measurement in Physical Education.* 2d ed. Boston, Mass. Allyn and Bacon, 1978.
30. Morris, P. R., and Whiting, H. T. A. *Motor Impairment and Compensatory Education.* Philadelphia: Lea & Febiger, 1971.
31. Rarick, G. Lawrence; Dobbins, D. Alan; and Broadhead, Geoffrey D. *The Motor Domain and Its Correlates in Educationally Handicapped Children.* Englewood Cliffs, N.J.: Prentice-Hall, 1976.
32. Ridenour, Marcella V., ed. *Motor Development Issues and Applications.* Princeton, N.J.: Princeton Book Company Publishers, 1978.
33. Santa Cruz County Board of Education. *The Behavioral Characteristics Progression.* Palo Alto, Calif.: VORT Corp., 1973. (order from: P.O. Box 11132, Palo Alto, Calif. 94306.)
34. Scott, M. Gladys, and French, Esther. *Measurement and Evaluation in Physical Education.* New York: Harper & Brothers, 1962.
35. Valett, R. E. *The Remediation of Learning Disabilities.* Palo Alto, Calif.: Fearon Publishers, 1967.
36. Vodola, Thomas M. *Individualized Physical Education Program for the Handicapped Child.* Englewood Cliffs, N.J.: Prentice-Hall, 1973. (order related materials from: Thomas M. Vodola, Director, Research and Evaluation, Township of Ocean School District, Oakhurst, N.J. 07755.)
37. Waugh, Kenneth W., and Bush, Wilma Jo. *Diagnosing Learning Disorders.* Columbus, Ohio: Charles E. Merrill Publishing Co., 1971.
38. Willgoose, Carl E., ed. *Evaluation in Health Education and Physical Education.* New York: McGraw-Hill, 1961.

Appendix B
DEVELOPMENT OF REFLEX BEHAVIOR

Human reflex behavior is observed partially at birth (depending on which reflexes are normal at that age) and is observed in varying degrees as the child grows older. Clinical personnel and educators often evaluate the reflex behavior of children suspected of having neurological dysfunction. In persons exhibiting overt neurological damage, or "hard signs," reflexes are elicited that should have been extinguished or integrated. For example, a physician might elicit the tonic neck reflex in a 25-year-old person with the spastic type of cerebral palsy even though this reflex should not be observed after six months of age. Neurological "soft signs," involving numerous minimal emotional, psychological, and behavior disorders, may also indicate a need for medical diagnostic examinations including testing reflex behavior.

This reflex behavior is essential to normal development. It is controlled at the spinal cord, brain stem, midbrain, and cortex levels of the central nervous system. With age, the spinal cord and brainstem reflexes gradually diminish so that the higher patterns of righting (midbrain) and equilibrium (cortical) reactions may become manifested. Neurological dysfunction is evident when the lower-level, more primitive reflexes continue to dominate to the exclusion of higher, integrated sensorimotor patterns.

SPINAL LEVEL REFLEXES

Flexor Withdrawal: Normal up to two months of age.
Stimulus: Painful stimulus given to bottom of the subject's foot.
Reflex: Flexion of the knee and hip. Dorsiflexion of the toes in that extremity.

Extensor Thrust: Normal up to two months of age.
Position: Flex one lower extremity at the hip and knee while extending the other lower extremity.
Stimulus: Stroke plantar surface of the foot of the flexed extremity.
Reflex: Flexed extremity will extend.

Crossed Extensor Reflex: Normal up to two months of age.

Type I Position: Flex one lower extremity and extend the other lower extremity.
Stimulus: Flex extended extremity.
Reflex: Opposite lower extremity will extend.

Type II Position: Both lower extremities are extended.
Stimulus: Tap the medial surface of one leg.
Reflex: Opposite leg will (1) extend at the knee and hip, (2) have foot dorsiflexion, and (3) have adduction and internal rotation of the hip.

BRAINSTEM LEVEL REFLEXES

Asymmetrical Tonic Neck Reflex: Normal from birth until four to six months of age.
Position: Subject lies supine.
Stimulus: Turn head to one side quickly.
Reflex: "Face-side" extremities will extend. "Skull-side" extremities will flex.

Symmetrical Tonic Neck Reflex: Normal from birth until four to six months of age.

Type I Position: Subject is placed over tester's knees.
Stimulus: Quickly flex head to chest.
Reflex: The upper extremities will flex and the lower extremities will extend.

Type II Position: Subject is placed over tester's knees.
Stimulus: Quickly extend head backward.
Reflex: The upper extremities will extend and the lower extremities will flex.

Tonic Labyrinthine Supine Reflex: Normal from birth until four to six months of age.
Position: Subject lies supine.
Stimulus: The supine position.
Reflex: Extension of all four extremities dominates.

Tonic Labyrinthine Prone Reflex: Normal from birth until four to six months of age.
Position: Subject lies prone.
Stimulus: The prone position.
Reflex: Flexion of all four extremities dominates.

Positive Supporting Reaction: Normal between the ages of three and eight months.
Position: Subject held under the arms.
Stimulus: Bounce subject on the soles of his feet several times.
Reflex: Increase in extensor tone, plantar flexion of the feet, and inversion of the ankles.

MIDBRAIN LEVEL REFLEXES

Neck Righting Reflex: Normal from birth until six months of age.
Position: Subject lies supine with arms and legs extended.
Stimulus: Head is turned quickly to one side.
Reflex: The body follows turning segmentally.

Body Righting Acting on the Body: Normal from about six months until eighteen months of age.
Position: Subject lies in a supine position with arms and legs extended.
Stimulus: Head is turned quickly to either side.
Reflex: The whole body follows in the same direction.

Labyrinthine Righting Acting on the Head #1: Normal from one to two months of age and continues throughout life.
Position: Subject is held prone in tester's arms with the head down, and blindfolded.
Stimulus: The prone position.
Reflex: The head raises so the child faces forward.
Note: There are other labryinthine righting acting on the head reflexes.

Optical Righting #1: Appears soon after the labyrinthine righting acting on the head (one to two months) and continues throughout life.
Position: Tester holds the subject in space in prone position.
Stimulus: The prone position.
Reflex: The head raises to a vertical position.
Note: There are other optical righting reflexes.

AUTOMATIC MOVEMENT REACTIONS

Moro Reflex: Normal until four months of age.
Position: Subject is held in a semireclined position.
Stimulus: Head is dropped backward.
Reflex: Abduction and extension (or flexion) of the arms and the fingers.

Landau Reflex: Normal from six months until two or two and one-half years of age.
Position: Subject is held in space, supporting the thorax in the prone position.
Stimulus: Head is raised actively or passively, or is lowered into a flexed position.
Reflex: When head is extended, the spine and legs will extend, and when the head is flexed, the spine and legs will flex.

Protective Extensor Thrust—Parachute Reation: Normal from six months of age and continues throughout life.
Position: Subject is suspended in air by ankles or pelvis in a prone position and with arms extended overhead.
Stimulus: Move head quickly toward floor.
Reflex: Immediate extension of the arms with extension and abduction of the fingers to protect the head.

CORTICAL LEVEL REFLEXES

Equilibrium Reactions
Supine: Normal from six months of age and continues throughout life.
Position: Subject is in a supine position on a tilt board wih arms and legs extended.
Stimulus: Board is tilted to one side.
Reflex: The arm and leg on the raised side will extend and abduct in an equilibrium reaction and the head and thorax will right themselves. There will be a protective reaction on the lowered side of the board.

Prone: Normal from six months of age and continues throughout life.
Position: Subject is in a prone position on a tilt board with arms and legs extended.
Stimulus: Board is titled to one side.
Reflex: The arm and leg on the raised side will extend and abduct. The lowered side will elicit a protective reaction.

Four-Foot Kneeling: Normal from eight months of age and continues throughout life.
Position: Examiner holds subject in a quadrupled position.
Stimulus: Subject is tilted to one side.
Reflex: The arm and leg will extend on the raised side while eliciting a protective reaction on the lowered side.

Kneel-Standing: Normal from fifteen months of age and continues throughout life.
Position: Subject is in a kneel-standing position.
Stimulus: Subject is tilted to one side.
Reflex: The arm and leg on the raised side will extend and abduct, and a protective reaction will be elicited on the lowered side.

Hopping 1: Normal from fifteen to eighteen months of age and continues throughout life.
Position: Subject is held by the upper arms in a standing position.
Stimulus: Subject is moved to right or left.
Reflex: Subject will hop sideways to maintain equilibrium, and head and thorax will return to normal position.
Note: There are other hopping reflexes.

Dorsiflexion: Normal from fifteen to eighteen months of age and continues throughout life.
Position: Holding under the axillae while in a standing position.
Stimulus: Tilt subject backward.
Reflex: Feet will dorsiflex, and the head and thorax return to a normal position.

See-Saw: Normal from fifteen to eighteen months of age and continues throughout life.
Position: In a standing position, tester holds subject's hand and foot, which is flexed at hip and knee.
Stimulus: Arm is pulled forward and slightly lateral.
Reflex: The flexed knee should abduct slightly and extend to maintain equilibrium. The head and thorax will return to normal position.

Simian Position: Normal from fifteen to eighteen months of age and continues throughout life.
Position: Squat-sitting position.
Stimulus: Subject is tilted to one side.
Reflex: The arm and leg on the raised side will abduct and extend while the lowered side will elicit a protective reaction.

Appendix C

BLANK FORM FOR PSYCHOMOTOR DEVELOPMENT ACTIVITIES

__________ **LEVEL**

Performance Competency (list)	*GPI p. #*	*Activities**

*Equipment: As indicated or items underlined.

INDEX